THE CATHAR VIEW

EDITED BY DAVE PATRICK

Dave Patrick is a writer and Certified Quantum-Touch® Practitioner and Instructor (www.quantumtouch.com), based in Nairn on Scotland's Moray Firth, midway between Findhorn and the Highland capital of Inverness.

His interest in the life and works of Sir Arthur Conan Doyle ('ACD') led him to join the White Eagle Lodge in 2008 (after reading THE RETURN OF ARTHUR CONAN DOYLE by Ivan Cooke), and the following year to edit his first book, THE VIEW: FROM CONAN DOYLE TO CONVERSATIONS WITH GOD, in collaboration with Colum Hayward of Polair Publishing.

Their next book project, THE VIEW BEYOND: SIR FRANCIS BACON — ALCHEMY, SCIENCE, MYSTERY (2011), resulted in Dave joining the Francis Bacon Society, founded in 1886, where he has also been a regular invited guest speaker. The Francis Bacon Society is understood to be the oldest still-active English national literary society.

Research undertaken for THE CATHAR VIEW: THE MYSTERIOUS LEGACY OF MONTSÉGUR has provided the opportunity to visit the Languedoc in South West France, including places like Rennes-le-Château and Montségur, something he has always wanted to do since first reading HOLY BLOOD, HOLY GRAIL (Henry Lincoln *et al*) in the early 1980s. It is a region he now loves to visit, drawn by his connection to the 'French spirit of light'.

Dave is a member of the British Society of Dowsers (BSD) and is interested in the development of other psychic skills such as remote viewing. He can be contacted by email via dave@healthyenterprise.com and via his websites at www.powerintheheart.com and www.thevitalmessage.wordpress.com.

In series with this title

THE VIEW
From Conan Doyle to CONVERSATIONS WITH GOD
edited by Dave Patrick

THE VIEW BEYOND
Sir Francis Bacon: Alchemy, Science, Mystery
edited by Dave Patrick

THE *CATHAR* VIEW

THE MYSTERIOUS LEGACY OF MONTSÉGUR

Edited by Dave Patrick

Polair Publishing Polair London
Publishing
www.polairpublishing.co.uk

First published October 20th, 2012
by Polair Publishing, P. O. Box 34886, London W8 6YR

British Library Cataloguing-in-Publication Data
A catalogue record for this book is
available from the British Library

ISBN 978-1-905398-28-7

Extracts from THE SHINING PRESENCE and THE LIVING WORD, and also from the magazine *Angelus*, are reproduced by kind permission of the White Eagle Publishing Trust, Liss, Hampshire. The extract from Walter Birks' book THE TREASURE OF MONTSÉGUR is by kind permission of the publisher, Thorsons (Harper Collins). Photos are reproduced courtesy of the original copyright holder.

Set in Monotype Dante by the Publisher and
Printed and bound in the UK by Biddles, part of the
MPG Books Group, Bodmin and King's Lynn

CONTENTS

Illustrations

Poems, Prayers and Songs

INTRODUCTION

WHO WERE the Cathars? Why have they become such a focus of attention? And what does their legacy, crystallised from their beliefs and lifestyles over seven centuries ago, mean for us today?

THE CATHAR VIEW seeks to offer some very diverse answers to these questions. Following in the footsteps of the Cathars, contributors shine their light into murky passages of long-gone history as they weave together an incredible story of dedication, passion, betrayal, ruthlessness, resilience, synchronicity and, above all, unconditional Love. A Love which has never gone away.

1 Perspectives

Colum Hayward in 'Cathar Joy' argues that although the history of the Cathars is characterised by ruthless suppression, they may provide us with an example to follow, one of heroic transformation and one which is ultimately joyful precisely because of a treasure those individuals found. In 'Imagining the Cathars in Late-Twentieth-Century Languedoc', researcher *Emily McCaffrey* investigates academic 'History' and popular 'history' as they pertain to the Cathars in a modern context, revealing what Catharism seems to offer today.

2 Travel

American harpist and singer *Ani Williams* invites us to join her on 'A Troubadour's Journey in Cathar Country', accompanied by her friend Henry Lincoln (HOLY BLOOD, HOLY GRAIL). 'The best way to get to know Cathar country is to walk it!'. *John Merrill* took his own advice, as described in 'Walking the Cathar Way'. Best known for her books on connecting the esoteric histories of Girona in Catalan Spain with Rennes-le-Château (CITY OF SECRETS, THE PORTAL), *Patrice Chaplin* links the Cathars with other pilgrims in the Pyrenees area and asks about the meaning of apparent reincarnational memory in 'Crossing Paths'. Irish writer *Deirdre Ryan,* in 'Cathar Tracking', takes us on a mystical journey of synchronicity and puzzling personal relationships, both current and from Cathar times, as she endeavours to develop a deeper understanding of her own spiritual identity.

3 History

Nick Lambert in 'The Appeal of the Cathars then and now' examines the historical and contemporary dimensions of this phenomenon, from the perspective of a broader Gnostic worldview; while in 'An Introduction to Bogomilism', *Dimitar Mulushev* investigates the connection between the Bogomils and the Cathars. *Roger Shorter*, in 'From the Cathars to the Reformation', looks at the Cathars' legacy in the context of the struggle to have the Bible available in the vernaculsr.

4 Legend

Hristo Madjarov takes another angle on the Bogomil/Cathar connection in 'Bogomils – Cathars: One Source and One Purpose', conjecturing that the traditions that begin with Jesus' ministry and the Essenes have been kept alive by Peter Deunov's White Brotherhood. *Val Wineyard* weaves a masterly tale of intrigue and surprise in 'An Alternative History', while Anthroposophist *Sylvia Francke* unravels the legends surrounding Christian Rosenkreutz, founder of the Rosicrucians, and his connection with the Languedoc, asking an enthralling question in 'Christian Rosenkreutz, Cathar'?

5 Search

Grace Cooke (1892-1979), the medium for spirit guide White Eagle, writes about her visit to Lordat in 1931 in 'A Vision of a Cathar Brother'. *L. Shannon Andersen* acted upon 'The Call of the Cathars' and it changed her life. Author of THE MAGDALENE AWAKENING, Shannon shares with us the extraordinary synchronicities and twists that followed her. *Jeanne D'Août* is the pen name of Anneke Koremans, author of the novel WHITE LIE, which involves the Cathars, Otto Rahn, and a huge timeframe: in this article she goes 'Back to the Source', searching for the Gospel of Love.

6 Rediscovery

Colum Hayward gives a unique glimpse into the Lordat expedition, written from a personal family perspective, narrating what really occurred during his grandparents' trip with the Polaires in their supposed search for 'hidden treasure'; *Maurice Magre* (1877–1941), an enthusiastic student of the Cathars, gives us 'Considerations on the Cathars and Their Doctrines', reproduced from the *Bulletin des Polaires*; and *Walter Birks* (1912–1999), whose experiences led him to reject neo-Cathar esotericism, nonetheless felt he had found something – not in France but in Syria. He offers 'A Personal Reminiscence', reprinted from THE TREASURE OF MONTSÉGUR.

7 Memory

The conquest of fear is the theme of *Anna Hayward*'s chapter 'Montségur'. It tells how she found the courage to face those fears, rooted in past-life Cathar memories; *Sylvia Francke* shares her deeply personal story of loss and bereavement, centred on the death through cancer of her daughter Helen, aged 11, in 1982. 'Helen's Story' provides a remarkable insight into Helen's Cathar connections 'on the other side'. In 'Cathar', poet and singer-songwriter *Jehanne Mehta* shares a short poem, and a memory of being burned at the stake at Montségur in 1244. 'The Cathars, Mary Magdalene and the Truth?' is by *Alphedia* (Fiona Murray). Via a question-and-answer session, Alphedia invites the spirit of Mary Magdalene to answer searching questions relating to the Cathars. Meanwhile *Val Wineyard* gives an intensely personal insight into her past-life experiences in 'Mingling of the Centuries'. Her memories connect her to lives and events dating back to Cathar times.

8 Belief

The work of Arthur Guirdham played a big part in bringing the history of the Cathars to wider public attention. *Margaret Long* knew Guirdham well, and 'Rediscovering the Cathars' takes a reflective look at his influence on contemporary Cathar studies. *Jaap Rameijer* considers the influence of Mary Magdalene on the flowering of Catharism in the Languedoc in 'Gnostic Christianity Reborn'; *Morag Foster* asks about the atrocities committed against the Cathars and in 'To Go to the Wall' wonders whether such events could happen again. *Simon Bentley*, in 'Some Astrological Notes', highlights the long-term significance of events at Montségur – the astrological chart for March 16th, 1244, 'shows not an ending but a beginning', shedding further light on the Cathars' resurgence today.

9 Connections

Lastly, in 'The ABC of Initiation' I attempt to 'connect the dots' between the Cathars and the subjects of our two previous books in the VIEW series in my own 'Journey of Synchronicity'.

DAVE PATRICK, Nairn, Scotland, September 2012

ACKNOWLEDGMENTS

The publisher and editor thank the White Eagle Lodge Mother for permission to use Grace Cooke's papers in the White Eagle Lodge archive.

They are also grateful to the White Eagle Publishing Trust for permission to use the major extract from the 1949 edition of THE LIVING WORD and HarperCollins for the excerpt from THE TREASURE OF MONTSÉGUR by Walter Birks and R. A. Gilbert (Thorsons Aquarian).

We have made every effort to give identify and give credit to photographers and quoted authorities, including their translators, but if any acknowledgment is missing we offer our apologies as well as our thanks.

★

Our grateful thanks go not only to the writers in this book for their written contributions, but to those who have contributed photographs as well: Jeanne D'Août, Hristo Madjarov, John Merrill, Jaap Rameijer, Deirdre Ryan, Ani Williams and Val Wineyard.

Additional translation and proofing help was provided by Maria Petkova and Nadia Leu. We thank them too.

The cover was made possible by the skills of Morgan Hesmondalgh and the photo on the back is by Deirdre Ryan.

The publisher, Colum Hayward (for Polair Publishing) would like to thank those who attended his Cathar Discussion Group at the White Eagle Lodge in Kensington, London, who provided much of the inspiration to commission this book, as well as those who joined the party he led to the Department of Ariège in May 2012 (and our hosts there, Jon and Debbie Stoelker in the village of Bédeilhac). He is also grateful to the White Eagle Lodge for overall encouragement in his own Cathar studies.

NOTE

The photograph which forms the headpiece for each section is a view of the Château de Lordat, taken by Ian Sumter and used by kind permission.

I. PERSPECTIVES : 1

CATHAR JOY

COLUM HAYWARD

Writing about the Cathars requires objectivity, but it is difficulty to understand them without a degree of subjectivity, too. One thing on which we will then be informed is what life and death both meant to them.

*I*F THE Cathars hadn't existed, we'd have had to invent them. Progressively, these so-called heretics of the Middle Ages have come to hold more and more for us. Seven or eight hundred years on from when they lived, they provide a receptacle for us in which to hold our total freedom of choice in belief – something unavailable to the mediaeval worshipper, as he or she found out, agonisingly. They provide us with a peg on which to hang ideals about our conduct among ourselves – ideals such as truthful response and non-violence, and respect for all. The ideas we choose from their list are very beneficial to all society, though in many – such as diet, many would-be Cathars of today are strikingly less strict than their thirteenth-century forbears set themselves to be. The history of Catharism also provides us

Colum Hayward is the recent author of THE MEDITATION LIFESTYLE and, earlier, EYES OF THE SPIRIT: WORKING WITH A SPIRITUAL TEACHER; he has also edited ARTHUR CONAN DOYLE'S BOOK OF THE BEYOND and ASIA MYSTERIOSA. He has provided spiritual care in the London White Eagle Lodge since 1980. That was the year he gained a PhD from Cambridge University. In 1999 he survived a very long mountaineering fall and has also rowed competitively on London's Thames. He lectures on esoteric spirituality and its history and launched Polair Publishing in 2004.

a place to store, and possibly to release, some of our deepest pain, when correctly or incorrectly we attach it to memories of death on the pyre of flames, or in a walled-up cave. And if we are attentive, they may provide us with an example that is heroic, transformative and actually (as I shall argue in this chapter) joyful.

What if they really hadn't existed? It is an extraordinary suggestion, yet the last fifty years of scholarship have sought to repudiate a Cathar myth and replace it with studies that are rigidly factual and empirical. On top of this, the most uptodate historical consensus is profoundly re-evaluative of who and how many the Cathars were – almost, of the existence of anything we can properly call 'Catharism'. How much we need to readjust our views will depend on what our own assumptions previously were. The most recent study, by R. I. Moore,[1] plays down any thought of a unified and organized sect spread across southern France and joined in rebellion against a powerful Church. It recognises in the burnings and in the reports of Inquisitors huge social and economic forces in turmoil, a revolution in Church discipline and massive political rivalries that catastrophically affected both the 'Cathar' towns of northern Italy and the relatively unreconstructed 'Cathar' territory of the Count of Toulouse and his neighbours, as they fell prey not only to land grabs from the North but also movements of modernisation. All this makes the reason for many burnings socio-economic and political, or one arising from plain score-settling within damaged communities. Moore makes it obvious that the road from Béziers and Carcassonne to the Guelphs and Ghibellines who fight it out in *Romeo and Juliet* is quite a short one. His ideas will be contested, but our understanding of the Cathars is actually enhanced by his work, and if we avoid the sense of a unified and proselytizing heresy, and instead think in terms of local reactions and connections, different congregations all trying in their own way to imitate the church of the very early days, before Constantine and before the Council of Nicaea, and certainly not thinking of themselves with a title other than *bons hommes*, we shall not be very far away from the developing scholarship.

What the new historians compel us to do is to think in terms of the 'Cathar' regions spawning an uncountable number of sects, some with the strong belief that God created the heavens and Satan the earth, and others simply contesting whether a corrupt priest still held the power to save their souls. Sometimes rightly and sometimes wrongly, the names 'Albigeois',

'Cathar' or 'Patarene' are used by their detractors to describe numerous reforming congregations – and to demonise all sorts of enemies.

Typically, but not universally, these congregations, groups and sects also possessed and used bibles and New Testaments in their own tongue – something which in itself was enough in the later period of their history to send them to the flames. They had differing views about Jesus but many saw him as never completely having incarnated on earth, so that the crucifixion was a crucifixion of something less than the whole being of Jesus. Some venerated the Epistles of Paul because they gave such clear evidence of an 'apostolic life' which could serve as an ideal for thousands and thousands who revolted against the anything-but-apostolic example of the Popes and clergy; yet the special place that writings of St John the Evangelist held in surviving records is paramount. Something I want to bring out is the power that St John's Gospel held for so many, and just what a force in belief it was for the supposed heretics actually to be able to read the New Testament for themselves.

In this chapter I want to work imaginatively from that sort of proposition to recapture what is an avowedly subjective view, but one which embraces something historical research can never quite do justice to. That is the power of the spoken word, and the things people felt in their hearts. To put it another way, what made it worth you going to the flames for your beliefs?

Let me first stay a little longer with the picture painted by scholars such as Moore of an extraordinary diversity of belief across lands where Church control had never been fully systematised, the lands primarily of the Count of Toulouse. Central papal control was the major achievement (for better or worse) of the mediaeval Church, but reached this area last, and bloodily. The heterodoxy among the communities means that there may quite appropriately be different Cathars for each one of us. Some that we link to will be radical dualists, for instance – people who believe in two gods, continually in conflict – while for others dualism may hold very little force. An organisation and a hierarchy holding Cathars together, Moore says, only began to exist when there was no alternative but to hold and strictly control admission to secret meetings. Prior to this, Cathar religion (religion in this context meaning the way people are bound together in one persuasion) was almost certainly much looser. It is however quite fair for us to talk about 'Cathar communities' before and after the onset of the organising process; what historians deny is that they saw themselves as anything other than simply true Christians, maintaining a tradition. Progressively, that age-old tradition was under threat, and more and more those who maintained it needed to communicate secretly with one another in order to survive. Coming from a background in esoteric religion, I was brought up to hear the word 'brotherhood' in a Cathar connection; as a network of 'Good Men' they perhaps fit that title just a little better now than once they did (except that it is wrong to make them all male by using these terms).

Alongside this, modern history also tends to play down the idea that a coherent packet of ideas conveniently reached the Languedoc and else-where in the mid-twelfth century – say from the Bogomil Balkans, or from fourth-century Mesopotamia, or anywhere else. The ideas we must now more loosely call Cathar are as a result much more easily viewed as some-thing arising spontaneously, unsystematically and yet strangely naturally, from ideas already embedded within the culture and character of local landscapes. At the same time we may underestimate the extent to which ideas travelled later in the period.

*

Although we take liberties with history when we claim our own private access to Catharism, there may actually be something to be gained from a more subjective approach to the functioning of these diverse minds and hearts. If in no other respect, Cathars were united in experiencing un-timely death, which is nothing if not a subjective experience. They were also very practised at bringing consolation to the dying, albeit by a ritual unknown in the Church. Their ceremonies were rituals to be experienced, not heard and obeyed. Somewhere, amid all this, they seem to have faced untimely death more easily, or maybe more resolutely, than most. How do we understand this to be?

Life ended sooner and more often violently for most people of the middle ages than today, and many went to the flames who were not Ca-thars in belief. To die for one's beliefs has always had something of a lux-ury to it – at no time so much as today, in certain parts of the world – and can as easily be achieved on the battlefield as upon the pyre. To go into the flames singing, as some sources suggest Cathars did, also speaks of the perceived advantages of reciprocated solidarity. We *want* them to have gone out of the world singing, too, for it confirms their heroism when we are trying to peg ours upon it. In fact, if they believed utterly in the evil of earth life, death was release. Maybe this has encouraged us traditionally to concentrate on the deaths of Cathars rather than the lives of Cathars.

One of the aspects of 'Catharism' that historians who deal in movements and stories have difficulty concentrating on is the ceremony of the *consolamentum*, because on paper it struggles to hold much colour or force. Yet it is to be remembered that communities are defined as well – indeed better – by their rituals and traditions as by their structures, and maybe more than by their written documents. What does the *consolamentum* feel like when it is enacted?

The *consolamentum* ritual properly follows the *abstinentia*, a period of one to two years of fasting and purification. An Occitan version of the ceremony, dating from quite late in the period (1250–80),[2] is led by the *ancia*, the elder among the *parfaits*. It begins with prayers and the first seventeen verses of St John's Gospel. There is then a general confession. Next comes the 'ministration' of the Lord's Prayer, in which the believer, or postulant, received 'the Book' – effectively, the power to use the Lord's Prayer. The postulant makes his *melioramentum* with prostrations or genuflections: his acknowledgment of the presence of the Holy Spirit in the elder who stands before him, and the elder delivers an allocution which sets out the scriptural basis behind the rite, and emphasises the solemnity of it. Next there is the *consolamentum* itself, which is a form of baptism by the laying on of hands. The believer hears of the responsibilities of – in effect – being received into the apostolic tradition, and prays for strength. The elder takes the Bible or Gospel and places it on the postulant's head, while three other *parfaits* place their right hand on him or her, and say the 'pardon' and *adoremus*, and a prayer of reception into the faith. There are then no less than six recitations of the Lord's Prayer, interspersed with the *adoremus* ('Let us adore....') and followed by the Act or Kiss of Peace. From other sources we know that as the new *parfait* rose from kneeling, he or she was clothed in the dark robe of the Cathar.

I have myself, while leading retreats, on three occasions taken the words that have come down to us and led a live enactment of them. As I have hinted, the texts are deceptive. On paper, they do not excite as much as the rediscovery of a seven-hunded-year-old ceremony might. When we read them it takes a great deal of imagination to realise what a distance we are from the Catholic liturgy. Nonetheless there is a kind of directness and simplicity; the closeness of aspects of this ceremony to what we know of practice in the church immediately after the death of Christ, lost to the papal church, is something Walter Birks has described particularly well for us in THE TREASURE OF MONTSÉGUR (he makes the same comment as I do, that in print, the words do not easily come to life).[3]

Enacted, they take on a new character. The ritual of kneeling, in context, has touched something in me that I cannot quite explain. There is a dignity in the movement when it comes, and a deep simplicity in the way the simple act contains so much. It is the same with the Kiss of Peace. Rituals can hold memories much better than words at times; here, the ritual action stirs something profound, at a level beneath the conscious, and on all three occasions those present have shared that experience with each other afterwards. The laying on of hands, which Cathars rightly claimed connected them with apostolic times and which the Church felt undermined priestly authority, has felt to me to be the real transmission of a power words do not quite convey. The initiation into the use of the Lord's Prayer, too, requires our imagination to understand it. To someone used only to hearing the liturgy, and the Gospel, through the mouth of a maybe corrupt priest, we must imagine the absolute exultation, within a container of reverence, accruing from the new possession of the very words (whether in Latin or the Occitan vernacular) that the Teacher sent by God – not the human being, for Cathar belief generally denied that, but the one beyond mortality – spoke to his disciples. To the new *parfait* or *parfaite* those words were released, given to them. Direct means of communication, between the earthly plane and something higher, between the individual and God, were opened to him or her.

In speaking of my own personal experience I am, as I warned, moving outside the normal rules of scholarship. I am abandoning objectivity. Yet I must find a way of feeling what this ceremony meant to the postulant – indeed to all present, else my historical record will be imperfect. How can scholarship understand or even describe something that we can deduce was subjectively thrilling to participants, avowedly real and, to the feeling self, transformative – unless it commits to the subjective area itself? Such a question was one that faced Réné Guénon in the late 1920s and it led him to insist that immersion in its rituals and traditions is the only way to understand any system of belief. There is a strange relevance in mentioning Guénon and what was effectively the birth of the Traditionalist School in anthropology, because at this very time his associates in the Polaire Brotherhood – men like Maurice Magre and Otto Rahn – were rediscovering Catharism, and although the materials they had to study it were small compared with today's, in many ways I deeply admire the imaginative sympathy they brought to the subject. There are aspects of their understanding that I think for this reason are preferable to today's analyses and studies of much more detailed records.[4]

When Pierre and Jacques Authié had the sudden revelation that led them to an organised revival of Cathar belief in the last few years of the thirteenth century, it was said to be the result of reading a single book.[5] That may be something now lost; it might be the longest Cathar text, *The Book of the Two Principles*; it might be the *Interrogio Johannis*, purportedly a dialogue (on the theme of Satan's role in the history of the world) between Jesus and St John at the Last Supper. It just might be the Book of Revelation, or the apocryphal Acts of John, but it is quite likely that it was simply St John's Gospel, read in the vernacular for the first time. We ignore at our peril the sheer astonishment that a first reading of a vernacular gospel must have brought out in the mind of a mediaeval man or woman; if we take Keats' 'On first looking into Chapman's Homer' and its reference to 'stout Cortez' crossing Central America and seeing the Pacific for the first time and add the two together, we probably still underestimate the power of the Gospel read for the first time in the vernacular.

Nor is St John's Gospel any ordinary document. One of the most luminous literary products of the ninth-century Celtic Church is John Scotus Eriugena's commentary on the Prologue to the Gospel (i.e., the first seventeen verses, those that were the favourite Cathar text). Orthodox in theology it nonetheless resorts to hyperbole to treat John as more than merely human, as it reminds us of how fitting is the choice of the Eagle as St John's symbol:

'John, therefore, was not a human being but more than a human being when he flew above himself and all things that are.'[6]

The same verses of the Gospel, particularly the first five, provided Cathar believers with the most crucial scriptural basis for their dualism. The words 'And the light shineth in the darkness, and the darkness comprehended it not' ring down to us from the first century AD, via the King James translators, with a freshness and a breadth of meaning that is infinitely memorable. How much more so to an *Ariégois* of the thirteenth century, reading them for him or herself for the first time, and in Occitan? More than we do, that *Ariégois* may have found that darkness to be an active thing, something to combat rather than illumine – and maybe that light a more real and more tangible thing too?

Phrases from St John's Gospel more than any other source pepper the *consolamentum* ceremony in support of Cathar belief. But the key passage from St John for understanding the *consolamentum* is the profoundly moving fourteenth chapter, which includes the verses: 'If ye love me, keep my commandments. And I will pray the Father, and he shall give you another Comforter, that he may abide with you for ever; Even the Spirit of truth; whom the world cannot receive, because it seeth him not, neither knoweth him: but ye know him; for he dwelleth with you, and shall be in you. I will not leave you comfortless: I will come to you.' In the texts of the *consolamentum* we have, the fourteenth chapter was not included in full, but the Occitan text uses this very quotation and two other verses, separately, in support of the ritual. This chapter is the best in the whole Bible for our comprehension of precisely what the Holy Spirit is, and we must assume from it that whatever consolation the *consolamentum* offered, it must broadly speaking have been a revelation of the Holy Spirit. We understand from this chapter that the Comforter and the Holy Spirit are one and the same. To receive the *consolamentum* is to receive the full force of the love of God. To the one who had received it, there was given the same power to hand it on to another.[7]

This is the reason neo-Catharism, the twentieth-century 'revival', has chosen to see the *consolamentum* as a love feast, a transmission of love. Today's devotees have made their own interpretation of what a love feast is, but the term is ancient. In the beginnings of Christianity the Eucharist was part of a ceremony known as the *agape*. Because of abuses in the early Church, the two were separated and the *agape* or Love Feast had fallen into disuse by the mid-second century. It included the Kiss of Peace.[8] In effectively reviving it Catharism can not only be seen as taking the lead in authenticity but also as reviving a sense in which the community were one, rather than people with limited access to the truth revealed to them, reliant on priests as intermediaries. Yet to talk about a revival begs a huge question: we simply cannot say with confidence whether we might really be talking of revival, or of unbroken tradition.

★

For all that the promises the Cathar novice made were severe indeed, the sense of real community bonding together as the Apostles were perceived to have done, must have been a wonderful compensation for the loss of things such as sexual relations. Bound in good fellowship to each other, they had no need to fear other minority communities. One of the charges against Languedocian Cathars was their employment of Jews, and we know that further south they had no more problem in their connection with Moorish communities – particularly if those communities offered a more gnostic consciousness, which some (such as Sufism) did. Troubadour music is believed to have some origins that lie in Moorish Spain, acquiring from it not only form but also the mystical idealisation of the feminine, and it is not hard to see the vibrancy of counter-ideals such as this, contrasting with marriages that held doubtful joys. How far the Troubadours and the Cathar movement are interconnected is another contentious question for scholars, but they run side by side. The troubadours give a gaiety to the life of the Cathar châteaux, at the least.

My overriding point in this article is that the contemporary thrill of Catharism lay in actual spiritual experience enjoyed by individuals: revelation, an experience of the manifestation of light in earthly life, exchanged for remote promises of salvation offered by priests. If Catharism is truly as dualistic as has sometimes been asserted, we might expect its proponents to be miserable life-haters, hanging around for death; even taking opportunities to shorten their lives. Although there was the phenomenon of the *endura*, an end-of-life starvation, there is actually very little evidence indeed that suicide was anywhere embedded in the tradition. Moreover, there is no record at all of those gloomy lives we might expect: the Good Men by contrast seem to have had an enviable reputation in their communities not only as those who brought succour and help, but enjoyed doing so. There is not the slightest hint that they did so reluctantly.

The boundaries of Cathar dualism have, therefore, to be carefully scrutinised. It is one thing to regard the earth as evil; another so to reject everything in life that life is permanently odious and unbearable. Where is the evidence that Cathars hated their lives? It has rarely been suggested, but there are two ways of dealing with dualism. One is to feel powerless before it and simply to await a death that brought release. There have been plenty of life-denying sects that have preached a doctrine of gloom, but there is no evidence that the Cathars were one of those. The other is to take that most crucial phrase from St John, 'The light shineth in the darkness, and the darkness comprehended it not' and see it as a token of their power and ours. *Embracing light, we are part of its shining into the darkness.* It is not entirely possible to substantiate that Cathars took this maybe very modern view, but we must remember that post-*consolamentum* the *parfait* was fire and air, not baser nature.

I am not completely original in making this suggestion. Like newspapers that sell bad news so much more profitably than good, scholars can write easily of the 'evil world' aspect of Catharism, but with much more difficulty of the divine perfection of the spirit realm. Maurice Magre, who wrote THE RETURN OF THE MAGI (as MAGICIENS ET ILLUMINÉS, 1930) and Otto Rahn, who offered CRUSADE AGAINST THE GRAIL in 1933, are creative writers as well as historians, and so have been largely dismissed by scholars. In the latter case, further complication arises from Rahn's association – chosen or unchosen – with the SS. Yet both books contain some suggestions I believe may hold some rewards if we pursue them imaginatively, such as Rahn's association of Catharism with the old pagan landscape of the Languedoc that he loved so intensely. The suggestion that is relevant at this point, though, is Rahn's description of what made a Cathar life one 'not lived in vain', which he said depended on three desires:

'First, to love your fellow man like yourself, which meant not to let your neighbour suffer when you have it in your power to bring him consolation and help. Second, not to cause harm to your fellow man, and above all not to kill him. Third: to spiritualize yourself, which means to divinize life in such a way that at the moment of death, the body abandons this world without regrets. Otherwise, the soul will not find any rest at all.'[10]

One of the things Magre said (without supportive reference, but eloquently), is that

'Never has any people been so deeply versed in magical rites concerning death. The *consolamentum* must have possessed a power that to us is quite inconceivable.... The sublime secret of the *consolamentum*, which allowed a man to die cheerfully because he was identified by the inspiration of love with the God within him, has been forever lost.'[10]

Maybe. I have wanted to suggest in this article that Catharism may have had – among some of its believers at least – a way of looking at life and death that gave a real ability to transcend death. Being burnt at the stake, if you believed yourself already free of the mortal world, was not such a great deal – which may explain some of the stories that have come down to us of a joyful approach to the flames, and the widespread choice of death rather than renunciation of belief. Whatever Cathars believed, they certainly must have believed it deeply.

It is all too easy for us, centuries afterwards, to attribute to Cathars a Buddhist doctrine of non-attachment (as Magre, himself a Buddhist, did in 1930),[11] or for me (brought up within a spiritual teaching that taught that part of the reason for incarnation was to bring light into the darkness by virtue of our own intermediate role between spirit and matter) to see something similar to my own beliefs in Catharism. Cathar belief had its own intellectual context, very mediaeval, one markedly different from to-day's. And so, always at risk of special pleading, I would rather concentrate on what renunciation of earthly connection might mean for a Cathar. For if you have a dualist belief, then you must renounce the earth or else attach yourself to evil. That renunciation might be contained in a binding decla-ration, but a truly enduring renunciation would have to be more gradual, hence the long months of the *abstinentia*. Even renunciation vows may have not only an external validity but also an inner or esoteric reality, so it may be we are only talking about a small number of people who really understood the ways in which renunciation might be so well achieved.

Walter Birks writes of the one who took the *consolamentum*:
'The good man was once more an angel and as such an object of ven-eration to his fellow-men, among whom he moved like another Christ. But if he had achieved the privileges of Christhood he had also in-curred the obligation to live like Christ and to devote himself entirely to the salvation of his fellows still in [earth's] prison. His renunciation of the world must be entire.'[12]

What is interesting about Cathar renunciation is that it did not take the form a withdrawal from the world into some hermetic or monastic retreat – not even a hiding away in nature, which would have been a more likely retreat for a Cathar than a building. On the contrary, the *bons hom-mes* normally engaged with society; they were a part of the community, acting within it once visibly and later secretly. They offered consolation not because it was their job to offer it, but where it was needed and sought. We do not know how far ordinary Cathars prepared themselves for *abstinentia* with partial or incremental abstinence, but even if each one of them put off the moment of total renunciation as late as possible, the example was constantly before them.

Abstinence and renunciation have power in themselves, yet the understanding that goes with the abstinence may be more powerful than the act, and the most powerful technique of all must surely be not just to reject the world of darkness, but really to embrace the world of light. There is no literature about this from the thirteenth century, yet I believe it is the logical outcome of detachment from the earth and constant focus on the divine world. Actively to explore and so welcome the latter is a spiritual technique in itself and not too far from the rest of Christian mysticism. Truly to touch that sphere in all its joy is a form of gnosis.

I want to end on an even more subjective note than I have hitherto allowed myself. First of all, although I am not one of those who has significant memories of a Cathar life (I certainly don't remember flames!) the effect any real concentration of the Cathar beliefs has in me is to evoke and release a feeling of joy – sheer, unbridled joy of the sort that comes from a deep sense of discovery. If it relates to anything, it has the character of gnosis too, the detail of which is now lost but the emotion and the realization are still current. Rahn, who was deeply passionate about the Cathars, may not only have had a sense of this gnosis, but actively sought a Cathar life – and faced death stripped of everything – but if he truly had enjoyed this revelation then he faced it joyfully.

My own mother died last September. She had spent many years in the role of Mother – spiritual leader – of the movement promoting healing and brotherhood between all human beings and with all levels of life that is known by the name, the White Eagle Lodge. Ninety-five years of life on the earth had taken her through many levels of experience, and finally had taken from her almost everything except her coherence and the loving smile and loving hand she held out for almost everyone. Her life therefore ended in the utmost simplicity (those who cared for her with all the paraphernalia of old age might not have seen it as simple!). What she most certainly did not lose was a sense of the reality of spirit operating in and through physical life, a sense of the universal presence of love. As progressively she slipped out of consciousness, it became more and more important for her to sing with us songs that reminded her of that presence. She loved 'For all the saints', with its clear images of a heaven world; but her favourites were not just hymns – they were even secular songs such as 'It's a long way to Tipperary'. I doubt the hospital ward with whom she spent her last days ever quite realised what she meant when she sang out

'But my heart's right there' at the top of her voice! But we knew. As she slipped out of life, I had a sensation of a truly welcoming fire, but a fire of initiation and joy, not of pain. We can all be Cathars.

Notes:

[1] R. I. Moore, THE WAR AGAINST HERESY. London (Profile Books), 2012

[2] We have the record of the *consolamentum* only from the Inquisition, in an Occitan form and a Latin one, but they are of quite different provenance, yet seem to derive from a common root, a manuscript now lost. The *rituel de Lyon*, named after its archival location, and described here, is in Occitan (but with quotation in Latin). I have used the authoritative text in Walter L. Wakefield and Austin P. Evans, HERESIES OF THE HIGH MIDDLE AGES, New York, NY (Columbia University Press), 1991. Most of it is reproduced in translation both by Walter Birks and Richard Gilbert (THE TREASURE OF MONTSÉGUR, Wellingborough, 1987, pp. 92-8) and Jonathan Sumption (THE ALBIGENSIAN CRUSADE, London, 2nd edn., 1999);

[3] Birks and Gilbert, pp. 98-9

[4] My later article in this volume, 'A visit to Ariège in 1931', offers more detail of the Polaires, while the translation of Maurice Magre's 'Considerations on the Cathars' shows one of the group introducing the whole topic to the readership of their journal. I have written of René Guénon further in a preface introducing the Oracle of the Polaires, in ASIA MYSTERIOSA by Zam Bhotiva (London, Polair, 2012).

[5] The story is told in René Weis, THE YELLOW CROSS: THE STORY OF THE LAST CATHARS, 1290–1329. London: Penguin, 2001.

[6] See Christopher Bamford, THE VOICE OF THE EAGLE, THE HEART OF CELTIC CHRISTIANITY: JOHN SCOTUS ERIUGENA'S HOMILY ON THE PROLOGUE TO THE GOSPEL OF ST JOHN, Great Barrington, MA: Lindisfarne Books, 2nd edn, 2000.

[7] Compare Birks, p. 82, citing what he refers to as the *Book of John*, which is the *Interrogio Johannis* mentioned earlier.

[8] See Birks and Gilbert, pp. 98-9.

[9] Otto Rahn, CRUSADE AGAINST THE GRAIL, translated by Christopher Jones. Rochester, VT: Inner Traditions, 2006, p. 90. The English translation of Magre's most popular book this side of the Channel is by Reginald Merton, and was first published in 1931; it is now available in the print-on-demand edition of Kessinger Press.

[10] THE RETURN OF THE MAGI, London: Philip Allan, 1931, p. 98.

[11] See THE RETURN OF THE MAGI, pp. 96–7.

[12] p. 84.

I : 2

IMAGINING THE CATHARS IN LATE-TWENTIETH-CENTURY LANGUEDOC

EMILY McCAFFREY

There has been a Catharism for every generation – including today's consumerist society, not just those who seek a new spirituality.

I

ONE OF THE most spectacularly successful examples of a scholarly history that has enjoyed genuine popular interest is Emmanuel Le Roy Ladurie's MONTAILLOU, VILLAGE OCCITAN DE 1294–1324 (1978). Using the Inquisition Register of Bishop Jacques Fournier, Le Roy Ladurie reconstructed the world of a thirteenth-century Cathar village in Languedoc, south-western France, giving an extraordinarily detailed and vivid picture of everyday life. His book recalled a pivotal moment in the history of Languedoc in which the Cathar, or Albigensian, heresy was violently repressed by the Albigensian Crusade (1208-1229).[1] More than this, however, the reception of Le Roy Ladurie's cultural history was part of a remarkable resurgence of local interest in the 1970s in the events of the thirteenth century in Languedoc itself. While it seems that a popular memory of the heresy and the Crusade had all but disappeared by the nineteenth century, today they are central to local collective identity and its expressions.[2] In the process, moreover, professional historians have found themselves lured into the attractive but awkward role of mediators between academic History and popular history.

After a brief description of Catharism, this article surveys the historiography of the heresy and, in particular, the development of a self-con-

Emily McCaffrey completed a PhD in History at the University of Melbourne in 1999. She subsequently worked as a Research Assistant in the Department of History at the same university and published a series of articles on Memory and History. In 2005 she moved to the UK with her family and now works as a freelance Editor.

sciously scholarly and rigorous methodology since 1950. This has been paralleled, however, by a remarkable flowering of popular interest in Catharism and of commercial and associational initiatives which have both met and encouraged this interest. Today Catharism and its memorialisation is at the heart of collective identity in Languedoc within a 'Europe des régions'. While a central element of the project of scholarly historians has been to contest what they see as the superficial myth-making intrinsic to this popular 'history', this article concludes by suggesting that the distinction between scholarly and popular history is often blurred.

II

Catharism first appeared in Languedoc in the first half of the twelfth century. Essentially a dualist religion that probably originated in the Balkans, Catharism was predicated on the opposition of light and darkness, of God and Satan, of the spiritual world and the temporal world. From an orthodox Catholic theological perspective, Catharism was plainly heretical: according to its doctrine, God did not create the temporal world, Christ never took on human form, nor suffered on the Cross, and baptism by water would not bring salvation. The only sacrament practised by the Cathars was the *consolamentum*, or baptism by the Holy Spirit, and it was the only means of salvation. The Cathar clergy, or Perfects, were those who had already received the *consolamentum* as part of their ritual of ordination. Once 'hereticated', a Perfect had to remain pure, abstaining from meat and sexual intercourse. The lay Cathars, or Believers, were also required to receive the same sacrament before death in order to be saved. The Cathars rejected ecclesiastical authority in an effort to return to the values of simplicity and abstinence from which they believed the Roman Church had departed.[3] As many of the local lords sympathised with the Cathars, the heresy also seemed to pose a threat to the potential establishment of royal power in the region.[4]

In 1208, Pierre de Castelnau, a papal legate, was assassinated in the town of Saint Gilles in Languedoc. His murder was attributed to the Cathars and prompted Pope Innocent III to launch a crusade against them. The Church, together with an army of northern French nobles led by Simon de Montfort, conducted a series of raids, sieges and battles, seeking out heretics and Cathar sympathisers. The Crusade was violent and merciless – heretics and their sympathisers were often either slaughtered or burned alive at the stake. After the death of de Montfort in 1218, Pope Honorious III launched a second Crusade, this time led by King Louis VIII. Ultimately, Languedoc was subordinated to the kingdom of France under Philip Augustus and his successors in 1229 with the Treaty of Paris, and the Cathar heresy was repressed after the siege of the castle at Montségur in 1244 and the establishment of the Inquisition.[5]

Historians began writing about the Cathars and the Crusade from as early as the thirteenth century. Until the twentieth century, however, written representations of the Cathars had been created essentially amongst elite literary circles and generally appeared as a function of other religious, political or cultural concerns. During the period of the Reformation, for example, the history of the Cathars was debated within the context of the religious conflict between Catholics and Protestants. Catholic polemicists used the Cathars as the misguided ancestors of the contemporary Protestant heresy. For their part, Protestant polemicists used a similar argument based on religious lineage to link Catharism with Protestantism to create and promote the *rêve albigeois*, or the insistence on the historical continuity of 'true' faith in the face of papal persecution.[6]

The Revolution of 1789 shifted the focus of the history of the Cathars from religious debate to that of nation-building in France and to providing a historical precedent for the political legitimacy of the nation. The secular nationalist view saw in thirteenth-century Occitanie a society of democracy, tolerance and freedom, and transformed the Cathars from heretics into free men. In other words, for liberal historians such as Augustin Thierry and Jules Michelet, the modern French tradition of democracy and political legitimacy had originated in the south.[7] In this way, they presented the French nation in its historical continuity: that is, the battle between democracy and absolute monarchy for which the origins were to be found in the events surrounding the Albigensian Crusade.

Then, towards the end of the nineteenth century, the memory of the Cathars was reinvented as a romantic legend in Napoléon Peyrat's epic HISTOIRE DES ALBIGEOIS (1870-82). Peyrat was a Protestant preacher from Languedoc, well known for his radicalism and anticlericalism, who also wrote poetry and history. In his HISTOIRE DES ALBIGEOIS, Peyrat lavishly recreated the Cathars as heroes and martyrs. He also transformed the castle at Montségur into a sacred monument to the Cathars which gave meaning to their sacrifice as defenders of the values of liberty, democracy and truth:

'Montségur is the Albigensian sanctuary, fortress and sepulchre. Its name dominates this history's entire landscape.... Montségur had been forgotten for six hundred years.... I resolved to visit the cradle of our people and the grave of our homeland.... Before writing about the martyrdom of the Albigensians, I went to seek inspiration from the holy mountain in the clouds.'[8]

Throughout the twentieth century mystics, Occitan nationalists, historians, and commercial and tourist entrepreneurs have all used these romanticised and heroic images of the Cathars for their own very different purposes.[9] Most especially, it is the invention of thirteenth-century Occitanie as a richly civilised and humane society, where the values of tolerance, independence and freedom were relentlessly defended, that has proved to be so resonant among them.[10]

In contrast, the most recent generation of historians of the Cathars has, over the last fifty years, dedicated itself to a new approach to writing history. It is self consciously scholarly and claims to be sceptical towards the mythological and romantic images of the Cathars that have dominated previous centuries. With a new and vigorous insistence on scholarship and the use of historical material, it has sought to reveal the 'truth' about Catharism. The discovery of original Cathar manuscripts earlier this century supplemented longstanding Catholic orthodox interpretations of Catharism from Inquisitorial records.[11] For the first time it was possible to study the essential tenets of Cathar belief and liturgy as a religious phenomenon on its own, and outside the dialectic of heresy and orthodoxy. Importantly, too, these documents prompted an interest in studying Catharism from 'within' and created a new methodological approach, following the trend in the *histoire des mentalités*, in which Catharism was reconsidered within its own historical, religious and sociological contexts.

The discovery of these original Cathar texts notwithstanding, the task of writing an accurate and scholarly account of Catharism in Languedoc remains difficult. The sources that are used to analyse Cathar doctrine, for example, originated in northern Italy, whilst ethnographic descriptions of Catharism as it was lived by families and villages come from readings of the Inquisition Register for Occitanie. In this genre, Le Roy Ladurie's has been both the most successful and the most contentious for its imaginative use of sources. Most commonly, however, recent historians have sought to document closely the details of Catharism.

Among the pioneers of this new, empirically based approach to writing the history of Catharism were the German Arno Borst and the Italian Raoul Manselli. By studying the *Livre de deux principes*, a doctrinal text on dualism that was discovered by Antoine Dondaine in 1939, Arno Borst examined the doctrinal origins of Catharism in south-eastern Europe and attempted to link it with its appearance in the west. Borst's method of inquiry allowed him to formulate some conclusions about how Catharism became attractive to many European Christians, and contributed to the debate about whether or not Catharism could be regarded as a Christian movement. He became a specialist in Cathar religion and his DIE KATHARER (1953) was one of the first scholarly texts to examine Catharism as a religious phenomenon. Like Borst, Raoul Manselli studied the original Cathar documents in order to examine Cathar religiosity. A professor of history at the universities of Rome and Turin, Manselli was particularly interested in the incidence of Catharism in northern Italy.[12] He wrote extensively about the sociology of Catharism in twelfth- and thirteenth-century northern urban Italian societies, attempting to demonstrate that, as more than a theological phenomenon, Catharism was able to respond to the spiritual insecurities of those who lived in a world of perceived injustices.[13]

The first French historians to follow this empirical method of inquiry into the origins and religious doctrine of Catharism were Christine Thouzellier and Jean Duvernoy. Thouzellier edited, translated and commented on a number of original Cathar texts, including the *Livre des deux principes*, the *Rituel cathare latin*, and the *Liber contra Manicheos*. Thouzellier was especially interested in examining these texts to understand and explain thirteenth-century heresies and the doctrinal controversies about them. For his part, Jean Duvernoy has been widely praised for his insightful reading of the Inquisitorial records. Not only did he extensively translate and edit the Inquisitorial Register of Jacques Fournier and several judicial depositions and interrogations, he also used his investigations to produce an impressive body of his own work. In the tradition of Emmanuel Le Roy Ladurie's anthropological study of Montaillou, Duvernoy also used the Inquisition Register to construct a rich description of daily life among Cathars in Languedoc.[14]

This new method of writing Cathar history has also embraced Catholic theological historians within the Church. In an effort to move away from the previously partisan nature of Catholic historiography, they have consciously devoted their work to the pursuit of historical veracity and scholarship. Monseigneur Elie Griffe, in particular, was among the first

French pioneers of the new Cathar history. Despite being a cleric, Griffe presented an independent and well researched historical and chronological account of Catharism in Languedoc and of the Crusade.[15] Rather than follow his predecessors in trying to justify the Church's actions throughout the Crusade, Griffe acknowledged that the Church's involvement in temporal affairs had been questionable and he denounced 'the close collaboration between the church and secular authorities that appears today to be not only unfortunate but absolutely absurd'.[16]

In 1965, another Catholic historian, Etienne Delaruelle,[17] launched a series of conferences at Fanjeaux, a hill town west of Carcassonne, that were dedicated to studying the religious history of medieval Languedoc.[18] Whilst the earlier conferences were dominated by Dominican speakers, a growing number of lay historians and specialists of religious history have participated in more recent years. In this way, the three conferences that have been dedicated exclusively to Catharism in Languedoc have covered a wide range of associated religious, historical and sociological themes.[19] The participation of an increasing number of non-Catholic professional historians points to the way in which shared assumptions of a common historical agenda have bridged an earlier polarisation between Catholic and secular interpretations of Catharism.

The work of these and other historians has not, of course, amounted to a definitive history of Catharism, but their contributions have allowed the most recent scholars to continue to build on what they had established. The precise methodological approach that they used to place Catharism in its medieval religious and sociological contexts remains a legacy for the work of the most recent generation of Cathar historians. The heart of the new Cathar scholarship is now located in Carcassonne at the Centre National d'Etudes Cathares (CNEC). This organisation encourages the scholarly study of Catharism in particular and of medieval heresiology in general, and supports a very impressive collection of erudite studies and documentation about Catharism. It claims that its main function is to source and to restore – through original documents – historical research in an area in which the proliferation of esoteric and commercial works only ever misrepresent it.[20] Today, the CNEC, as well as the scholars who are associated with it, enjoy local and international respect within both academic and popular circles.

One of the most prominent of the new generation of Cathar historians to be associated with the CNEC, and a popular local identity, is Michel Roquebert.[21] Roquebert actually began writing about the Cathars and the Crusade as a journalist for a local Languedoc newspaper.[22] In summer 1964 he wrote a three-page article on the various Cathar castles that could be visited during the holiday period. Then, for the same daily newspaper in 1966 and 1967, Roquebert ran a series of almost seventy articles on the epic history of the Cathars, from the origins of Catharism to a detailed chronology of the events of the Crusade. This series of articles proved to be the means by which Roquebert was able to move from journalism into the field of history. It also formed the basis for his highly acclaimed multi-volume history of the Cathars and the Crusade, L'ÉPOPÉE CATHARE (1970-96).[23] Roquebert's multi-volume work is the result of the study and analysis of original Cathar documents and the Inquisition Register to present an almost day-to-day account of the history of the Crusade. In this way, it is clearly situated within the field of *histoire événementielle*. Because it examines the social, cultural and economic problems of thirteenth century Languedoc, it could also be situated within the field of *histoire des mentalités*. Indeed L'ÉPOPÉE CATHARE has become an important reference for any inquiry into the history of the Cathars and the Crusade and represents the work of one of the first in the new generation of Cathar historians.

Whilst completing the L'ÉPOPÉE CATHARE series, Michel Roquebert also wrote works of a very different order. The Toulouse publishing house Privat has published these under its exclusive *Collection Domaine Cathare*, a series directed by Roquebert himself. As one of the new generation of historians, he appears to have held with the commitment to reveal the truth about Catharism. Not surprisingly, his interest in archaeology and his position as president of the Groupement de Recherches Archéologiques de Montségur et des Environs (GRAME) have converged in MONTSÉGUR, LES CENDRES DE LA LIBERTÉ (1992).[24] The dustjacket of this work claims that 'Michel Roquebert has raised Montségur above the myths that obstruct and distort it, and has endeavoured to rediscover the truth ... the reality of a time and a place.' Indeed, Roquebert's specific aim was to denounce many of the myths that, in large part, were created by Napoléon Peyrat: 'The history of Montségur, free of abstraction, legend, myth and literary fantasy.'[25] With reference to archaeological investigation and to original documentation,[26] he claimed that Montségur was never a temple of the sun, that it was never mounted upon a subterranean village, and that it was never the castle of the Holy Grail.[27]

Today, however, even more than Michel Roquebert, Anne Brenon appears at the forefront of the historical study of Catharism. A former state archivist, in 1982 she became the director of the CNEC and in 1991 she was promoted to president, a position she continues to hold. One of Brenon's most successful major works on Catharism, LE VRAI VISAGE DU CATHARISME (1989), was written as a result of extensive analyses of both the *Livre de deux principes* and the judicial inquiries made by the Catholic Church during the Inquisition. She refuted the notion of Catharism as heresy and redefined it instead as a form of ancient Christianity. She asserted that the Cathars, or *Bon Chrétiens*, lived by the teachings of the New Testament (especially the gospel of St John) but that, in contrast to orthodox Catholic dogma, they had a specifically dualist interpretation of the bible. By attempting to return to the original values of the primitive Church, she believed that Catharism was a 'Christian movement of its time, dissident but innovative in the wave of evangelical revival that was going to challenge the Church'.[28] What was most important for Brenon in this work, however, was that, in keeping with the claims of the new generation of Cathar historians, she unveiled the 'truth' about Catharism and deconstructed the myth of the Cathars as heretics. Not only has she sought to explain Cathar doctrine, she has also sought to reveal the nature of the urban life of the Cathars, of their economy, society and culture. Again, by drawing on information gleaned from the Inquisition Register, Brenon constructed a *histoire des mentalités* in her work LES FEMMES CATHARES (1992). Here, she pursued an analysis of the daily life of Cathar women and provided a wealth of anecdotes about marriage, motherhood, family and home life, and prayer life.

The result of all her investigations, she claims, facilitates her presentation of authentic Catharism 'from within'. This historical method, she concludes, is exceptionally satisfying: 'It was much more rewarding, both intellectually and emotionally, to ask the Cathars themselves to speak about Catharism, than to waste paper, effort and the reader's attention, by referring to contemporary commercial Cathar mythology.[29] In addition to distancing their 'new history' from centuries of polemic and myth then, Roquebert and Brenon are also, in their capacity as scholarly historians, attempting to dissociate themselves from an unprecedented popularisation of the Cathars in the decades since 1960.

III

One of the most significant turning points in the rise of the popularisation of Catharism occurred in 1966 with the national screening of a two-part television series, *Les Cathares*. The series seemed to draw heavily on the romantic mythology and legend that Peyrat had created in his HISTOIRE DES ALBIGEOIS, in that it brought magical, mythical and mysterious images of the Cathars into the homes of millions of French people. Across the board, both local and national newspapers reported that it was an excellent series and that it had successfully recreated the drama of the Crusade.[30] It was not necessarily 'authentic' Catharism which seemed to be so important to viewers. Rather, the drama associated with the sacred site at Montségur, where hundreds of Cathars were burned alive after the fortress was taken in 1244, provided the focus for interest. In addition to its entertainment value, the series recalled the reinvention of a unique past that explained and legitimised some of the contemporary claims for southern political and cultural identity. The national daily, *Le Monde*, predicted that henceforth the Cathars would be the subject of intense interest and ongoing discussion; indeed, the immediate effect of the television series was dramatic.

The resurgence of popular and commercial interest in nos ancêtres les Cathares coincided – and was indirectly connected with – a new appeal to collective identity in Languedoc. Here, as in other regions with claims to linguistic and ethnic specificity, the revolt of May 1968 against the perceived rigidity and autocracy of the Gaullist state took on a radical and autonomist tone. In the case of the south, a growing sense of economic malaise was blamed on the concentration of economic and political power in Paris and the north. In the context of a more radical Occitan discourse in the 1960s and 1970s, the Albigensian Crusade became a more widespread collective memory of political, economic and cultural oppression by the north and of the south's continuing struggle for liberation. To define themselves and legitimise their claims against the state, radical regionalists had to construct a specific regional identity. The problem of constructing a national consciousness for Occitanie, however, is that Occitanie has never existed as a political entity, only ever comprising several shifting, conflicting and independent territories. Occitanie never constituted a kingdom: it was only ever, at best, a group of disparate principalities.[31] The collective memory of an imagined historical struggle against the French state therefore became central to the construction of southern identity.[32]

Today, the memory of this particular moment in the south's history is even more popular and diffuse, and extends well beyond the field of regional politics to include the commodification of Catharism through publishing, commerce, advertising and multimedia. Indeed, Catharism has become a product of mass consumption. Publishing houses reacted first to the powerful interest in the Cathar myth and published pocket books and guidebooks, simplified reference books and picture books about the Cathars. Novels based on the Cathars and the Crusade also appeared on the market. These new publications formed a burgeoning category of commercial, mainly fictional, literature. Commercial publishing houses in particular sought to satisfy the increasing popular fascination with the dramatic excitement and mystery of the Cathar legend after the 1966 screening of *Les Cathares*.[33] In other words, these commercial novels featured more and more of the sensational and less and less of the historical, what the historian Charles-Olivier Carbonnell subsequently dismissed as a 'profanation of History.'[34]

In local newspaper reports, popular images of the Cathars are often made relevant to contemporary popular discourse in Languedoc. When reporting the exploits of local sporting teams, for example, newspapers regularly evoke the memory of the Cathars to characterise what they perceive to be the superior qualities of strength and resistance in local players. In October 1992, for example, one newspaper reported that the Languedoc rugby team was characterised by 'Pride, bravery, valour ... all permanent traits of the Cathar character'.[35] Sporting events even adopt the Cathar theme for little more than the geographical reference it recalls. The medical motorcyclists' club, for example, conducted a tour of the Cathar castles in 1992,[36] an annual football clinic is held at a campsite called 'The Cathar',[37] an army training programme at Carcassonne was baptised as 'Operation Cathar 3',[38] and a local fun run is called 'The Cathar fun run.'[39] There is even a leisure centre at Aigues-Vives called 'The Kart'Are', where go-karting is the main attraction.

Through communicating the details of the region's increasing number of specific Cathar events, local newspapers have also played a very important role in promoting a popular collective memory of Catharism. At Limoux, south of Carcassonne, for example, there is a short film about the Cathar phenomenon that one newspaper has promoted as 'Catharama on

the big screen'.[40] Another local newspaper reported on a conference held
in October 1991 by the novelist and Occitan nationalist Yves Rouquette
and headed the article 'How to become a Cathar'.[41] It was a title which
not only reflected a public awareness of Catharism, but it also suggested
the timelessness of the phenomenon in Languedoc, inasmuch as there is
always an opportunity to become 'Cathar'. In much the same way, a local
Audois who wrote an article about Montségur that appeared in the travel
section of the national daily, *Le Figaro*, in July 1992, claimed to have Cathar
ancestry and he even appended a short bibliography of Catharism to his
article 'for those who wish to convert to Catharism'.[42]

At Minerve, north-east of Carcassonne, a museum of figurines which
recaptures the story of the Crusade was reported for its significance to the
region because 'The epic story of the Occitan Cathars is still very much alive
in the region's memory . . . The museum will tell you the history of the
region with originality and . . . with lots of talent.'[43] At Leucate-Village, the
Young Cathar Movement organised a ball for singles and *La Dépêche du Midi*
announced that 'The Cathars ... will get together.' It clarified, however, that
'No, there will be no pyre for the Young Cathar Movement', but 'a great ball
for singles'. Finally, the announcement finished with a quip: 'There will be no
need for Simon de Montfort, the Cathars are going into battle'.[44] More pejora-
tive perhaps, was the name given to Mlle Moretto, a local girl who achieved
third place in the 1994 Miss France competition. Reversing the story of the
northern Crusade, the same newspaper reported that 'with great panache,
Carole Moretto, alias Miss Albigeois, led her beauty crusade to Paris'.[45]

Similarly, in the field of advertising, the popular expression of Catharism seems to appeal to a large clientele. These appeals range from CDs
and DVDs on Catharism and Languedoc to a unique collection of eight
Cathar castle brooches, and to washing powder that claims: 'In the Midi-
Pyrenees region, you have an exceptional choice: twelve Cathar castles and
eight varieties of Ariel.'[46] More enterprising again, perhaps, is that a French
sugar company has produced sugar cubes in 'Cathar castle' wrappings. In
the area of food and wine, and arts and crafts the Cathar theme also appears time and time again. There even exists a communications business
called 'Cathar, the Perfect Communicator'. More broadly, the globalisa-
tion of communication and information systems in multimedia and on the
World Wide Web means that information about the Cathars can now be
disseminated well beyond the region. Indeed, a search of 'Cathars' on the

Internet reveals more than one thousand web sites, including titles such as 'Cathars Online: What's New', 'The legend of the Cathars' and 'Cycling in search of the Cathars'. The range of Cathar-related information available on the Internet is astounding: from scholarly studies of Cathar doctrine to chat rooms in cyberspace about the legend of the Holy Grail at Montségur. Moreover, free market access to the Internet has often compromised historical veracity, as the website 'Cathar Mega Links to Pages on the Web' clearly highlights: 'Now in the comfort of your own home you can pick and choose the conspiracy theory or attributed heretical doctrine that best suits your denominational, personal or political agenda. Why bother with facts when 'the truth is out there'?'.[47] Possible link sites include 'Cathars and the secret bloodline of Christ', 'Cathars, Conspiracies and Crazies', and 'Cathars, Satanists and Magicians'!

Not surprisingly, the local tourist market also thrives on popular images of the Cathars. The museum of thirteenth-century methods of torture in Carcassonne, for example, exploits the mystery surrounding medieval Inquisition and methods of torture. Moreover, the presentation of the artifacts is melodramatic and of poor quality – unkempt mannequins provide victims for the ghoulish methods of torture on display, medieval music plays sombrely in the background, the light is dim and it is dusty.[48] Once the visitor has toured the museum, local vendors have plenty to offer in the way of souvenirs, such as fluorescent plastic swords, miniature models of besieged castles, miniature chocolate reproductions of Montségur, Cathar bread and Cathar wine.

More recently, however, local government bodies have worked closely with the CNEC, among others, in order to formulate a less brash tourist programme for the area, because it feels that the issue of authenticity is as important for the identity of the region as advertising and promotion. One of the most important undertakings of regional government was to develop the Cathar theme within the framework of its historical and cultural significance to the local population.[49] Again, drawing on the medieval history of the troubadours and the Cathars and the attendant myths of independence, tolerance and resistance, locals have been encouraged to be proud of their feeling of cultural otherness and to project this as a tourist attraction. Catharism in the south has proved to be very attractive to the local population because it provides the opportunity to awaken and enrich a lost identity. By re-imagining the Cathars, southerners can transform the condescending stereotype of the southern sausage-scoffing, lovable simpleton into the more positive image of the southerner as a timeless, hardy democrat.[50] Behind the local government's insistence on authenticity lies the tension that exists between efforts to maintain historical authenticity and the pressures to restructure the local economy. Despite the undertaking to prevent a 'cultural Disneyland' in the area, economic imperatives often mean that compromises are inevitable. The most recent effort to extend the successful Cathar tourist programme to Gruissan, a small seaside town in Languedoc with absolutely no historical evidence of the Cathars ever having passed through there, is one example.

Clearly then, there exists a distinct tension between efforts of those who wish to pursue an 'authentic' historical account of Catharism for some tourists and locals, and those who wish to commercialise and commodify the myth to satisfy the demands of others. Interestingly, a similar tension appears between the work of recent historians of Catharism such as Michel Roquebert and Anne Brenon and their role as popular intellectuals. As a reaction to the unprecedented mythical and commercial popularisation of Catharism since the 1960s, Roquebert and Brenon are, they claim, committed to revealing the 'truth' about Catharism in Languedoc to the local community as part of their unique heritage. In this way, the public is encouraged to move away from more popular commercialism and myth and to respond positively to issues of authenticity and local identity. In recent years, each of their publications has been widely acclaimed in the local media for bringing these issues to the forefront of debate. For the release in 1989 of Roquebert's fourth volume in the ÉPOPÉE CATHARE series, MOURIR À MONTSÉGUR, for example, the *Indépendant* newspaper hailed it as being 'A regional and national event . . . this time history speaks the truth'.[51] To commemorate the same occasion, another local paper, *La Dépêche du Midi*, posed a rhetorical question as a way of confirming him as a historian of repute: 'Roquebert is far from being unknown in the department of the Aude.... Besides, is he not a member of the CNEC?'[52]

Brenon's works have also been widely reported in a way that seeks to make her academic knowledge of Catharism available to the wider public. The publication of LES FEMMES CATHARES was reported in the *Midi Libre* newspaper as being a significant event for the entire *Audois* population: 'The Cathar drama will remain forever etched in our memory. All children of the Aude whether here or elsewhere must know the true face of these courageous women.'[53] Moreover, in order to bring the human face of Brenon closer to the public, the same article emphasised that:

> 'To write this account, Anne Brenon consulted the manuscripts of the Inquisitorial Register. The young woman emerged from the journey . . . bruised, wounded. To let myself be carried away ... I am a woman. I could not remain indifferent. I am neither a believer nor a mystic, but these men and women became a part of me.'

Michel Gardére wrote with similar effect in the French current affairs magazine, *L'Evénement du Jeudi*. He commented that, collectively, the historians of the CNEC, including Roquebert and Brenon, have the ability to bring the Cathar phenomenon alive and to make it attractive to the wider public. He wrote that they 'patiently collect documents on Catharism. Each day they meet with the Perfects, almost living among them, they know their names, skills, their anguish and their experiences.' He also pointed out that they 'know so much [about the Cathars], and write about them in books that obviously do not sell as well as those books with invented mysteries.... The Cathars, even though they are long dead, still warm the hearts and souls of Southerners.'[54]

While the media has played an important role in promoting these historians as the public faces of Cathar scholarship, the historians themselves have also cultivated their own popular image. In this way, their public participation in the promotion of Cathar history has often had the effect of underscoring the perpetuation of a popular, mythical Catharism. In particular, it is their promotion of the Cathars as heroes and martyrs and their recreation of them as democratic and pluralistic that has proved to be so popular. For his part, Roquebert appears happy to participate in more light-hearted celebrations of the Cathars. In 1993, for example, *La Dépêche du Midi* was thrilled to secure Roquebert's participation in its 'Cathar Gold' competition. The opportunity to win 1,000 gold coins was launched using the myth of Cathar treasure. Effectively the entrants (there were about 10,000) had to fill out correctly an incomplete sentence, the winning version of which was, 'The Perfects, Mathieu and Pierre Bonnet, carried the treasure from Montségur and hid it in a cave in the county of Foix.' Roquebert agreed to devise the sentence for the competition and the newspaper was clearly grateful for the contribution of such a high-profile historian. 'Michel Roquebert', it wrote, 'winner of the Académie Française's award for history in 1970, is considered to be one of the greatest historians of Catharism.'[55] His status as an eminent historian notwithstanding, Roquebert's enthusiastic contribution to the competition was the very means by which the Cathar myth of hidden treasure could be promoted and strengthened.

The legend surrounding the castle at Montségur is another theme which frequently appears in Roquebert's historical and archeological work. Most especially, he does not seem to be able to resist borrowing from the rich poetic description that made Peyrat's HISTOIRE DES ALBIGEOIS a classic romantic work. Of Montségur, Roquebert writes:

'The setting is wonderful, with this huge Pyrenean rock standing at more than 1,200 metres, like a gesture of imposing elevation, the castle ruins, a hieratic and silent sentinel at the entrance to a lost valley surrounded by forest, dotted with small lakes, and dominated by high mountain tops that are covered with snow late in the season and trace in the sky the arch of a great amphitheatre where shuddering floods burst forth.'[56]

Moreover, he seems to repeat Peyrat's myth itself by commemorating the sacredness of the site: 'But history has made this mountain much more than simply an excuse for charming walks: a sanctuary. One doesn't only come here to visit old rocks. One comes here to meet the ghosts of a lost religion, to search amongst the setting of a seven-hundred-year-old drama.'[57]

Similarly, Brenon's insistence that we remember the Cathars with love and affection is indicative of her tendency to be seduced by Peyrat's myth of the martyrdom and heroism of the Cathars. Writing LE VRAI VISAGE DU CATHARISME, she suggests, was an emotionally exhausting task for this very reason. She concluded this book with a dramatic image, demonstrating that, like Peyrat, she too is inclined to imagine the Cathars as peaceful and harmonious people and to link their legacy to the present: 'It is time for quiet. It is dark outside and the turtledoves are cooing. We will never know which of the Cathars listened to them with more love in their hearts.'[58]

Whilst they have participated in the recent appeal of Catharism at the popular level and enjoy the status of local celebrities, Roquebert and Brenon claim that their function in public life is much like the one they pursue in scholarship, that is, to educate the public with the truth about Catharism. Indeed, they are active participants in meetings centred on popular yet, they claim, truthful Catharism.[59] Despite their successful role as public intellectuals, however, there still exists a very real tension between public perceptions of Catharism and historical scholarship. Even if, in general, Roquebert and Brenon have sustained the delicate balance between historical scholarship and popular memorialisation, at times their willingness to be public intellectuals has seriously compromised them.

In June 1986, for example, the 'Ronde Cathare', an 800-kilometre four-wheel drive pilgrimage throughout Cathar country, was held for the second time. Roquebert and Brenon were recruited as highly esteemed representatives from the CNEC to present historical dissertations on various Cathar castles. The publicity for the four-wheel-drive adventure was not well received by others at the CNEC.

Both Roquebert and Brenon must have contributed to the statement issued to the public, which insisted that the CNEC 'is not at all implicated in the organisation of the rally: not only do we not sponsor it – how would we anyway? – but, conversely, none of us will get a centime for the information that we will be able to contribute.' The statement subsequently reiterated the CNEC's essential and unchanging public function in the face of a growing consumer culture centred on Catharism:

> 'Our mission is to deliver a de-mythified image of Catharism, and we consider that it is our duty to make this information available to everyone. Our work is to communicate information, the right information, in a particularly difficult area. The tourist and commercial markets of Catharism are completely controlled by traders in esotericism who carry with them the means with which to sensationalise it.'[60]

Significantly, it appears that some representatives from the CNEC have complained about the local press on more than one occasion. In Limoux in 1992, at the launch of the CNEC's regular series of conferences on Catharism, Brenon was heard to complain about the way in which the local press was disseminating information to the public. 'It seems', La Dépêche du Midi stated sarcastically after hearing what it must have considered a trivial complaint, 'that we haven't been nice to her. What a disaster!'[61] More seriously, however, La Dépêche du Midi also sought to defend its public role in the face of such criticism from Brenon:

> 'We have given lots of space to the presentation of this event that will see Limoux come alive…. We published, in great detail, the programme of festivities. We even listed the menu and price for the festival dinner and the telephone number for making reservations, and all that without Anne Brenon even bothering to give us a single telephone call. So, if Anne Brenon intends to complain publicly about the local press, she will, in future, be looking for someone else to promote her public appearances.'[62]

Clearly then, the local press has a very powerful and influential role in bringing the faces of historians such as Roquebert and Brenon before the public. Whilst the press appears to function as a bridge between scholars of Catharism and the public, the tension between the message that the scholars wish to convey and the liberties with which the press can interpret them for the public, is significant. Indeed the press has been able to dictate the terms for the public's perception of a particular figure. Consider, for example, the journalist Jacques Bertin's rather cynical comments on Roquebert's fascination and love for Montségur: 'He goes back to Montségur again and again: 'Up there is THE magic mountain!' And, as soon as he realises that, once again, he has opened the door to a world of myth, he corrects himself: 'MY magic mountain'.' But, observes the journalist, 'it's too late'.'[63] For a Cathar historian who claims to be so devoted to separating truth from myth, perhaps this kind of publicity does not serve to underwrite his own carefully constructed image. On the contrary, it seems to perpetuate the very same myths that he claims to deconstruct.

The tendency for the distinction between scholarly and popular Cathar history to become blurred was apparent at a conference on Catharism and troubadours, held in the small town of Baziège in late 1996. The conference was organised to commemorate one of the Albigensian Crusade's battles at Baziège in 1219. Historians, Roquebert and Brenon among them, presented various papers on subjects ranging from Catharism, troubadours, and local agricultural development to the Occitan language.[64] The conference proceedings were held in a great hall, generously decorated with billowing Occitan flags and, during the breaks, participants were invited to purchase from a selection of popular and historical books available on Catharism. During one of these breaks, scheduled after a lecture on Montségur as a solar temple, the two hundred participants were invited to put on special protective sunglasses and to witness an eclipse of the sun. The conference closed with a huge 'Cathar' feast including: 'Perfect' terrine, 'Montségur' cheese, and 'Cathar' cake. The austere vegetarian dietary regime followed by practising Cathar Perfects would not, of course, have allowed them to eat cheese and cake, much less terrine!

IV

Particularly since the screening of the 1966 television series, *Les Cathares*, the collective memory of the Cathars and the Crusade has become more popular and widespread, and has lent itself extensively to a range of literary, artistic and commercial interpretations. Indeed, the possibilities for commodifying and selling a specific moment in the south's history have been impressive. Museums, theatrical reconstructions, television series, novels and memorabilia have, over the last thirty years, contributed to the production of Catharism as entertainment. This process, in which the past, the south and the Cathar ideology of democratic tolerance have become commodities, is also linked to the movements of cultural and political nationalism that animated political life in France in the decades after 1968. At least in the south and in terms of a specific discourse based on colonisation by the north, a reworked past has legitimised some of the radical claims for political and cultural separatism or autonomy. Here, the question of whether history is or should be entertainment recalls other issues about commemoration, collective memory and the political uses of history.

If today southerners know about the story of the Cathars and the Crusade (however historically correct or incorrect in substance), it is due in large part to more recent consumer practices where the dramatic and fictional reconstruction of events has taken place in the media and in literature, art, and commerce. And if the collective memory of the Cathars has changed as a result of recent consumer practices and historical practices to become more entrenched in myth and mystery, it still provides the greater society of the south with a link to its past. What has remained consistent, however, is the positive representation of the Cathars as belonging to a legendary society of tolerance and democracy, of culture and wealth. It is a heritage of which southerners can be proud. It is the message that historians like Roquebert and Brenon are seeking to authenticate and promote, even though they too often do this in such a way as to anchor the Cathar myth more firmly in public consciousness.

In other words, in addition to Roquebert and Brenon's recognised achievements in the field of scholarly Cathar history, their local success recreates them as the public faces of popular Catharism. By sharing their knowledge of Catharism and by promoting the Cathars as people to admire, even to love, they are, on one level, demonstrating that the Cathars can be explained in both religious and sociological terms. But, on another, more subtle level, Roquebert and Brenon are also mythologising the Cathars and feeding the need of both themselves and the local Languedoc community to establish links with the past and to explain their identity by reinventing the Occitan historical narrative. In this way, they are challenging the traditional classification of cultural practices as either 'elite' or 'popular'. As Roger Chartier has pointed out, the relationship between 'elite' and 'popular' is complex: in reality, he argues the relationship between them can no longer be understood as it once was, as relations of exteriority between two juxtaposed but autonomous worlds (one elite and the other popular). Instead, both are producers of cultural or intellectual 'alloys' whose elements (codes of expression, systems of representation) are as solidly incorporated in each other as in metal alloys.[65] Whilst the achievements that Roquebert, Brenon and Le Roy Ladurie have made in the area of historical scholarship should not be questioned, they are also necessarily part of their society and not immune from personal responses to specific social and political contexts. It is therefore not surprising that their popularity underscores the wider community's commitment to (re) discovering legitimate links with the past.[66]

The process of remembering the Cathars and the Crusade in late-twentieth century Languedoc exemplifies the interplay between academic History and popular history. Whilst tensions can arise as a result of this interplay, particularly on the part of 'scholarly' historians committed to empirical rigour, both approaches have contributed to the reconstruction of a popular identity at a time when the concept of a 'Europe des régions' has become more widely appreciated and accepted.

Indeed, the interplay between academic History and popular history has facilitated the means by which local and regional groups have been able to imagine a community for themselves.[67]

Notes:

[1] Emmanuel Le Roy Ladurie's MONTAILLOU, VILLAGE OCCITAN DE 1294–1324 (Paris: Gallimard, 1978), enjoyed spectacular success inside France, and was translated into many other languages. For an analysis of this success, see Natalie Zemon Davis, 'Les Conteurs de Montaillou', *Annales, économies, sociétés, civilisations*, 1 (Jan.–Feb. 1979), 61-73.

[2] For the ways in which society constructs collective memories see Maurice Halbwachs, ON COLLECTIVE MEMORY (Chicago and London: University of Chicago Press, 1992); for a semantic analysis of the term 'collective memory' see Noa Gedi and Yigal Elam, 'Collective Memory – What is it?', *History & Memory: Studies in representations of the past*, 1, 1 (Spring/Summer 1996), 30-50.

[3] For more details on the religion of Catharism, see Anne Brenon, LE VRAI

VISAGE DU CATHARISME (Portet-sur-Garonne: Editions Loubatières, 1995); Jean Duvernoy, LE CATHARISME: L'HISTOIRE DES CATHARES (Toulouse: Privat, 1976); and Jean Duvernoy, LE CATHARISME: LA RELIGION DES CATHARES (Toulouse: Privat, 1979)

[4] On why the elite might be drawn to Catharism, see Charles Bru, 'Eléments pour une interprétation sociologique du Catharisme occitan', in René Nelli, ed., SPIRITUALITÉ DE L'HÉRÉSIE: LE CATHARISME (Paris: Presses universitaires de France, 1953), 25-59; Jean-Louis Biget, 'Notes sur le système féodale en Languedoc et son ouverture é l'hérésie', *Hérésies*, 11 (Carcassonne: 1988), 7-16; and Annie Cazenave, 'Hérésie et société', in Anne Brenon and Nicolas Gouzy, eds., CHRISTIANISME MÉDIÉVAL, MOUVEMENTS DISSIDENTS ET NOVATEURS (Villegly: CNEC/ Centre René Nelli, 1990), 7-61.

[5] For more details about Catharism and the Crusade see Guillaume de Tudèle, THE SONG OF THE CATHAR WARS: A HISTORY OF THE ALBIGENSIAN CRUSADE, translated by Janet Shirley (Aldershot: Scolar Press, 1996); Elie Griffe, LES DÉBUTS DE L'AVENTURE CATHARE EN LANGUEDOC, LE LANGUEDOC CATHARE DE 1190 À 1210 (Paris: Letouzey et Ané, 1971); Elie Griffe, LE LANGUEDOC CATHARE AU TEMPS DE LA CROISADE, 1209-1229 (Paris: Letouzey et Ané , 1973); and his posthumously published LE LANGUEDOC CATHARE ET L'INQUISITION, 1229–1329 (Paris: Letouzey et Ané , 1980); and Michel Roquebert, L'EPOPÉE CATHARE, L'INVASION 1198-1212, Vol. 1 (Toulouse: Privat, 1970); L'ÉPOPÉE CATHARE, MURET OU LA DÉ POSSESSION 1213-1216, Vol. 2 (Toulouse: Privat, 1977); L'ÉPOPÉE CATHARE, Le lys et le croix 1216-1229, Vol. 3 (Toulouse: Privat, 1986); L'ÉPOPÉE CATHARE, MOURIR À MONTSÉGUR 1229-1244, Vol. 4 (Toulouse: Privat, 1989); and L'ÉPOPÉE CATHARE, LA NUIT DES ENFANTS DE DIEU 1249-1321, Vol. 5 (Toulouse: Privat, 1996).

[6] The origins of the *rêve albigeois* can be attributed to Matthias Flacius Illyricus, *Catalogus testium veritatis: qui, ante nostram aetatem, Pontificum Romanorum primatui variisque papismi superstitionibus, erroribus, ac impiis fraudibus reclamarunt* (Geneva: Iacobi Stoer & Iacobi Chouét, 1608).

[7] Augustin Thierry, LETTRES SUR L'HISTOIRE DE FRANCE POUR SERVIR D'INTRODUCTION É L'ÉTUDE DE CETTE HISTOIRE (Paris: Furne, 1874); and Jules Michelet, HISTOIRE DE FRANCE, 17 vols. (Paris: Marpon et Flammarion, 1879-1884).

[8] Napoléon Peyrat, HISTOIRE DES ALBIGEOIS, Vol. 5 (Paris: G. Fischbacher, 1882), Epilogue. All translations from French are my own.

[9] Twentieth-century mystics have been fascinated by the legend of the Cathars. Some spiritual groups such as the Rose-Croix, Gnosticism, Manicheanism and Anthroposophism transformed Montségur into a sacred site, at times identifying it as the castle of the Holy Grail. Montségur also inspired a number of individual mystics. The German writer Otto Rahn, for example, used the legend of the Holy Grail at Montségur to establish a link between Romantic and Germanic traditions in his book LA CROISADE CONTRE LE GRAAL (Paris: Stock, 1934). Rahn went so far as to claim that the Cathars were ancestors of the Nazis and part of an elite community of the Aryan race! In political discourse, some

radical Occitan nationalists and historians, Robert Lafont among them, have tended to explain their history of political, economic and cultural 'colonisation' by northern France as having its origins in the Albigensian Crusade. For a critical analysis of the writing of Occitan history, see Emmanuel Le Roy Ladurie, 'Occitania in historical perspective', *Review*, 1, 1 (Summer 1977), 28-9; and Gérard Cholvy, 'Histoires contemporaines en pays d'Oc', *Annales, économies, sociétés, civilisations*, 34 (July-Aug. 1978), 863-79.

[10]'Christopher Hill's essay, 'The Norman Yoke', in his PURITANISM AND REVOLUTION: STUDIES IN THE INTERPRETATION OF THE ENGLISH REVOLUTION OF THE SEVENTEENTH CENTURY (New York: Schocken Books, 1958), 50-122, provides a similar example of the process of remembering because, like the Albigensian Crusade, whilst there is meaning in the legend of a Golden Age in which the Anglo-Saxons were free, there is actually an absence of meaning. That is to say that because both legends embody so many connotations and romantic notions they become so malleable as to be constantly applied and reapplied to various situations and political climates. In this way, they escape any set of specific meanings.

[11] See especially the manuscripts discovered and edited by Antoine Dondaine in 1939, LE LIBER DE DUOBUS PRINCIPIIS: UN TRAITÉ NÉO-MANICHÉ EN DU XLIIE SIÉ CLE; SUIVI D'UN FRAGMENT DE RITUEL CATHARE (Rome: S. Sabina, 1939). See also Christine Thouzellier's UN TRAITÉ CATHARE INÉDIT DU DÉBUT DU XIIIE SIÉCLE D'APRÈS LE '*LIBER CONTRA MANICHEOS*' DE DURAND DE HUESCA (Louvain: Bibliothé que de l'Université , Bureaux de la Revue, 1961).

[12] See Raoul Manselli, SPIRITUALI ET BEGHINI IN PROVENZA (Rome: Nella sede dell'Istituto, 1959) and SAN FRANCESCO D'ASSISI (Rome: Bulzoni, 1980).

[13] In particular he argued that evangelism and myth distinguished the success of Catharism in the community from Catholicism. The apparent absence of evangelism within the Church and the excesses of wealth among the clergy contrasted sharply with the ascetic, itinerant and evangelical lifestyle of the Perfects: see Raoul Manselli, 'Evangélisme et mythe dans la foi cathare', HÉRÉSIES, 5 (Carcassonne: 1985), 7–9.

[14] See Duvernoy, L'HISTOIRE DES CATHARES; LA RELIGION DES CATHARES.

[15] See Griffe, LES DÉBUTS DE L'AVENTURE CATHARE EN LANGUEDOC; LE LANGUEDOC CATHARE AU TEMPS DE LA CROISADE; and LE LANGUEDOC CATHARE ET L'INQUISITION.

[16] Griffe, LE LANGUEDOC CATHARE AU TEMPS DE LA CROISADE, 231.

[17] Etienne Delaruelle is Professor of History at the Catholic University of Toulouse and canon of the Catholic Church.

[18] Fanjeaux is where the house of Saint Dominic is located. Saint Dominic was the first of the clerics to try to convert Cathars to Catholicism before the Crusade. The conferences at Fanjeaux have been held annually since 1965.

[19]'Les Cathares en Languedoc', *Cahiers de Fanjeaux*, 3 (Toulouse, 1968); 'Historiographie du Catharisme', *Cahiers de Fanjeaux*, 14 (Toulouse, 1979); 'Effacement

du Catharismeé (XVIIIe à XIXe siécles)', *Cahiers de Fanjeaux*, 20 (Toulouse, 1985).

[20] Presentation booklet for the CNEC (Carcassonne, 1995), 4.

[21] Roquebert was born in Bordeaux but claims to have ancestors in the Ariège and Comminges. He pursued tertiary studies in philosophy, then taught in schools for some years before turning to a career in journalism. Today, he is a well-known member of the CNEC and president of the Groupement de Recherches Archéologiques de Montségur et des Environs (GRAME).

[22] Roquebert was *La Dépêche du Midi*'s editor-in-chief of a regular section on the arts until 1983.

[23] Roquebert's first volume, L'INVASION, was awarded the Académie Française's prize for history in 1970, and his third volume, LE LYS ET LE CROIX, was awarded the literary Grand Prix from Toulouse in 1986.

[24] This work is an abridged version of the fourth volume in Roquebert's 'Epopée, Mourir à Montségur'.

[25] Michel Roquebert, MONTSÉGUR, LES CENDRES DE LA LIBERTÉ (Toulouse: Privat, 1992), 16.

[26] See the excavation reports published in the Bulletin du Groupe de recherches archéologiques de Montségur et des environs (Carcassonne: GRAME, 1973, 1974 and 1975); see also Montségur, treize ans de recherche archéologique (Carcassonne: GRAME, 1980). Roquebert also claims to have consulted the Inquisition Register for this book.

[27] He further developed the theme of how the legend of the Holy Grail became wrongly associated with the incidence of Catharism in the thirteenth century in LES CATHARES ET LE GRAAL (Toulouse: Editions Privat, 1994).

[28] Anne Brenon, 'Les Cathares: Bons Chrétiens et hérétiques', *Hérésies* (Carcassonne: 1990), 154.

[29] Brenon, LE VRAI VISAGE DU CATHARISME, 315.

[30] In *Le Monde*, for example, Maurice Denuzié re commented that 'If the evocative power of the television no longer needs to be proven, it can still sometimes surprise us. The two screenings reminded millions of television viewers and informed millions of others about this Albigensian Crusade that, as a result of a war that was not only religious, helped to create unity for the kingdom of France.' 'La Revanche des Cathares', *Le Monde*, 31 March 1966.

[31] Pierre Bonnassie, 'L'Occitanie, un état manqué?', *Histoire*, 14 (July-Aug. 1979).

[32] For examinations of the ways in which the south has used the Albigensian Crusade in the reconstruction of its historical narrative, see Le Roy Ladurie, 'Occitania in historical perpective'; Cholvy, 'Histoires Contemporaines en Pays d'Oc'; and Andrew Roach, 'Occitania Past and Present: Southern Consciousness in Medieval and Modern French Polities', *History Workshop Journal*, 43 (Spring 1997), 1–22. On a more theoretical level, Michel de Certeau has discussed the writing of history and what he called 'the other'. He pointed out that a

striking aspect of current historical research was the confrontation between an imperative method and its 'other', or, more precisely, the manifestation of the relation that a mode of comprehension (e.g. French national history) holds with the incomprehensible dimensions that it 'brings forth' (e.g. regional history): Michel de Certeau, THE WRITING OF HISTORY, trans, by Tom Conley (New York: Columbia University Press, 1998), 38.

[33] See for example, Zoé Oldenbourg, LES BRÉLÉS (Paris: Gallimard, 1960); Gérard de Séde, Le Trésor cathare (Paris: Julliard, 1966); Jean Markale, MONTSÉGUR ET L'ÉNIGME CATHARE (Paris: Pygmalion, 1999); and Dominic Paladhile, SIMON DE MONTFORT ET LE DRAME CATHARE (Paris: Librarie académique Perrin, 1988).

[34] Charles-Olivier Carbonnell, 'Vulgarisation et récupération: le catharisme à travers les mass média', Cahiers de Fanjeaux, 14 (Toulouse, 1979), 364.

[35] 'Le défi cathare', L'Indépendant, 20 Oct. 1992.

[36] 'Le moto club medical à l'assaut des châteaux cathares', Le Généraliste, 1396 (11 Dec. 1992).

[37] 'Les cathares préférent le cassoulet', La Dépêche du Midi, 23 Aug. 1991.

[38] 'Cathare 3 s'achève à Carcassonne', L'Indépendant, 10 Dec. 1994.

[39] 'La foulée cathare', L'Indépendant, 22 July 1992.

[40] 'Catharama sur écran géant', L'Indépendant, 15 April 1994.

[41] La Dépêche du Midi, 20 Oct. 1991.

[42] 'Voyage en douce France: Jean Cau à Montségur', Le Figaro, 15 July 1992.

[43] 'Parfait', L'Indépendant, 26 July 1993.

[44] La Dépêche du Midi, no specific date. Found in a special collection of photocopied material at the CNEC Archives, Carcassonne.

[45] 'La Croisade de beauté de Miss Albigeois', La Dépêche du Midi, 29 Dec. 1993.

[46] Television supplement to La Dépêche du Midi, 8-14 Nov. 1993.

[47] http://www. surfsup. net/cathar/links.htm.

[48] Other museums in the cité that are similarly evocative of myth and mystery include: Musée Mémoires Moyen-Age (a miniature model of a medieval city under siege); le moyen-age dans la cité (an exhibition about medieval weapons, costumes, Templars, Cathars, etc.); and Le Feu Sacré (although the Cathars do not feature at all, fire-breathing dragons, swords, and knights in armour evoke an image of bloody battle).

[49] For an examination of a parallel development in the heritage industries of America and Britain particularly, see David Lowenthal, THE PAST IS A FOREIGN COUNTRY (Cambridge and New York: Cambridge University Press, 1985). See also Eric Hobsbawm and Terence Ranger, eds., THE INVENTION OF TRADITION (Cambridge and New York: Cambridge University Press, 1983), for an insight into the way in which society seeks to preserve the past.

[50] Roland Barthes argued that descriptions of the 'characteristics', or stereotypes, of ethnic minorities have often been adopted by the locals because of a subconscious

desire to be faithful to this image. He explained that 'a conjuring trick has taken place; it has turned reality inside out; it has emptied it of history and has filled it with nature'. Roland Barthes, MYTHOLOGIES, trans, by A. Lavers (London: J. Cape, 1972), 142. This time, however, southerners are seeking to project their own image rather than to fulfil one that is imposed upon them from outside.

[51] *L'Indépendant*, 2 Nov. 1989.

[52] *La Dépêche du Midi*, 31 Oct. 1989.

[53] *Le Midi Libre*, no specific date. Found in a special collection of photocopied material at the CNEC Archives, Carcassonne.

[54] Michel Gardères, 'Ces Nazillons qui se prennent pour des Cathares', *L'Evénement du Jeudi*, 10 April 1991, 53.

[55] 'Ils vont se partager mille piéces d'or', *La Dépêche du Midi*, 4 Jan. 1993.

[56] Roquebert, Monstségur, LES CENDRES DE LA LIBERTÉ, 11.

[57] Ibid.

[58] Brenon, LE VRAI VISAGE DU CATHARISME, 324.

[59] Specifically, these include the CNEC's conferences held to inform the public about Catharism, as well as historical conferences on Catharism which are open to public audiences.

[60] 'Centre national d'études cathares et rallaye', *L'Indépendant*, 26 June 1986.

[61] 'Les Cathares débarquent', *La Dépêche du Midi*, 5 Aug. 1992. [62] Ibid.

[63] Jacques Bertin, Le Grand Zoom, no specific date. Found in the special collection of photocopied material at the CNEC Archives, Carcassonne.

[64] Michel Roquebert presented a paper called 'Le Catharisme en Lauragais', and Anne Brenon was scheduled to give a paper on 'La Maison Cathare (Communauté de Parfaits ou de Parfaites)'. I understand that Brenon was unable to attend the conference on the day but the fact that she had agreed to attend is sufficient for my example. Rémy Pech, Professor of History at the Université du Mirail, Toulouse, and Jean Duvernoy also presented papers.

[65] Roger Chartier, 'Intellectual history or sociocultural historyé', in Dominick La Capra and Steven L. Kaplan, eds., MODERN EUROPEAN INTELLECTUAL HISTORY: REAPPRAISALS AND NEW PERSPECTIVES (Ithaca and London: Cornell University Press, 1982), 33-4.

[66] Although, of course, Le Roy Ladurie is regarded in France as a national historian and has actively sought to distance himself from the political agendas of many militant Occitanistes: see Le Roy Ladurie, 'Occitania in Historical Perspective'.

[67] The expression is taken from Benedict Anderson, IMAGINED COMMUNITIES: REFLECTIONS ON THE ORIGIN AND SPREAD OF NATIONALISM (London: Verso, 1983).

FROM THE HISTORIOGRAPHY OF THE CATHARS AND NEO-CATHARS
(clockwise from top left): Déodat Roché and friend; the 'pog' of Montségur; signature of Maurice Magre; René Nelli, Cathar historian; Château de Peyrepertuse; memorial to the Cathars who died at Montségur, erected by Déodat Roché in 1960; Otto Rahn's signature. See pp. 24–47 and 129–136. (Pictures *Val Wineyard*, apart from the signatures.)

II. TRAVEL : 1

A TROUBADOUR'S JOURNEY
IN CATHAR COUNTRY

ANI WILLIAMS

For author C.S. Lewis, the troubadours 'effected a change which has left no corner of our ethics, our imagination, or our daily life untouched…'.

ECHOES of the troubadour's song can still be heard across the lands of Oc, ringing in the silence and the song of the nightingale, in the melody of flowing springs and sometimes a chanson from a modern minstrel. Since the beginning of time, the music of nature and of muse wove a spell that sustained the harmonious patterns across the landscape and be-

Ani Williams is world-renowned harpist and singer, and has recorded more than two dozen albums of original sacred music based on ancient spiritual traditions. She has given concerts in Central and South America, England, Holland, Scotland, Ireland, France and Egypt, in such venues as Troyes Cathedral, and various churches and châteaux in France, Saint James's Church in London, the Findhorn Foundation in Scotland, the Giza Pyramids, Den Rus in Amsterdam, Centro de Cultura in Mexico City, and in the United States. She has done seminal work in the study of sound healing and the relationship between musical tones, the human voice and healing. In 1994 she developed Songaia Sound Medicine and Voice Spectrum Analysis, a system of using specific musical frequencies as therapy. Ani also leads pilgrimages to ancient sacred sites, and is a contributing writer to various international publications. *Note: Ani's photographs for this article are to be found on pp. 2 & 3 of the colour section*

tween earth and heaven. Enchantments woven by the troubadour poetry and songs nourished the land and all its creatures.

Oc is the region of Southern France reaching from the great mountain range of the Pyrenees, across land and rushing rivers to the Mediterranean Sea. The language of Oc was spoken in this region called Occitania or Languedoc (langue d'Oc) during the medieval era, and songs and poems still survive today in this language of the muse and the poet. The word Oc means *yes*, and the people of this region stood strong for the positive life giving principles of love, beauty and equality.

> 'There is no day on which I grow not
> Finer and more pure,
> For this world holds no nobler lady
> Than she whom I do serve and I adore.
> And these – the words I speak –
> Come singing from an open heart.'
>
> *Troubadour Arnaut Daniel, 1180–1200 (translation by Henry Lincoln)*

The quest for the grail, the return of beauty and the elevation of the feminine arose out of a deep longing held within the heart of the people and troubadours carried this impulse between medieval châteaux, mountain fortresses and across the land. Troubadours were also messengers carrying news and keeping alive the network of secret factions, such as the Templars, Cathars, and gnostic groups. The word *troubadour* comes from the roots *trouver* in French and *trobar* in Occitan, meaning one who finds or discovers and also one who invents. Troubadours can be seen as the ones who are recovering the seeds of truth, flowering into the songs which stretch our minds and hearts, and weaving a new cultural matrix for a new era.

> 'Whatever the gods do, they do by song.... Things are summoned by this praise song and encouraged to come joyfully into being.'
>
> *Marius Schneider, Cologne University*

For several decades, I have been a questing troubadour journeying in many lands of the world and learning from the ancient cultures, from the people and through observing nature. I found a shared thread of wisdom and knowledge that streams like a river, connecting like tributaries, all religions and ancient traditions. The job of the troubadour is to strive to bring these essences alive in stories and songs to reawaken the magic and mystery of life, re-enchanting our world. The following accounts are a few fragments of this harper's journey through the ancient sites of the Land of Oc.

A Land of Heretics

'...the Grail is a living force, it will never die; it may indeed sink out of sight, and for centuries even, disappear ... but it will rise to the surface again and become once more a theme of vital importance....'

FROM RITUAL TO ROMANCE, *by Jessie L. Weston*

In the summer of 1987 I visited Southern France for the first time and spent three weeks in a friend's family farmhouse in Cahors in the region of Lot, site of an important Templar commandery during the medieval era. At that time, I had never heard of Templars or Cathars and was a travelling troubadour, making my way from South America and Britain, on to Egypt. During that short stay I sang to Black Madonnas, serenaded the stones in Neolithic circles and huts and explored the wonders of the beauty inside the earth in Magdalenian era grottos and their underground rivers. I was not yet aware of the tragic history of the many factions who inhabited this region, yet sensed a deep memory of multiple layers of poignant stories remaining in the land that was entirely overwhelming. That was the beginning of a long quest for threads of truth and wisdom resonating in Southern France and the sacred covenant that was formed by a people's love of freedom and freedom to love.

The various groups who have resided there have perennially been labelled heretics: Cathars, Templars, Jewish refugees, Kabbalists, gnostics, troubadours and more. The etymology of the word 'heretic', or *hérétique* in French, is from the Greek *hairetikos*, 'able to choose'. These groups were all labelled as heretics and yet, they were the ones who chose to be true to their authentic path, unwilling to compromise their values and succumb to the agendas of the ruling kings or the Church of Rome. Perhaps it is for this reason that so many people are drawn to study and understand these groups today. We all hunger for freedom in a world that has become severely incapacitated by its fascination with material success and power. The Languedoc has always been a refuge for the rebellious and the free-spirited.

Throughout history, the quest for beauty, love and truth has struggled to survive amid the quest for dominance and greed. During the medieval era, the dominant powers of church and state burned the last Templars. They burned thousands of Cathars, and they burned Joan of Arc, who tried to liberate her people from foreign rule. They even tried to ban the poetry and songs of the troubadours. But the spirit of truth would not be silenced and rose again and again, from the dust and ashes, rising from the half remembered promise patterned in the blood, held in the heart. Always they return, with the flame of hope for a better world filled with compassion, beauty and a song of love returning to the land.

Not only do we return, but we are stronger. Out of struggle and adversity, we give birth to something greater, more passion to adhere to our truth. Depth of soul can be born out of times of challenge and it is through the fight for survival that one is seasoned and ripened beyond what could have occurred in an environment of ease and docile comfort. The beginning of the first and second millennia were turning points, times of great change and chaos, such as our current entry into a new millennium, a New Earth and a return to Beauty.

Meeting of Two Troubadours in the Pyrenees

> 'The supreme goal of Catharism…. to disengage the divine essence that sleeps in the heart of matter.'
>
> THE GRAIL, *by Jean Markale*

After reading Walter Birks' THE TREASURE OF MONTSÉGUR in 2007, I felt a strong impulse to visit the Sabarthez caves and nearby châteaux said to be connected with the Cathars and with the grail mysteries. The Sabarthez region is a narrow valley of the Pyrenees with the Ariège River cascading abundant clear waters from the mountains above. The high walls of the canyon host voluminous caverns, some reaching ten kilometers or more in length. My intention was to somehow find the caves mentioned by Walter Birks and Antonin Gadal, but finding accommodation for that night was first on the list.

I parked the rental car in the little village of Ussat-les-Bains. Even the name of the village is fascinating, as numerous thermal spas in the region were developed by the Romans during the first and second centuries CE, during which time Romans practised adoration of Isis. Often there are clues to be found in the old names of sites and Ussat is phonetically similar to *Ausset, Iset*, her Egyptian name. The Coptic word for her is *Usat* and the Greco-Romans called her Isis.

As I walked through the village looking for a nice *chambre d'hôte*, I came to a strange sign saying, 'Maison de Flutes de Pan'. Not only did the place offer cheap rooms, but the owner apparently was a musician. I had heard Panpipes in the Andes, but not in the Pyrenees! Intrigued, I knocked on the door and Christian Koenig answered, a tall man with a deep and intense gaze, and it felt as if I was meeting a familiar old friend. With my scant French, about equal to his English skills, we discovered within the first ten minutes that we both played numerous instruments, including the troubadour harp. I was excited to learn that Christian was an expert in medieval Cathar and troubadour *chansons*. Through the universal language of music and after exchanging several songs, we agreed that he would guide me to a Cathar initiation cave that afternoon. I did not know at that time that Christian had inherited some of the texts and artefacts from Antonin Gadal, a man who was born in Ussat-les-Bains and dedicated his life to the study of the Cathars and the caves in the region. Certainly I had knocked on the right door!

Two images were impressed on my memory from that first meeting. In the stairway of Christian's home was a large pentagram carved in stone. I was to learn the following day that the Cathar initiation cave called Bethlehem is located on the hill directly opposite his home. Within the small double exit cave is a pentagonal shaped recess in the wall, just large enough for a human body with legs and arms extended to form a pentagram, similar to Da Vinci's Vitruvian Man. Also within the cave is a large rectangular altar stone, or sun stone, thought to have been used by ancient Celtic and Mithraic sun worshipping traditions. Several have been found in the Pyrenees region; one that I had visited is near Saint Michel de Cuxa near Mt Canigou and the other is at Rennes-le-Château.

The pentagram I noticed that day was the first of many to be discovered in the French churches and carved in the stones, and seemed to relate to an ancient stream of Hermetic knowledge that emerges in Templar, Cathar, gnostic and grail traditions. The pentagram is a shape associated with perfection, harmony, music and beauty. The Cathars called themselves the Pure and their 'priests' travelled in pairs, living a life of fasting and prayer. They ministered to the poor and healed the sick and sang in the ancient languages, continuing the traditions and practices of the first Christians, Essenes and Nazareans.

Cathar priests were both male and female and called *parfaits* or Perfects. In his book THE GRAIL, Jean Markale relates the quest for the grail in Wolfram von Eschenbach's epic 'Parzival' to the 'Purity that leads to perfection, the supreme goal of Catharism'. He continues that the grail ritual in *Parzival* is essentially Cathar and concerns an alchemical goal to 'disengage the divine essence that sleeps in the heart of matter. This is pure Catharism'.

The second thing in Christian's home that intrigued me was the Bible over the fireplace opened to the Gospel of John, which begins, 'In the beginning was the Word,' the sound of creation. This is the gospel which was used almost exclusively by the Cathars. Above the Bible was a piece of art portraying the resurrection mysteries and a caduceus within the Christed human. (A caduceus is the 'herald's staff' carried by Hermes and is depicted with two entwined serpents and wings. This image was used in ancient alchemy and is still the modern symbol for medicine and healing.) The Hermetic science of resurrection combining sacred music and Eastern purification practices used by ancient gnostics would become a central theme in my continuing quest and research.

I returned at the appointed hour for the promised visit to the grotto, but Christian was not yet finished with his day's work and the hours dragged on until it was twilight and soon to be very dark. I was quite concerned about navigating the mountain paths at night, not to mention the unknown twists and turns of a large cave. Finally he appeared with two miners' headlamps and said, 'Okay, let's go'. What did I get myself into this time? Yes, I had wanted to visit the Cathar initiation cave, but this was turning out to be my own initiation. I tried to walk without the headlamp bouncing too wildly, trying to focus the limited light on the narrow and steep path. As we ascended the mountain, keeping the light focused on the path became a metaphor for my life. I had always walked a razor's edge, choosing adventure over comfort as a modern troubadour. But more than once the quest took me dangerously close to the limits of human endurance.

Once inside the enormous cavern, we turned off our headlamps and were immersed in total darkness. I began seeing strange lights moving and had a strong feeling that we were not alone.

Christian played an old Cathar melody on his panpipes, which was haunting, and with the expanded acoustics of the large grotto, the song seemed to open a door between dimensions of time. Then I played and sang the Aramaic Lord's Prayer and again sensed the spirit of the place and the people who had made this a place of refuge grow more present and palpable. Aramaic was called the language of the angels and was spoken by Jesus and his followers, and most likely by Cathars when saying this ancient prayer. A phrase kept singing within me during that experience in the dark cave, 'Heart of the dove, the way of love.' Perhaps like Saint John says in his gospel, *Lux lucet in tenebris*, 'the light shines in the darkness'.

'Penetrate to the caves, for in the cave you will find the secret of a brotherhood.... He would have to work in the dark with only the light of his own spirit.... Treasure lies in wisdom and love, remember.'

September 29, 1937, White Eagle, quoted in THE TREASURE OF MONTSÉGUR, *by Walter Birks and R. A. Gilbert.*

Montréal de Sos—Grail Castle

On a subsequent visit to the Ariège and Ussat-les-Bains, Christian suggested that we visit the ruins of Montréal-de-Sos, a 'Grail Castle'. The valley of Vicdessos is south-west of Tarascon-sur-Ariège and leads into the Pyrenees; there is still a path at the end of the valley in use for thousands of years that is travelled by modern pilgrims as well as smugglers passing between Spain and France. The fortification château of Montréal de Sos was built in the twelfth century within the region and rule of Raymond-Roger, Count of Foix. The Count was sympathetic to the Templar and Cathar cause and his wife ultimately became a member of the Cathar church.

Raymond's sister was Esclarmonde, meaning 'light of the world', and one of the greatest Cathar priests. She was responsible for the rebuilding of Montségur and records tell us that she received the Cathar sacrament, the *consolamentum*, to become a *parfait* or Perfect in 1204 AD. In a local legend, it is said that Esclarmonde took the form of a dove in order to carry the Holy Grail to safety during the Cathar persecution at Montségur. After climbing to the top of the ruins on my first visit to Montségur, I felt the presence of a great white bird wrapping its wings around our small circle of pilgrims as we were chanting softly ... perhaps an imprinted memory held within the stones of the château.

Driving to Montréal-de-Sos through the narrow winding valley road from Tarascon-sur-Ariège toward Vicdessos, the opening to the extensive caverns of Niaux can be seen on the left. Niaux is a Paleolithic era cavern that hosts paintings of bison, horses, auroch, ibex and fish, more than twelve thousand years old. One passes the medieval château ruins of Miglos and the nearby Neolithic dolmen called Sem. (Interestingly, Sem was the name of the Egyptian priests who performed rituals to Osiris and also one of the sons of Noah).

What is in a name? If one looks at the etymology of names of ancient places, especially in areas that host a concentrated number of sacred sites, the name can provide clues about the nature of the place. The phonetic resonance of a word tends to carry more meaning than just the spelling, as this can change dramatically in a short time. The sound of a name can also identify essential qualities of the thing or place named.

'Mithraic liturgy contained magical formulas held to be 'root-sounds' … every object is related to a subtle sound which, when uttered, can destroy, modify or bring into being the corresponding object.'

MANTRAS: SACRED WORDS OF POWER *by John Blofeld*

One of my Tibetan teachers once said that in a language predating Sanskrit, Hebrew, Sumerian and Egyptian languages, there was no separation between the sound and the root resonance of that to which it referred. (This reminds us of modern physics and string theory.) When a word was uttered, the material or state which related to that resonance was called forth. This is the same science practised in the relationship between a *mantra* (a combination of *bija* seed syllables) and its corresponding shape or design, called in Sanskrit *yantra*. This sound science was practised by Thoth-Hermes and Isis, both of whom ruled over Egyptian temple music and chant.

From the base of the medieval château of Montréal, the easiest access is through one of the short passage caves that open just below the fortification. On the day that Christian Koenig and I arrived, there was an archeological excavation in process. I asked what sorts of things they were finding and the men replied that there were pottery fragments, various knights' gear, and coins dating to the mediaeval era, when the Knights Templar were active in this region.

From the top of this castle ruin, one can see Canigou, the highest peak of the Pyrenees in this area. Canigou has mysterious legends of secret Cabalistic groups from Spain, including Salvador Dali, performing rituals and chant to 'call down the grail'. Christian led the way down to a small initiation cave on the eastern slope of the hill beneath the château. There he pointed out an unusual painting on the stone wall depicting what looked like six red crosses, a red lance or dagger, a red tool or paddle/oar, a solar disc, and a large rectangular platter with six drops of blood. The platter, dagger and drops of blood are common grail themes and are represented in the procession at the Grail Castle in Wolfram von Eschenbach's epic of the grail, 'Parzival'.

Déodat Roché, considered to be the last Cathar 'pope', believed the most important site for the Cathars was Montréal de Sos and compared it to the grail castle Montsalvesch (Mount Salvation) mentioned in Wolfram's *Parzival*. When Roché was shown a painting of the scene depicted on the cave wall of Montréal, he recognized it as being identical with an illustration found in a manuscript of the thirteenth century, 'La Queste del Saint Graal' edited by Albert Pauphilet (Paris, 1923). Interestingly, there is a triangular alignment in the Vicdessos valley formed between the ruins of Montréal de Sos, the Neolithic dolmen Sem and a peak named Col de Grail.

A Time for Burning—A Time to Return

Al cap dels sèt cent ans, verdejara lo laurèl.
(The laurel will flourish again in seven hundred years)

This prophecy was said to have been given by a Cathar *Parfait* in the thirteenth century. Seven centuries after the 1244 massacre at Montségur, many souls would be reborn to take up the torch and return to this land called Languedoc, to find the fragments of the Cathar church of love, the peaceful way of the dove.

In 2006 I rented a flat in Rennes-le-Château right next to the Magdalene Chapel. The apartment shared a stone wall with the Magdalene grotto and garden and I soon became the self-appointed gardener and caretaker. Shortly after my arrival, I met Henry Lincoln – while I was playing my troubadour harp in the village restaurant, which was run at that time by Rennes researcher and author Jean-Luc Robin. Over the ensuing years, Henry and I have developed a fond friendship.

Most readers will know of Henry from his co-authored book, THE HOLY BLOOD AND THE HOLY GRAIL, although if you mention it to him, he will now insist, 'it's nothing more than an hypothesis'. But the book certainly sparked a marked resurgence of interest in the Magdalene mystery, the grail quest and Rennes-le-Château. These days, the village is filled with tourists, seekers and wishful diggers for treasure, but more than this, it is a place for dreaming and remembering, a meeting place for writers, researchers and pilgrims on the grail trail.

In the 1970s, Henry produced with the BBC and TV2 Danmark a series of films and documentaries, on the Cathars, Nostradamus, Egypt and

Rennes-le-Château. Since 1982, when THE HOLY BLOOD AND THE HOLY GRAIL was first published, Henry has written KEY TO THE SACRED PATTERN and THE HOLY PLACE, in which he presents his discovery of a perfect pentagram in the Rennes-le-Château landscape. It is quite extraordinary, as the measurements are exact, identifying five Templar sites and high points in the landscape. The pentagram embodies the divine harmonic proportion, sometimes called the Golden Section. Henry describes this region as a place where Venus' perfect harmony and beauty touch the earth as Mary Magdalene.

These sites forming a pentagram lie right in the heart of Cathar country and nearby is one of Henry's favorite places, Montségur – the last stronghold of the Cathars and the site of the burning in 1244 AD of hundreds of 'the pure'. In KEY TO THE SACRED PATTERN, Henry compares Montségur to Masada in Israel, where another persecuted people chose to perish rather than renounce their faith. He writes there:

'Even today, as one walks the rocky pathway, it is impossible not to sense the presence of those two hundred brave souls who made the bitter choice. For them, the hideous torture of the flames was less painful than abjuring their beliefs. Hand in hand and singing, they walked that fearsome road into Eternity.

'Each time I tread those stones, I am aware that I am filling the space of a certainty and a strength of faith which is all but incomprehensible in our more 'enlightened' age. But across the centuries, the flame still burns at Montségur and the martyrs have not been forgotten.'

In 1972, Henry Lincoln was on location at the high mountain fortress of Montségur to film a BBC Chronicle documentary on the Cathars and the fateful burning of the faithful; those who chose to walk into the flames rather than forsake their beliefs. On the final day of filming, Henry stood in the doorway of the great château describing how the Cathars descended the path leading to the pyre two by two and singing.

A few days after the BBC crew had returned to London, Henry received a frantic phone call from the director, saying that they needed to return to Montségur immediately to do a re-shoot. None of the footage from the last scene was usable, as during Henry's scene describing the Cathar procession to the fire, he appeared to be surrounded by flames. I asked Henry if the BBC had kept any of this discarded film, but sadly it had been destroyed. What a shame that no one at the studio had a sense of the significance of that strange footage!

Few people know another side of Henry, that he is a troubadour at heart – and has written poetry since childhood. The poem overleaf, 'There Is A Time For Burning', is one Henry wrote in 1972. He argues that it was not inspired by the Cathar story, but by the simple turning of the seasons in rural England. I wonder, though, how much of it springs from another time and a deep memory impressed upon the soul.

During his research of the Cathar history and legacy for his first BBC 'Chronicle' film, Henry visited the home of Déodat Roché, known as 'the last Pope of the Cathars'. Roché was a dedicated researcher and sincere believer in the lofty ideals of Catharism. In his quest for spiritual truth, Déodat had studied Buddhism, Gnosticism, Anthroposophy, Manichaeism, and vegetarianism, but after all of these 'isms' Roché settled on Catharism as the way that best fitted his deep sensibilities and values. He wrote,

> 'Before Christ, who was at its Dawning, Catharism had shone its light upon the Brahmans of India, the Magi of Persia, the Essenes of Judea and in Greece upon Pythagoras and Plato.'

Roché was one hundred years young when Henry last visited him in 1977 at his home in Arques, near Rennes-le-Château. Recently I asked Henry what he could remember of those meetings with Roché. As we sat in Henry's garden above the thermal spa village of Rennes-les-Bains on a hot summer's afternoon, he shared with me the following:

> 'Roché was very quiet and self-contained, which made him curiously powerful. His tiniest gesture became incredibly potent. Much of the time we just sat, enjoying one another's presence. A very tall, thin, yet distinguished-looking man, he looked rather other-worldly, translucent as if he was ordained with a special quality of light.

> 'He told me that the Cathars preferred to hold their services or rites in the open air, in nature and not in enclosed spaces or churches. He spoke of the *parfaits*' laying-on of hands for healing and how they believed that the source of their curative gifts resided in the level of spirit and came from God, not the physical realm.'

Henry explained that although people assume that the Cathars disappeared in 1244 with the fall of Montségur, there are still remnants of Cathar families throughout this region and the traditions were handed down throughout the centuries. For example, the family Bonzom in Quillan is a homophone of the French word *bonshommes*, the good men of the Cathar way. And another Cathar name is rue Marty in the nearby town of Couiza.

There is a Time for Burning

There is a time for Burning.
The Earth yields up its life
And when the Gathering has borne all away
And nothing remains but what seems dead and useless
Then....

Then the Earth catches fire
Blazing the fierceness of its cleansing time
Into the sky
Purging
Purging the dead, decaying-seeming dross
To purest, flame-burning, self-consuming ash
The better to prepare for newness after sleep.

There is a time for Burning.
A man's soul also yields up its Breath
Year after year in blind unknowing

There is a time for Burning.
Somehow – some time – some souls
Ignite to a joy of flame gold life.

There is a time for Burning.
But first some hand must strike the spark,
Or else the time may slip.

There is a time for Burning.
Ah! There is Blessing in the fire
For those who know the burning
For those who know the meaning in the flame.

There is a time for Burning.
There is a time...
There is a Time.

                                                Henry Lincoln

Like Henry and many other lovers of Occitan Catharism, Roché was also a troubadour poet:

La Chanson du Silence

Come, we shall hear this eventide the Song of Silence
The song which begins
When, in the night, the song of the nightingale draws to its close;
The song which is heard with the gentle growing of the grass,
The song of the living waters,
Which rest, for a moment, against the reed's reflexion;
The song of the branch
Which trembles and which dances
When freed from the loving burden of a bird;
The secret song cradling the blue-tinged shadow
Of the lily, fading from its springtime promise,
And awaiting, ere it flowers, for a sign from the bright azure sky.

'Réalmont: Summer 1941'. English translation by Henry Lincoln, 2012

A Visit to the Déodat Roché Museum

'Throughout my life, I have never ceased to search for a religion of faith and of justice and with no dogma. For me, it is the spirituality of Catharism which comes closest to this natural religion.'

Déodat Roché

In June of 2012, Henry and I visited the Déodat Roché Museum in Arques, a little village in the Aude *Département* of the Languedoc, and where Roché began and ended his centurion years. After much prodding, I finally persuaded Henry to venture into this self-imposed 'forbidden territory'. He was quite upset that the new museum had totally destroyed the character of Roché's lovely village home and turned it into a sterile, modern edifice. Once inside though, Henry was impressed with the library of Roché's books and articles and found the gallery of photographs of him brought back fond memories of their visits together.

We found ourselves perusing the Cathar Bible, which the Cathars had translated into their own Occitan language. It was illustrated with lovely medieval images and one that caught our eye was a large red fish. The caption under the copy of the bible indicated it was from the *Rituel Cathare de Lyon* in the Bibliotheque Municipale de Lyon. Next, Henry spotted something unusual inscribed underneath a carved cross which was perhaps a tombstone or marker stone of a Cathar family. He said the lines formed the Egyptian hieroglyphs *nefer*, meaning God, and *meri*, meaning 'beloved', and so – 'Beloved of God'.

These hieroglyphs were surrounding a glyph that looked like a fish … possible clues to the Cathar awareness of Jesus' knowledge received from his time in Egypt's temples? I remembered Henry telling me about that moment so many years ago when he had a first meeting with Michael Baigent and Richard Leigh in the garden of his home in the English countryside. They were discussing their respective research on the Rennes-le-Château mystery and the possibility of a royal bloodline from the House of David. During this meeting, Henry had said, 'There is something 'fishy' going on here'. That moment and statement was the seed which would grow into the pivotal book in this modern grail quest, THE HOLY BLOOD AND THE HOLY GRAIL.

Images of various other artifacts in the Roché Museum included a metal pentagon and a twelfth-century stone 'colombe' or dove. There are many references to the pentagram being a significant symbol in Catharism. Firstly, that it represents perfection, the goal of the Pure Ones. The pentagram embodies the Divine Proportion, sometimes called the Golden Section. This is the proportion found in the graceful spiralling forms of nature, the harmonics of music and is basically the principle of beauty within all of creation. The pentagram is also a reference to the Hermetic wisdom of Egypt and embraced by Platonists and Pythagoreans and the Kabbalists. Perfection as it refers to one's spiritual path was often called The Way, and was termed by Hermes the path of initiation, the Ancient Road, according to Victoria LePage in her book MYSTERIES OF THE BRIDECHAMBER.

Elizabeth Van Buren speaks about the import of the pentagram in her book THE SIGN OF THE DOVE:

'The Gnostics taught that the pentagram was the "Passport to the Kingdom of Light".'

In the Roché museum there was a small stone carving of a white dove, said to have been found at Montségur. We often see the dove representing Holy Spirit, or *ruach* in Hebrew, descending in the Baptism, bathing the initiate in pure light and in the waters of the spirit. The dove is associated with Sophia, purity and the feminine wisdom. In ancient Sumerian the word for dove is *Hu*. The Egyptian hieroglyph *Hu* is depicted as a dove and *Iahu* is listed as a name for Isis in Deimel's Akkadian-Sumerian Glossary. *Ia Hu* is a Sumerian phrase meaning 'exalted dove'.

> 'The Moon-goddess of Asiatic Palestine was worshipped with doves, like her counterparts of Egyptian Thebes, Dodona, Hierapolis, Crete and Cyprus... *Ia-Hu* stands for the Moon-goddess as ruler of the whole course of the solar year.'
>
> THE WHITE GODDESS *by Robert Graves*

The dove has a long association through many eons and cultures with the spirit of purity and love. Yona or Ionah, also meaning dove, is also the name Jonah or Ionnes, John. We can relate the dove to John, and perhaps for the Cathar, the secret *Book of John*. Many legends speak of the lost treasure of Montségur that was carried over the mountains to the grottos or châteaux of the Sabarthez. Some say the precious treasure was a lost gospel of Saint John.

Château de Lordat and Visions of John

> 'Magdalene and John the Virgin will tower over all my disciples and all men who shall receive the mysteries.'
>
> *Pistis Sophia*

The process of unravelling the tangled mass of broken threads that history has left us often requires a visionary view, to see the patterns and to find the essence of truth waiting just beneath the surface. Often when visiting a place for the first time, one will receive an impression or sense of the energies there, which obviously will be mostly subjective and coloured by our own beliefs and agendas. But sometimes there is an insight that is greater than one's self and can be sensed in the site as an imprint reaching through time, left 'for those with eyes to see and ears to hear'.

On my first visit to the Castle of Lordat, I had a distinct vision of what I call the Holy Family travelling from Tarascon-sur-Rhône to the western Tarascon on the great Ariège River in the Pyrenees. This river lies at the bottom of a steep and narrow valley with sheer mountain faces on either side, dotted with countless caves, some weaving through the mountains for many miles. These are the grottos well known to Cathars, centuries earlier to the Visigoths and stretching through time through the Romans, Greeks, Phoenicians, Mithraic sun cults and further back to Celtic, Neolithic and Paleolithic peoples.

After the crucifixion, the members of Jesus' family and inner circle of disciples were in danger of being persecuted and fled from Palestine. According to legend they came to the shores of France in a boat without sails or oars and there is an old tradition in Europe that said that travelling in a boat without oars would signify that the boat was actually being guided by God and would be carrying a royal bloodline or the inheritors of a kingdom. Mary Magdalene, Mary Salome, Mary Jacobe, John / Lazarus, Martha and Sarah were said to be on that boat and settled in the region now generally know as Provence, in Marseilles, Arles and up the Rhone River to Tarascon. And if Jesus was married to Mary Magdalene, John-Lazarus would be his brother-in-law and Martha, his sister-in-law.

In a vision during my first visit to Provence, I saw the Roman presence near Marseilles becoming threatening to the Holy Family, who had become, in effect, Jewish refugees. I saw them retreating further west into the Pyrenees, where they could rest in relative safety. Looking East from the Château of Lordat, past the Pic de St-Barthélémy towards the Cathar castle of Montségur, I could imagine the family of Jesus walking through these rugged mountain passes: Mary Magdalene, Martha, John Lazarus and others. Ultimately it would be the Cathars who used the same paths to move between the mountain fortresses. These have been places of refuge throughout the centuries, wild and barely accessible, where people could live and practise for a time, before the next threat to their safety arose.

As I sat one afternoon at the Château de Lordat in deep contemplation, I could hear a ringing in the air, like thousands of tiny bells. I perceived the light within growing more intense and heard a voice of one named John. He said that yes, the memory of his presence was there at Lordat and the surrounding region, but that he could be called upon anywhere and was not limited to any particular place. 'Wherever you are, whenever you ask, I am there', I heard. And, 'Be still, be empty – breathe deeply and drink this eternal light and allow your cup to be filled.' I sensed the imprint of light and love that John and the Holy Family had left in the land.

'He is grace-giving grace, not because he possesses it, but because he gives the immeasurable, incomprehensible light.'

Secret Book of John, Nag Hammadi Library, translated by Frederik Wisse

Two villages near Lordat are named Luzenac (*luz* meaning light) and Lassur (*Lassare* is French for Lazarus) or 'light of Lazarus'? And a hill next to the nearby château of Montréal-de-Sos, is called Col de Grail. Biblical and gnostic texts tell us of the house at Bethany near Jerusalem, where Jesus often visited the family of Mary Magdalene, Martha and John-Lazarus. In the depictions of John and Magdalene across Europe and beyond, they are the ones shown holding a cup, or grail vessel, guardians of a secret tradition.

Lestelle-Betharram—Star of the High House

> 'Glance at the sun. See the moon and the stars…
> All nature is at the disposal of humankind.
> We are to work with it.
> For without it we cannot survive.'
>
> *Hildegard von Bingen*

On the river Gave de Pau, nestled in the rugged Pyrenees of France, there is a village called Lestelle-Betharram. Although it is only fifteen kilometers from the famous pilgrims' destination of Lourdes, it is not as well-known. However, during the seventeenth and eighteenth centuries it was one of the most popular pilgrimage sites in Europe. During the medieval era, pilgrims would stop at this ancient sanctuary as a station on the Camino de Compostella and knights returning from their campaigns against the Moors in Spain would rest here to pay homage to Our Lady. The name of the village is intriguing, *Lestelle*, or *l'estelle*, meaning 'the star' in old French, from the Latin *stella*; *center* means house in Hebrew; *arram* is a Hebrew word meaning high or elevated, hence 'Star of the High House'.

The local church of Our Lady of Betharram was built to honour her numerous visitations over the centuries and is overlooking the river where she appeared. Entering the church one is greeted by a large painting of Mary Magdalene anointing the feet of Jesus with her vase of spikenard. Both Jesus and a male disciple are pointing at her as 'The One who knew the All'. The painting shows Magdalene as one who truly understood the inner mysteries:

> 'Mariham, Mariham, the beloved … speak in boldness, because thou art she whose heart stretches toward the Kingdom of the heavens … you who will give light upon everything in accuracy and in exactness.'
>
> *Pistis Sophia*

Could Lestelle-Betharram also hint at 'Star of Bethany'? As mentioned earlier, the home of Mary Magdalene and her brother John-Lazarus was in Bethany; both Mary and John are traditionally portrayed with grail vessels – John with a cup, often with a snake, and Mary with her jar or vase of un-guents for the Messianic anointing ritual. The cup is the container which holds the light of initiation and I propose that they were at the centre of those who were guardians of the secrets of ascension and resurrection.

Opposite and facing this painting of the anointing of Jesus by Magda-lene is a large painted sculpture of Saint John holding a cup with a snake coiled around the rim. John is standing on the eagle, the other symbol normally associated with him. The assumed authors of the other three synoptic gospels of Matthew, Mark and Luke are represented by the hu-man, the lion and the bull respectively. John's is the gospel that stands out as unique among them and begins with the words *In Principio Erat Verbum*, 'In the Beginning was the Word', indicating a knowledge of sound science and the creative power of resonance. The serpent grail held by John is an alchemical symbol of the science of ascension and John-Lazarus was the one who received the resurrection mysteries teaching from Yeshua as recorded in the 'Secret Gospel of Mark'. John's symbols of the eagle and the serpent represent the above and below, sky and earth, indicating the Hermetic 'As Above, So Below' tradition.

Cathar researcher and author Walter Birks was stationed in Syria during the Second World War and appointed to gather intelligence in the region (the old name for Syria is *Arram*). Birks became friends with a leader of the mysteri-ous Nosairi sect. Numerous scholars have written that the Nosairis are a mys-tical branch of pure Christianity, and may still practise the ritual of drinking the light from the chalice, the cup of John. The Nosairi leader confided with Walter that when a worshipper takes the cup, he says, 'I drink to the Light'.

> 'The grail you speak of is a symbol and it stands for the doctrine which
> Christ taught to John the Beloved alone. We have it still.'
>
> THE TREASURE OF MONTSÉGUR, *Walter Birks and R. A. Gilbert.*

For Walter Birks, this information connected the puzzle pieces of his years of travels and research of Catharism with the first Christians. It seems likely that the Nosairi tradition of Syria must have been related to the early Christian Nazoreans or Nassenes, a first century Gnostic group, said to honour the ancient serpent wisdom. Having also travelled the world over several decades as a troubadour, I had noticed that many of the cultures I observed used a similar linguistic in the root syllable *NA* and its meaning of serpent, wisdom or 'godliness'.

The Hebrew word for snake is *na'asch*; Sanskrit *nagas* are serpent wisdom deities; *nadi* in Sanskrit is the serpent path of the human chakra system; in Mayan, *Na Chan* means House of the Serpent, the old name for the pyramid-temple city of Palenque; in Yaqui language (a Mesoamerican tribe), *nagual* is the term for shaman, wisdom keeper; *Nana* or *Inanna* is the ancient Sumerian Mother Goddess; the Egyptian hieroglyph for the 'N' sound is a wave form like the serpent path (even though it signifies water); the Koran lists *Naz'ra* as the Arabic name for early Christians; a Gnostic sect during the time of Jesus were called Naassenes who honored Sophia, the Mother of Wisdom; and in John's Gospel, when the temple police in Jerusalem were looking for Jesus, they demanded, 'Where is the Nazorean'?

'And as Moses lifted up the serpent in the wilderness, even so must the Son of man be lifted up.' (John 3 : 14)

When seen from a visionary perspective as a matrix of related patterns, a story woven through time begins to reveal itself. The serpent glyph as depicted in Native American petroglyphs is an undulating line, and also symbolizes energy movement, water, wisdom, *kundalini* (yoga of inner resurrection), sound waves, and the sign for the current Age of Aquarius.

Some of the basic practices used to purify the body and mind, and common to all these 'Serpent Wisdom' cultures, were various forms of meditation, chant, sacred music, yoga or other specific movements, breathing exercises, fasting, sun gazing: a striving to live in balance and harmony with the 'Above and Below' of heavenly and earthly cycles.

These ancient cultures were the true guardians of the Grail and the inner mystery traditions, who knew the ways to awaken humanity from the dark cave of unconsciousness to their divine light essence, not denying the sometimes dark and dense journey through matter, but embracing the gifts of life's lessons and navigating one's way through consciously as a seed makes its way through dark soil toward the sun.

'Deliver us from these human forms and re-clothe us in light among the stars.'

Syrian Nosairi prayer, in THE TREASURE OF MONTSÉGUR *by Walter Birks and R. A. Gilbert.*

This is the Cathar Way, the path to perfection, the journey of purification and the Cathar Perfect's *con-sol-amentum*, 'with the sun in the mind'.

This is the path of the Egyptian initiate depicted by the cobra, *Ureaus* of awakening at the third eye, signifying mastery of the serpent movement within the body, mind and spirit. This is the illumination of *Re-Herakhty,* Horus of the Solar Horizon, as it appears at the brow of the adept in the dawning of wisdom. This is the truth of Thoth and Ma'at, who taught in Egypt that by continual singing of harmonious chants, humans grew like unto the Gods. This is the Great Work of alchemy symbolized by the unity of the Ouroboros snake eating its own tail. It is the above and the below, becoming One of Thoth-Hermes. This is the wisdom path of Sophia.

Now is the time of revelation of John's message, the time of the return of the troubadours, the return of the path of the heart and the wisdom that liberates. This is the time to remember our original intention and the time for the re-enchantment of our world.

Postscript, a Postcard from Paradise:

Dear Children,
Wish you were here.
Here we are all one.
Tree, Adam, Eve, Snake

Medhananda 'Archetypes of Liberation'

WALKING THE CATHAR WAY

REVD JOHN N. MERRILL

The best way to get to know Cathar country is to walk it! John Merrill walked the Sentier Cathare *East–West in the autumn of 2011 and plans next to tackle the* Chemin des Bonshommes *North–South in autumn 2012.*

THE *SENTIER Cathare*, or Cathar Way, stretches from near Narbonne on the Mediterranean to Foix in the Pyrenees and is a 250 km (150-mile) historical trail linking together some eleven castles where, in the thirteenth century, the Cathars were besieged and burnt at the stake. Some say this was the perfect heresy, others that they followed the true Christian faith. Their 'religion' spread from Turkey through to Italy and reached their major stronghold in the Languedoc region of France. They had their own hierarchy of perfects and bishops which threatened the Roman Catholic church. As a result, the Pope set up an Inquisition and an army led by Simon de Montfort, and spent forty years destroying their castles and killing them all. The King of France was also involved, as without intervention he had no power in this part of the country. The Cathars' story is one of suppressed freedom and man's inhumanity to man.

The route of the *Sentier Cathare* crosses the terrain where they lived and worshipped. Today the locals are ashamed of what happened six centuries ago and it is an area where birds do not sing.

When, once, I walked across Europe and all the Alps and the Pyrenees, I did not walk through this area. Something held me back. But having been

John has walked 205,000 miles and worn out 117 pairs of boots. This connection to Mother Earth and the sacredness of the landscape developed a deep spiritual understanding, and his connection to the Divine. He has never been lost, injured, or come to any harm … he has been guided. At the age of 65 he answered his inner voice, and trained to be an Interfaith Minister. He believes in looking at the whole and that is the reason he embraces and honours all faiths: all have their own beauty. *For John's photos, see colour section, p. 1.*

part of a Cathar discussion group in the Spring of 2011, and learning there was a waymarked path, I resolved to walk it and see at first hand where this ruthless campaign was waged. I decided on mid-September to start off, when it would it be warm and the campsites and the gites-d'étape would still be open. Gites are like former youth hostels, with bunk beds, showers and a fully-equipped kitchen. I flew from London Stansted to Carcassonne, which is today a complete walled town, once the home of the Trencavel family, leading supporters of the Cathars. The path doesn't pass through Carcassonne, but I could catch the train from here to Narbonne and on to Porto de Nouvelle where it begins, at the railway station. As I stepped out of the entrance there was my first of a long succession of blue and yellow blazes, which I would follow for the next ten days. The last two days, to Foix, were in another French region, and there the path is marked with red and white stripes.

A mile along the trail in the town I came to my first municipal campground and camped, it being early evening. I walked down to the sea later for a meal, and watched a full moon rise from the Mediterranean. I bought some food in the morning and set off on what is described as the hardest day: 29 km (18 miles) and 600 m of ascent. On it you cross four limestone plateaux and pass two wind farms. The path was well marked and defined but the heat was intense, 30°C. By mid-morning it was hot. I took it easy. I walked for ten hours, though, through to Durban Corbières, arriving at another municipal campground at 6.30 pm. I just had time to pitch the tent and get to the supermarket, which closed at 7.00 pm. Later I sat at a picnic table, the only camper there, and ate a full meal with the obligatory baguette and bottle of red wine.

The following day was equally hot and equally long, to Tuchan. As I walked, I passed many vineyards bursting with ripe grapes. Some were being picked by hand while other vineyards had a machine that went over the vines to get the grapes. Nearing Tuchan I came to my first Cathar castle – the Château d'Aguilar. Along the route, the path passes beneath each one in turn, and you have to leave the path and ascend 150 m or more to view the ruins. Usually you have to pay an entrance fee; I could leave my pack at the ticket office for the ascent. At Tuchan, I stayed in a cafe with rooms, and was given an unusual meal of a chicken leg in a bowl of peas!

The next day, to Duilhac-sous-Peyrepertuse, brought me first to Padern and a castle, but not one associated with the Cathars. Then began an ascent, passing the remains of Molhet Priory, to the Roc de Mouillet where there is a shrine. On the summit was a luxurious armchair. Here I sat in unbelievable comfort and admired the mountainous view!

Next was a long hot crossing to the base of Quéribus Castle, one of the most famous Cathar castles. Perched on a rock pinnacle, the castle was the last Cathar stronghold to surrender, in 1255. The ruins are well preserved and there is, surprisingly, a large amount of room. I pressed on later, with a steep descent to Duilhac and the town-run gite-d'étape, on the way passing an épicerie for food. I was the only occupant.

The following day, to Prugnanes, I considered the hardest, though it was only 17.5 km and reputedly 4½ hours of walking. But the guide was wrong in giving it 650m of ascent. It was more than double that, for instead of just ascending Pla de Brezou, and following a descending path down towards the famous limestone Galamus Gorge, you ascended through rugged mountains; the route had been changed! Shortly after leaving I passed the next castle – Peyrepertuse. This is a remarkable fortress which surrendered in 1240. The campsite in the gorge was closed – only open in July and August – and I pressed on to Prugnanes and a *gîte*, but no shop.

There is a variant of the route through the gorge, which has traffic, but you miss two castles, so I kept to the main path. The weather was now cooler, about 22°C, being in the mountains, as I walked onto the smaller and traffic-free St-Jaume Gorge. At the end were the two Fenouillet Castles, which had free access. Then a long ascent to Aigues-Bonnes began, and a long descent to the stage end at Puylaurens. Above was the next castle, but part of the next day's route. As there are no facilities at Puylaurens, I walked a kilometre down the road to Lapradelle. But, being Sunday, the shop was shut and the restaurant closed. Fortunately there was a *chambres-d'hôte* – bed and breakfast – and they obligingly cooked me a meal and gave me a bottle of wine, moments after arriving, to help me relax!

The morning brought the ascent to Puylaurens Castle, which wasn't open, but I walked through, like a couple ahead of me, to view the site. Here some of the Cathars went after the surrender of Montségur in 1244. It is well fortified and in a lofty position. The path then began a long ascent before descending to the attractive village of Axat and the River Aude. Fortunately the shop was still open and I bought food and sat by the flowing river. Then I continued on to Quirbajou, the end of the stage, which has no shop, but a *gîte*.

The early part of the next day, to Puivert, was through forest, with cool and shady walking to Coudons. Then I continued to Nébias and its fountain marking the watershed (dividing line) between the Atlantic and Mediterranean. I restocked on food, and continued with more ascent and descent to Puivert and its castle and campsite. The castle was taken after just three days in 1210.

The next stage, to Espezel, runs north to south unlike all the others, which run east to west. It was unusual too in that I crossed two flat farm-land areas, and here was a popular base for the French Resistance during the Second World War. And at 17 km it was an easy day with no castles! The following day was also quite short at 20 km but with more than 500m of ascent to reach the gite at Comus.

Again there was no shop: I had to carry all that I needed for two days. On the way I ascended to the Pas de l'Ours which, at 1352m, was the high-est point of the route. These two days were a nice breathing space before the climax of the expedition.

The day's route from Comus to Montségur is supposed to be a short one, only 15 km, but there is one long spectacular descent of the Frau Gorge (Gorges de la Frau), whose limestone sides rise up 1,000 feet or more. This is followed by a long ascent to Montségur. But it is all worth it, for there is camping, a shop, restaurants and a gite in Montségur. I stayed in the latter and caught the small shop before they closed for a week.

Above the medieval village is the castle of Montségur, the Cathars' nemesis. Here after a prolonged siege, in 1244, some two hundred perfects surrendered and were burnt at the stake below the castle. A monument marks the site (see the photograph in the colour section). I reached the castle in the morning and viewed its remoteness and steep cliffs. As many as five hundred lived in the castle and outside in homes built on the steep limestone precipice. Food and water were a constant problem. One can only marvel at the tenacity, faith and dedication of the Cathars – to live here despite the tragedy that was unfolding around them.

The penultimate day, a relatively short one, was to Roquefixade, a de-lightful unspoilt village, with a superb gite and a lofty Cathar castle above. Now I was following the red and white blazes of the Midi-Pyrenées region, first to Montferrier and its flowing river. Other walkers were at the shop here, as several routes pass through this point. Also a hiker with a donkey carrying his gear. I pressed on to Roquefixade.

The final day, first to the Château de Roquefixade in the early morning, with views to the neighbouring mountains of the Pyrenees and the valley, covered in silky mist. Then on along a fine ridge in beech woodland, where I disturbed a military manoeuvre. All the participants were dressed in camouflage gear and shouldering automatic rifles.

Half an hour later, the long descent to Foix began. After two hours I was in the Youth Hostel, with a fine view towards the castle: journey's end. In the evening I went to the abbey church and attended Mass, although it was in French I could understand it. I needed to say thank you for the walk.

In the morning I explored the castle that has changed little over the centuries and was a major player in the Cathar story. Then onto the train to Toulouse – which is again a major site of the Cathar story, with the Count of Toulouse trying to be friends with the King, Pope and Cathars. He eventually lost his land and was excommunicated. I spent three hours seeing the cathedral and the Cathar sights.

Toulouse is also on the southern French route to Santiago de Compostella. Running through the city is the Canal du Midi; it passes through Carcassonne, and when I arrived there later in the day, I camped beside it for my last night. The next day I caught the plane back to Stansted. As with all walks I learnt and saw a lot, but much remains to be explored, including the several other routes that I crossed. As one walk ends another comes into the frame!

As I sat beside the Canal du Midi on my last night, I asked myself a question. 'Now that you have seen where the Cathars lived, what has it meant to you?'

I was very glad that I been and walked through the area and seen at first hand where they lived and where history was made. I felt I had come to know them in a small way and that I had made a deep connection to a former life. As I mentioned at the beginning, I felt resistance to walk through the area on my long European Alpine walk. I still experienced a strong resistance as I did this walk: in fact I was amazed how badly I walked. At first I thought I was past it, now in my sixties – too old to ascend and descend mountain paths. But no, this was not correct: the legacy of the land and former life were acting as buffers to my progress. It wasn't until Montségur that I came alive; perhaps I was home? I know this now, having recently walked the Camino di Assisi, where nothing held me back and after each day I was not tired.

The more I walked this trail, the more I wanted to know about the

Cathars. I could only admire their lofty castles, which defended their faith: in many ways 'cathedrals in the skies'. I appreciated Cathar devotion and felt that their eradication had deprived the world of deep knowledge and wisdom. There must have been many grains of truth in their understanding, and in their appreciation of St John's Gospel, which they always carried. They had no churches but carried out their services in people's homes and in the fields. A simple but powerful natural faith without the trappings, ritual and glamour of the Catholics.

Of all the places I saw and walked, Montségur was the most sombre and astonishing place. Putting aside the terrible slaughter below the castle, as I wandered around the ruins and saw the lean-to shelters the besieged inhabitants had made over the steep drop, I could only admire their strength and courage to fight for what they believed in. Little remains of their own records, and most of what we know of the Cathars is gleaned from the Inquisition records. They are simply an enigma, and part of me wants to know more – a lot more. Since the walk I have read many more books about them, and I am still trying to analyse what I have learnt.

There is another walk, the *Chemin des Bonshommes* (Way of the Good Men, GR107), from Foix, over the Pyrenees, to Spain. It's a route the perfects used to escape from the Inquisition. On it you pass the village of Montaillou, one of the last bastions of Cathars in their late flowering (roughly 1295–1310). Very detailed books describe the life here and much remains as it was. I can't wait to get there.

Although the Pope and the King of France achieved their aims, it was a hollow victory. More than seven centuries later the area is untamed. It is still independent in its outlook and the castles remain. And the Cathar story is very much alive. The people still have appreciation of the Cathars and the terrible wrong that was done. As I said in the early part of this story, the land knows the wrong, for you rarely see or hear a bird sing. Even the earth is sorry for their demise.

Resources:

Guidebooks: THE CATHAR WAY by Alan Mattingly (Cicerone Press). The GR (*Grands Randonnées*) organisation produce a guide to the *Sentier Cathare*, and in Carcassonne and Toulouse there is a wealth of books on the Cathars and their castles.

Maps: there are numerous maps available, including one devoted to the *Sentier Cathare*.

CROSSING PATHS

PATRICE CHAPLIN

The final Cathars crossed the Pyrenees and briefly found sanctuary in what is now Spain. Patrice Chaplin links them with other pilgrims and asks what is the meaning for us all of apparent reincarnational memory.

ONE OF the most common past lives is Cathar, and those reincarnated in this time frequently have plausible even compelling recollections of the South of France in the thirteenth century. These often begin as déja vu glimpses or repetitive dreams and can for a while stir changes in everyday thought-patterns and manifest physically. The appearance of scorch marks on the skin, a fear of or unusual reaction to fire, vertigo, the urgent need to help those around, a strong desire to know more about this other reality that appears in dreams, all signal up a time that has gone. Once the cause is noted, the states of distress recede. The recipient often makes researches into that French past, finds pieces of information that could be familiar or a sense of what still needs to be resolved. Many become healers, teachers, alternative practitioners. Over time they are often drawn to others who have experienced not dissimilar symptoms and states of angoisse and this gives a reassurance, a validity. Whatever one's view of reincar-

---

Patrice Chaplin is internationally renowned for more than twenty-five books, plays and short stories. Her most notable work includes ALBANY PARK, SIESTA, INTO THE DARKNESS LAUGHING, HIDDEN STAR, NIGHT FISHING, DEATH TRAP, THE PORTAL and CITY OF SECRETS, which is the extraordinary true story of one woman's journey to the heart of the Grail legend.

Patrice's journey into the Holy Grail's mystery first began when she stumbled upon the Spanish city of Girona in 1955, as a fifteen-year-old girl who had left London in search of Bohemia. During the 1950s and 1960s, she spent time with Jean-Paul Sartre and Simone de Beauvoir. She was married to Charlie Chaplin's son Michael and her friends included Salvador Dali, Jean Cocteau, Lauren Bacall, Miles Davis and experts on the esoteric practices of the Kabbalah in Spain.

nation, I think to at least claim connection with these rare evolved beings in the thirteenth century can only be positive, giving substance to this so often vacuous present. It beats being Cleopatra!

After I wrote CITY OF SECRETS,[1] I took the Journey of Initiation from Gerona in NE Spain to Mt Canigou in the Pyrenees. When I first arrived in Gerona in the 1950s, they said parts of the wall of this ancient city were over 4000 years old. I was awed by its age. Now each time I go back there the city becomes ever older. Ten years ago, remains of artefacts dated back to 8000BC, when the region was inhabited by Celtic tribes, had been found. Recently a mandible was found in the pre-Neanderthal area of Banyuls supposedly dating from 20,000 years ago.

Gerona's architecture, pre-Roman, Roman, Gothic, offers a wealth of potential reincarnations on every corner. It has housed the mystical, the secret, the forbidden. A city touched by dreams, dreams from other centuries that appears in legends passed down in poetry and street stories, songs and even some say in the cries of the birds, a place of leylines and magnetism that held the rituals of initiation for this journey of the eleven sites across Catalunya.

Under the Constellation of the Great Bear and Seven Stars in a Venus Magic Square, the spiritual practice has been in existence for centuries. Its purpose is to uncover a stage of freedom, evolvement, resonance which allows a passage between time and space as we know it. At each site an ever-advancing practice of purification, surrender, reflection, acceptance, rebirth outside of earthly limitations – in some way very similar to the Cathar ministry. Priests are recorded to have taken this journey and as did poet priest Jacinto Verdaguer, they then chose to work away from the direction of the church, in some cases performing exorcism and laying on of hands—ending for Verdaguer in excommunication before his death .

The Cathars were condemned not for what they did, but for what they were, and for this they were prepared to die. The *parfaits* in the ceremony of Consolation reached a spiritual level of purity which allowed the Holy Spirit to dwell within and freed the recipient of reincarnation and further worldly suffering. I find this at variance with the profusion of reincarnates in this era. Were they in part retaining that Cathar past to resolve what had not been completed? There are echoes of Cathar practice along the Catalan journey of Initiation, but it is unlikely and there is no record that they would have taken this path, which does pass geographically through their area. Sites on the French side were Perpignan, Rennes-le-Château, Beziers, Carcassonne, and Foix. Did their paths cross during these cruel times?

It's known that Cathars, between 1310 and 1320, did wander in the west of Catalunya, Leida, Morellas, Prades, and some in exile from north of the mountains where Jacques Fournier, Bishop of Pamiers, was seeking to persecute them. There was no substantial sign of Cathars in Catalunya in the thirteenth century, but St Dominic, Founder of the Dominican Order, who preached against the Cathars from 1206 to 1216, came from Calervega Catalunya. Peter II of Aragon kept heresy out of Aragon Catalunya and was killed at the battle of Muret in 1213, which was seen as the beginning of the end of an independent Midi.

The Catalans today believe Cathars did escape into the mountains and forest of Gerona province. This was the golden time of the Jews of Gerona, rabbis, craftsmen, scholars, cabbalists, creating an excellence not since matched, and ending (as in the case of the Cathars most cruelly) with the Expulsion in 1492.

A concert of Cathar songs was organised two years ago in a village, St Miguel de Fluvia, and the priest recalled Cathar presence in the area .

As a Roman Catholic he offered penance by removing his clothes and, naked, beating himself ceremoniously. For many Catalans it was too extreme, but could anything be 'too' or 'extreme' after that destruction, never to be forgotten, that heralded centuries of rigidity and darkness? On the Catalan journey I followed, participants at the Perpignan site were aware during meditation of a yellow cross. That of the Cathars?

Another was aware of smoke and choking, and was back in a time he it seemed could only have experienced in actuality. His description of the fire strongly resembled the burning to death in Perpignan of Bertrand d'Alian in 1258 – a Cathar sympathiser and son-in-law of the Count of Foix. Reincarnation? Or being able to reach back through the veils of time?

Others felt a desire to heal, but was it for the present day or those events eight hundred years before? Surely it is by attunement possible to heal that which happened in the past and in some way appease that pain.

Notes:
[1]CITY OF SECRETS was published by Robinson Publishing in 2007. Patrice's latest novel is called MR. LAZARUS and is available as a Kindle eBook.

CATHAR TRACKING

DEIRDRE RYAN

Everyone's journey to Cathar country is a personal adventure.

WHEN I was asked about writing a chapter for my friend Dave's book on the Cathars, I instantly went to that place of feeling unworthy. I'm not an authority on the subject. Why would my trip around the Languedoc be of any interest to anyone? I didn't intend on berating myself but simply looked at the facts; I'm not a writer nor do I consider myself a highly realised spiritual being. If anything, I am stumbling along through life, still trying to figure myself out, like most people.

However, I decided – why not? This was a trip I truly embodied and an adventure I still hold dear many years later. We often overlook the magic in the mundane or fail to notice the spiritual being next to us sipping tea, listening compassionately while we unload our woes. In writing this short chapter I came to realise that you don't have to climb a mountain to have a great story. Everyone has a story, and there is validity in everyone's experience; often the most profound shifts occur within the small stuff of our day, if we're paying enough attention to notice. So without further ado I began to look at the photographs of that trip, unwind and let myself go.

From the outset this trip was one fuelled by curiosity and intrigue. I wanted in, I wanted full disclosure on the lives of the Cathars but, more

Deirdre Ryan is Dublin-born with a background in education. After working as a teacher in the primary school sector in Ireland, France and the UK, she found herself constrained by the lack of autonomy within the existing teaching structure. Upon leaving what was very much a stifling environment, she has followed her intuition and creative impulses leading into the fields of brain injury, rehabilitation and working with adults with learning difficulties.

She now lives in Scotland in Forres, Moray, with her husband, Ken, and four-year-old daughter, Alex Georgia. This first experience of being published, has been a joy, reminding her of the ideology she held as a child – *do what you love.*

than anything else, I wanted to sense something of relevance to me. Having read Kate Mosse's compelling novel LABYRINTH, I had flirted with the possibility of past lives. By the time I had read Arthur Guirdham's THE CATHARS AND REINCARNATION back in 2006 I had more than entertained the possibility: I was positively convinced that our journey as humans entails us having past lives. I began to entertain the possibility for myself, again flirting with notions such as my having been a Cathar. I needed to go to France and verify this somehow. However what I expected and what actually came to pass for me was ultimately a journey about who I am now, and not so much who I may have been in the past.

My fascination with the Cathar faith and their tragic demise was really inspired by Guirdham. I loved his book, and what's more I loved the scenario in which he himself was brought to the conclusion that we reincarnate. His client was just an ordinary housewife and yet somehow her story turns the tables, where unexpectedly the teacher becomes the student. From his propulsion back into thirteenth-century France, I also felt pulled into a journey. Is it possible I have had several lives too?

Having been raised a Catholic, I resonated from the start with Guirdham's difficulty in believing his client's nightmares to be anything pertaining to past life and his reluctance to accept these episodes as anything other than nightmares. In short the book was convincing. Disillusioned with my upbringing in the Catholic church from a very young age, this book was to enable me to name my own experience.

With LABYRINTH and Guirdham's work beside me, I was pointed in the direction of Carcassonne. So in late Spring 2007, with a boss telling me to take my annual leave, I found myself being lured once again to France but this time with a mission. What happened at Montségur? What really went on in Rennes-le-Château? Carcassonne was soon upon the horizon and an adventure I treasure to this day began in the mediaeval city and its château that was never taken by force!

Arriving in CARCASSONNE… Couldn't wait to leave…

Mid-March 2007 and a city filled with a bitter chill. I still to this day don't know what chased us out of that city. Was it just a case of the bitter cold or something else? My friend Caroline and I landed with the intention of spending two nights around Carcassonne but by the end of our first day, we had our minds made up to cancel our second night in the guest house. Instinctively – we just didn't feel good there. Bikshu Sangharakshita, in ALTERNATIVE TRADITIONS (published in 1986), refers to how

> 'hundreds of towns and villages were laid waste, and many thousands of men, women and children were massacred. The civilisation of Languedoc was destroyed, and the whole area so badly devastated that the effects persist, it is said, down to the present day.'

Here he describes the impact of Pope Innocent the Third's 1209 campaign to annihilate the Cathar faith and its followers based in the Languedoc. His campaign was one of the most effective, systematic and ruthless annihilations of human beings in history. His crusaders, a merciless force and a law unto themselves, were given exemption in the eyes of the church in their treatment of their fellow human beings. They extracted reports of heresy and confessions by whatever means, accurate or fictitious, it did not matter and many fell foul to their interrogations, guilty or not, with unspeakable consequences. Is it conceivable that those threads remain to be picked up in Carcassonne, woven into its walls of stone and ancient streets? It was time to move on. And onward we went, to a place called Nébias, located outside Quillan.

With snow all around, we were warmly invited into the home of Rayseen, a radiant and light lady known to my friend Caroline. An 'American gal', she had shared a beautiful home with her Irish husband Cathal who had recently passed on. She undertook the renovations they had planned together alone. She had installed beautiful wooden columns and beams throughout the space. Whitewashed walls flowed round to form a curvaceous opening that lead to her kitchen and open-plan living area. It was a haven after our experience in Carcassonne. We both could breathe with ease again. With introductions made and warm embraces, an unexpected invitation came our way by means of a phone call. At the other end of the line was a fellow American requesting Rayseen's attendance to an impromptu private violin concert to be performed by him and his fiancée at the local church in Saint-Polycarpe. By synchronicity, the invitation was extended to ourselves and we accepted with delight. A flask of cocoa and we were back in the car.

Being of no particular religious persuasion, these two wily Americans had cunningly managed to charm the keys of the local church from the elderly lady who tended to it. She proved an amusing character, with her head wrapped in a small scarf folded over to make a triangle, typical of what my grandmother wore on windy days. I am sure she wore two pairs of nylon tights under an even thicker pair of socks, a knee-length woollen skirt and a buttoned cardigan with an unfastened housecoat completing the ensemble. She was intrigued by our presence and quite the curious creature, although we all had French, not one of us could discern her colloquial tongue.

She had plenty to say and did not seem disconcerted or put off by the one-way flow (she continued to tell us many great things, I'm sure). However one thing we all understood clearly was the importance of the key, the time she expected it back, and that she was its stalwart custodian.

The church had been chosen by our new-found friends for its dome ceiling and the magic that that would infuse in the music. No sooner had we entered than their love affair that was music began, with an immediacy and intensity that reflected their passion. The bows touched the strings with a profound energy that raised the hairs upon my skin. It reached the dome and was sent back round to us as though it were a wild wind, dancing around our bodies. I can hear those strings still and how those two lovers played in unison, and although their music played like a symphony, it was two parts coming together. There was a distinguishable sense to it of the male and the female. The two complemented one another in a fusion of movement and music, almost as though they were each finishing the other's sentence.

Later, when hunger descended, we found ourselves seeking something light to eat. So after our serenade in the église, our newly-founded merry troupe regrouped at a local café and ate together. I believe it was in Limoux. It was while there that something of significance occurred between the man of the couple and me. In conversation he revealed that his fiancée was to be wife number five. Perhaps in the eyes of others – a little excessive! I asked him, 'Why so many marriages which ended in divorce?'.

When he replied 'They were all wenches', I burst into laughter. Here he was in his late fifties, several children later and returning to what was once his student to marry yet again.

I couldn't help feeling more than a little intrigued. Apparently, at the age of 16, she had been his violin student and he, a man more than ten years her senior, became her lover. What ensued was a story of a wild love affair in the barn where she had her violin lessons, her unwitting parents none the wiser. And now many years later and a lot of living, they had returned to one another. I have always been one for a story of forbidden fruit – or perhaps I'm just a sucker for a happy ending! As a couple, they were meant to be.

It took no longer than this story of clandestine love for me to find myself hooked on the energy of this man. We carried on chatting, laughed wholeheartedly, even outrageously, till it hurt. After a time it felt like we were no longer five but just us, two. The connection we shared felt so familiar and natural, there was an inexplicable fondness from the off. For that moment, I enjoyed it for what it was, two souls resonating and laughing together like old friends.

As it happens, I later had the opportunity to connect up with a lady who channelled in the United States called Catherine-Alexis. She drew my attention to many things during our lengthy conversation but, most intriguingly, she referenced my trip to France. When I asked about past lives and there being any Cathar link for me, she informed me that there was a gentleman in a café with whom I had had an amazing connection. By this time I had forgotten any man or any café and couldn't fathom what she meant. Then it dawned on me as she made reference to 'The man in the café, the one you had an instant rapport with and laughed with, he was with you as you were both pushed to your death. You were Cathar, both male, close friends, like brothers'.

I am never quick to trust what I cannot discern for myself, but this rang true. There was an immediate lightness upon hearing this. I let the knowledge pour over me and felt its authenticity. I reflected on the joyful giddiness we – this man and I – had shared together in that café, and sensed that it was the first in a series of things that were righted on this soul journey. I look back now with tenderness and think – what a reunion.

We spent three nights with Rayseen. Three women together, we spent the days sharing stories, laughing and cooking together. Both Rayseen and Caroline had lost their partners in the previous year or so and although both women forged onwards in their paths, there were still unanswered questions. Why had Sam not come back in some way and given 'a sign' that he hadn't left entirely? Caroline's loss had been more recent and this trip was a gift she'd given to herself to recover from the two years prior in which she had dedicated herself entirely to nursing him, until he passed in the Autumn of 2006. I mention this as, when we gathered on the floor that evening upon soft cushions scattered about the room, we chatted of Sam and his pact to let Caroline know that he would never be far away, even through death. The lights went crazy, flickering on and off like candles in a sudden draught. We giggled but there was no denying each of us were startled. Just as we spoke of him giving a sign, he went for the oldest trick in the book.

Over the evening we plotted our next day or two curled like cats in the cushions. Despite the thick snow, we were determined that a climb of Montségur would feature in our trip: after all we were here to satisfy curiosity and know more of this Cathar country. The following day we were driven, courtesy of Rayseen, to the foot of Montségur.

Montségur

We passed the monument there dedicated to those Cathars that occupied the final stronghold of their kind on top of Montségur. It left us in quiet contemplation.

We felt sadness only in the facts. Two hundred or more Cathars upon descending this mount were burned alive. Steadfast and unwavering, they refused to renounce their faith and spare themselves such a torturous demise.

We then began our ascent. Given the season it was surprising to meet other souls who felt compelled to make the hike to the top. They however had already been, while we were just starting out, unsure of what to expect, especially given that we were almost knee deep in snow. Rayseen stopped soon into the ascent and Caroline shortly after. For them just being present on this now sacred place was enough.

For me it wasn't. I had a need, a complete urge to make it to the top. The snowflakes danced down from the heavens in silence as I climbed. A mist had formed above making it difficult to discern how far I had to go. Always the one to hate every step of a Corbett or Munro (hills over a certain height back in Scotland, where I live now), I felt light going up the white-covered mountain. It was almost as though I was being lifted to the top. My heart felt light and with each step, I bathed in the soft flakes of snow, the stillness and the feeling of connection with this place. I reached the top alone without another soul.

There I observed the thick walls of stone that bore testament to the great fortress that was the final stronghold of the Cathars, although what is there today was built long after the Cathars had been thrown to their deaths or burned alive.

I thought about those poor souls descending into the abominable snare that waited below. What courage on their part and what an atrocity perpetrated upon them by the waiting army.

Most people find this pilgrimage a sacred experience, and I must say it is true for me too. The horror of what went on here was no longer palpable. Years of light-workers visiting and blessing this place have banished such energy, it seems. I loved being there, standing in awe and delighting in the solitude. In my memory now is the enduring sentiment of feeling that lovely connectedness while I stood there in the snow between the remnant walls of the fort.

Rennes-le-Château

Rayseen was certainly in the centre of things. Her location in Nébias was thirty minutes from everywhere of significance. Next stop: Rennes-le-Château. By this time we had heard about the mischievous goings on of a certain priest, Berenger Saunière: the theories and conspiracies. It felt great to be on his tail, to be tracking him down. What did he get up to? We entered the small church there and saw the devilish grin of the Satan-like creature that stood beneath the fount of holy water, its message of good triumphing over evil.

Here in the surrounding valley an English archaeologist, Graham Simmans, had dedicated much of his life to finding what it was that Saunière had discovered and had subsequently hidden. Convinced that the priest had buried something akin to the Holy Grail, he had commissioned secretive digs in the surrounding area, screened off in the chance that something of significance were to be unearthed. Prior to this he had worked in Egypt, Jordan and Israel tracing the origins of Christianity. He concluded that Christ survived the crucifixion and made his way to the South of France. He believed that here in the region of Rennes-le-Château the true essence of Christ's message flourished among the prevailing culture.

We were to knock on his door there in Rennes-le-Château only to discover that he had passed away the previous year; his widow received us. Yet again I couldn't overlook the uncanny coincidence that I was now in the company of three women who had each recently suffered the loss of their companion. Like Rayseen finishing the renovations they had planned together, Graham's widow was to see her late husband's book published – 'Jesus after the crucifixion: from Jerusalem to Rennes-le-Château' – revealing that Jesus never died on the cross. Although I had tried to ditch the Church at fourteen, the 'truths' I had been told were still hard to shirk. This came as another challenge to my almost 'catholic' faith, a welcome one nonetheless.

Standing in the living room of Graham's house, I observed the three women and how they formed a triangle as they stood in the room. They somehow appeared unified in their shared loss. A peculiar thing happened to me as I became conscious of the synchronistic meeting. A wave of energy passed up through my body like an electrical surge coming from the ground, through my legs and permeating the rest of my being. As I watched the three, a pace back from them, it was as though I was merely meant to be there in the capacity of observer.

In that house of strange and foreign artefacts that testified to Graham's life's purpose, there was conversation of angels, Jesus and his family, huh? Again that reference to our Lord who died on the cross to save us mere mortals, instead of threatening any belief it created a sense of excitement within me.

The vast number of artefacts was mystifying, strange masks and weapons used by various tribes around the world. I wish I'd had my camera so that I would have pictures to aid my recollection rather than a vague memory. However, it is enough for me to know that something of significance occurred within my being there. I looked at the three women, sure that they too had felt or experienced an energy surge pulse through their bodies, apparently not. I was on my own with that one to figure out. Perhaps it was a conscious awareness of the compassion I felt for them.

As I recollected this trip I found some forgotten aspects to it resurfacing, not realising that I had buried them deep down. I know that this trip not only excited me in terms of a magical adventure, I had come without my partner. Always living in each other's ear, I had relished the idea of a getaway with some girlfriends. I suddenly felt bereft as I was tossed into a sea of emotions. At one point I had to leave the company of my two lady companions and immerse myself in the shower where I let the water cascade over the torrent of tears that flooded my entire being. I suddenly felt what it was to be without my partner. And I ached.

Unable to hold back the tears, I felt as though I too were in mourning. It came like a bolt out of the blue. The next while of our time in sisterhood together with Rayseen was spent in conversation about my own relationship. Why was I suddenly grieving it, in turmoil without warning? Did I fear that one day I would inevitably experience the loss that they were both valiantly facing? In the presence of their story, I couldn't help going into my own 'what ifs'. I felt painfully confused around letting go of something, at the time I thought it was him but I realise now, it was something more than that.

I started out my journey to the Languedoc with some naive expectations. In the hazy mist of fact and fiction, I was hoping to discover a connection to a past life; surely I must have been a Cathar? Setting off, that certainly felt like the ultimate goal, some validation pertaining to having had a Cathar life. Up to that point, I had never dedicated a trip to anything of a spiritual nature, never taken a workshop in anything alternative, apart from my mother gently pushing me to try my hand at Reiki... ('Yes mam, I laid my hands on and his bald head felt like a bloody radiator, but that's just biochemistry, not healing.') My mocking Irish nature wouldn't let me go there; I remained halfheartedly committed and just read, censoring myself and choosing to ignore those inclinations towards opportunities that don't fit with the norm. I came to a simpler conclusion, that life is my workshop.

I had made a journey to Cathar country, a place steeped in history. Arriving with such expectations of discovery, I found it wasn't what I had hoped for, it was something even better. I never expected my journey to be one of sisterhood, compassion and healing – but ultimately it was. When you go in search of the truth, it's not unusual to discover yourself.

While I know that I didn't fully integrate my experience of the Languedoc back then, I realise now that I cried for more than my relationship that trip. I cried for my gorgeous companions. I cried for the earth beneath my feet and the trees that stretched into the sky that witnessed all the human suffering, fear and torture that took place there. I cleansed my body, releasing those tears and hopefully with them I released something from that very spot on which I stood, and hopefully more.

III. HISTORY : 1

THE APPEAL OF THE CATHARS THEN AND NOW

NICK LAMBERT

This article examines the historic and contemporary appeal of the Cathars, and more broadly the Gnostic worldview, in terms of its cosmology, heterodoxy, connections to antiquity and Eastern religions, and transcendent aspects. It considers the Cathars' evolution by way of the Manichaeans and Bogomils, and the effect this had on their development; and some outcomes of the Cathar movement.

'The dead filled the place murmuring and said:
'"Tell us of gods and devils, accursed one!"
'"The god-sun is the highest good; the devil is the opposite. Thus have ye two gods. But there are many high and good things and many great evils."'[1]

IF ONE believes in the cyclical nature of time, and certain recurrent themes in human history, then it seems quite natural that what was once suppressed or hidden should re-emerge and become the focus of our attention. Throughout the twentieth century, the study of the Cathars – and the broader area of Gnostic thought, within which they can be situated – came

Dr Nick Lambert is Lecturer in Digital Art and Culture at the Department of History of Art and Screen Media, Birkbeck, University of London. He researches the applications of technology in the arts and the history of this area. He also has a strong interest in aspects of hermetic and Gnostic philosophy, the work of Frances Yates, and medieval architecture.

to occupy the interests of a range of thinkers in Europe and America. Carl Jung, quoted above, is probably the most significant figure in this 'Gnostic Renaissance', but as Gilles Quispel notes in his review of Robert A Segal's THE GNOSTIC JUNG, streams of philosophical thought from this source have appeared from the Enlightenment onwards:

> 'Gnosticism is the third component of Western civilization. It originated in Alexandria just before the Common Era and in its Hermetic, Jewish, and Christian ramifications it profoundly influenced our religion and culture. Marc Chagall, the Chassidic painter, represented Jewish, Cabalistic Gnosis in our time. Goethe and William Blake were Christian Gnostics; Carl Gustav Jung venerated the Hermes Trismegistus of alchemy. Therefore ancient Alexandria is as important as Jerusalem, the origin of faith, and Athens, the cradle of reason. Until this day the churches preach the faith and the philosophers believe in *logos*, but the Gnostics trust their inner experiences and express them in imaginative symbols.'[2]

While mainstream philosophers and theologians are still notably suspicious of 'inner experiences' and 'imaginative symbols', the concepts of divine immanence, emanations and the illusory nature of the material world have found a ready home in art and literature, particularly in science fiction and comic books. Dealing as they do with speculative situations, sometimes set in the mundane world, or in the far future or the deep past, with modern superheroes taking the role of demi-gods and villains standing in for demons, the sci-fi and fantasy genres have recapitulated many Gnostic ideas.

The prime example is of course the film *The Matrix* (1999), which has attracted much comment on the similarities between the artificially-induced virtual reality in which its characters subsist, and the fallen material realm of Gnosticism. There are also elements of this in the modern concept of the Internet as a non-material realm of existence for those who participate in it. As cultural commentator Christopher Loring Knowles says in his article on the originator of cyberpunk, William Gibson, whose book NEUROMANCER began this line of contemporary thought:

> 'The Wachowskis [directors of *The Matrix*] didn't really understand Gibson's gnosis, in that Gibson's Cyberspace wasn't the prison, it was the escape from the prison. It was a place of endless freedom and possibility. [...] Gibson's obsession with dislocation and created environments ties into the Gnostic desire to escape the Demiurge's world.'[3]

Knowles is convinced that areas of pop culture, especially those touched by certain visionaries like comic book artist and writer Jack Kirby, are places where an unconscious awareness of the basic Gnostic tenets emerges into the modern world. Many of Kirby's scenarios, stripped of their futuristic accoutrements and superheroes, revisit the myth of the Demiurge, the flawed creation, and the possibility of gnosis through contact with extradimensional beings.[4] Extraordinary as this might sound, it seems to fit with the history of the early Gnostics, as Steven Runciman relates:

'The early heretical tradition was preserved [by] the literature of the Gnostics. The Gnostics always had a taste for fairy stories. Their familiar method of exegesis had been to publish a book of the vision of some famous Biblical character [such as Enoch] in which the seer described the heavens as being planned according to a Gnostic model. Or they would adopt some traditional fable and give it a Gnostic moral. [...] These stories were very much to the taste of the general public and remained in circulation.'[5]

In the case of the Cathars, the visionary text is of course the Vision of Isaiah, where the Old Testament prophet described his journey through the heavens and expounded on the cosmic struggle between God and the Devil:

'And we ascended, he and I, upon the firmament, and there I saw the great battle of Satan and his might opposing the loyal followers (honorantiae) of God, and one surpassed the other in envy. For just as it is on earth, so also is it in the firmament, because replicas of what are in the firmament are on earth.'[6]

Since the dualistic tradition to which the Cathars belonged – to a greater or lesser extent – is regularly traduced by many orthodox commentators as 'pessimistic' or 'elitist', it is curious that the imaginative output of both early Gnostics and their more recent heirs should actually be very popular. If one includes the medieval troubadours as part of this as well, given the mystical and often heterodox content of their tales, then stories with an essentially Gnostic character have been a central part of the Western literary tradition.

It is instructive to understand the appeal of an ancient, once-pervasive and still subversive worldview, broadly termed 'Gnostic', that even today arouses strong opposition from many quarters. For instance, Philip Pullman's trilogy, HIS DARK MATERIALS, which includes a strongly Gnostic cosmology despite Pullman's professed atheism, has roused much ire from traditionalist Catholics who cavil at a universe in which a flawed Demiurge poses as the god worshipped by a corrupt Church:

'Pullman's work is definitely anti-orthodox. And, because that is so, it is also anti-Christian since true Christianity is orthodox. Thus, one can only hold to her remark if he believes that Gnosticism is true Christianity. And, if that is the case, it follows logically, again, that Pullman is advocating and presenting a form of belief that is in opposition to Catholic teaching.'[7]

Clearly the spirit of the Inquisition lurks rather close to the surface in the orthodox psyche. But artists and writers consistently draw inspiration from this heterodox view of the universe, which does not in itself make them 'Gnostics' *per se*. Kirsten Grimstad proposes that even before Jung found analogues of his theories in Gnostic beliefs, and before the major discovery of the Nag Hammadi library in 1945, the late nineteenth-century 'religion of art' in the *fin-de-siècle* milieu of Paris gave rise to sentiments very close to those of Gnosticism. She considers this to have begun with Baudelaire as 'an extremist revolt against modernity' that reflects the fallen material world of Gnosticism:

'The so-called religion of art [Aestheticism] in effect rekindled a culturally subversive sectarian structure of thought that left its watermark on diverse literary texts of the period. [...] Moreover, the ancient Gnostic salvation through gnosis reappears in the *l'art pour l'art* ideal of an autonomous aesthetic utopia of absolute art as a medium for absolute reality and an escape from the social world and the perceived horrors of modernity. This movement culminated in modernist abstraction.'[8]

This is a bold claim, but Grimstad goes on to substantiate it with specific reference to Mann's DOKTOR FAUSTUS and the broader cultural context of the rediscovery of Gnostic thought, through reprints of the *Pistis Sophia* in the 1850s, G.R.S. Mead's extensive works in hermetic and theosophical thought (which might well have influenced Jung) and Hans Jonas's works that showed continuity between the Gnostics and Mandaeans. Indeed the role of Theosophy in promoting Gnosticism at the turn of the twentieth century resulted in its widely-acknowledged influence on Russian artists and musicians like Scriabin, whilst Mead's Quest Society, based at the Kensington Hall in London, brought together all kinds of luminaries:

'Yeats, Arthur Symons, Ezra Pound, Dorothy Shakespear, Wyndham Lewis, Rebecca West, T. E. Hulme, A. E. Waite, Evelyn Underhill, Gershom Scholem, Martin Buber, Jessie L. Weston, among others, attended the Quest lectures, which continued through the 1920s, and contributed to Mead's journal, *The Quest*.'[9]

In these names alone were the pioneers of Modernist art and poetry, the key researchers on the Kabbalah and Arthurian legend, and leading mystics and occultists. If they all subscribed in part, at least, to some aspect of the Gnostic worldview, what was it that fired their imaginations? Grimstad's summary of Gnostic beliefs provides a clue:

> 'Gnosticism features a radically pessimistic view of life and the world combined with a radically optimistic belief that the human spirit is itself divine, though lost in an alien and hostile world ruled by an evil deity.'[10]

It was both the spiritual rejection of the world and the powerful imagery of a dualistic cosmos that informed their interests, and this surely throws some light on the reasons for Cathar popularity too. Grimstad is surely right to balance the pessimism with optimism, for why should a faith that was wholly negative (as the Cathars are often said to have been) hold any kind of attraction for a rational human being? But if it was about reawakening the divine spark and escaping the cyclical terrors of history and the world, then this type of *gnosis* that informed the European *avant garde* of the 1900s might not be so far removed from the faith that inspired all levels of Occitan society seven centuries before.

In trying to comprehend this aspect of the Cathars, one must acknowledge the dearth of actual texts originating with them, as opposed to the writings of their medieval interrogators. Fortunately other areas in the Gnostic and Manichaean tradition have become better represented since the rediscovery of numerous Gnostic texts from the mid-nineteenth century onwards. Before that time, the principal sources of knowledge on Gnosticism were the detailed denunciations by the Church Fathers, particularly of the Dualist heresy of Manichaeism, and it is because of these early writings that the Cathars too were labelled as 'Manichees'.

Even the naming of the 'Cathars' as such is controversial, particularly as the nomenclature has shifted over time. Until the later nineteenth century they were routinely called Albigensians, after the district of Albi in which they were found, but when Henry Charles Lea published his magisterial study A HISTORY OF THE INQUISITION OF THE MIDDLE AGES in 1887, the term 'Cathar' came into vogue. Some recent historians are sceptical of using a term that even the Catholic authorities only rarely used; Pegg for instance lists a variety of synonyms used by the people of the Languedoc:

'No person, whether mendicant inquisitor or the men, women, and children they questioned, ever used the noun 'Cathar' to describe heretics in, for instance, the Toulousain, the Lauragais, or in the pays de Foix. Instead, it was always, with no exceptions, *boni homines, bone femine, bons omes, bonas femnas, good men and good women*; while the good men and good women themselves frequently referred to each other as "the friends of God".'

For the sake of simplicity this text will call them 'Cathars' as this has achieved a fairly universal currency in modern times and its medieval provenance is well attested, if only from the religion's enemies.

The Appeal of Dualism

The eternal battle of good and evil deities is at the centre of the Cathar worldview and although this belief came in a variety of forms, they were very similar to the dualistic faiths that were specifically prohibited by orthodox Christianity: the Gnostics, the Manicheans, the Paulicians and the Bogomils of the Balkans. It is upon the issue of dualism that much of the excitement and controversy around the Cathars rests. Absolute dualism is the position adopted in the *Book of Two Principles*:

'The good God is not the creator of the base and tangible elements of this world; another creator is responsible for them. God is almighty but not in the sense that He can create evil; what He does not desire He cannot do. He is omnipotent over all good things, but there must be another creator from whom all evils flow, who in no way derives from the good God. The evil one is eternal, as are his works.'[12]

Thus the Book argues very cogently for there being two Gods on the basis that a good Deity could not be the source of evil, nor could his creations become evil unless an external source of evil corrupted them. This is not only Dualist, it is also tinged by Gnostic thought and seems to indicate a wide-ranging heritage for the currents expressed in Catharism. The Manichaeans had anticipated this in the third century AD when Mani set out his dualist position:

The specifically dualist aspects of Mani's religion built upon existing elements of dualism in Zoroastrianism, setting out the basic terms for later dualists to follow:

'The material world, i.e. the realm of Ahrmen, king of darkness, is considered evil; on the other hand the spiritual world, i.e. the realm of the Father of Greatness (Zurwan) and of the gods of light, is good. From this novel perspective Mani modified the Iranian dualism. It was not however entirely new because the dualism of light and darkness was already in his time a commonplace in gnostic thought and teaching.'[13]

The reemergence of dualism in Western Europe was likely spurred by confusion in the Catholic Church about the origins and role of Satan, and Eva Weiling-Feldthusen points to the Fourth Lateran Council of 1214, where it was decreed

> 'that God had created angels and that '[…] the devil and the other demons were indeed created by God good in their nature but they became bad through themselves'.[14]

The dualist explanation of good and evil gods was less equivocal than this compromise, and the spread of the Cathars shows how compelling it was for many people. It was simply more consistent, given the state of the world, to attribute equal powers to the contending gods. Another factor was the disparity between the Jehovah of the Old Testament – the 'jealous god' of Moses and the Israelites – and the peaceful philosophy of Jesus and his Apostles. Many Gnostics held that the Old Testament deity was in fact the Demiurge, Samael (the blind god), and his flawed Creation came about through a misguided desire to ape the true Creator.

Strong echoes of this cosmology are found centuries later in William Blake's radical interpretations of the Bible. He outlined a Demiurge called Urizen, embodying the legalistic, hidebound and narrow-minded aspects of the Old Testament's Jehovah, and Blake cast him as an implacable figure, conveying something of his antithetical and flawed creative powers as the Cathars once saw them:

> 'Lo, a shadow of horror is risen
> In Eternity! Unknown, unprolific,
> Self-clos'd, all-repelling: what Demon
> Hath form'd this abominable void,
> This soul-shudd'ring vacuum? Some said:
> 'It is Urizen.' But unknown, abstracted,
> Brooding secret, the dark power hid.'[15]

In terms of the origins of Cathar dualism, Weiling-Feldthusen alludes to an ongoing debate in religious history between structuralists, who assert that similar belief systems could arise independently of each other because of fundamental similarities in the human mind and brain; and diffusionists who posit the continual spread of ideas from an identifiable source. She places the main Cathar historians – Dmitrii Obolensky, Steven Runciman, and Yuri Stoyanov – among this latter group, but says that they all have to account for the separation in time between the Manichaeans and the earliest accounts of the Paulicians.[16] Moreover, as the remnants of the Manichaean church were concentrated in Central Asia in the tenth century, it seems unlikely that they could have influenced developments in Bulgaria, where the Bogomils emerged around that time.

Instead, newer theories have picked up on ideas from the nineteenth century about a Zoroastrian influence on the Bulgarian tribes as they came through the Steppes, and also a pre-existing Thracian dualist religion; the cult of the twins that is mentioned by Greek writers.

> 'One popular theme is that of the cosmogonic tradition of the earth-diver, recorded in Eastern Europe, and which describes the world as being created by two primal figures moving about on the surface of the waters. Recently scholars have linked this tradition to the Bogomil creation myth and claimed that it was also developed under the influence of Iranian dualism, and modified afterwards in Gnostic and Manichaean circles.'[17]

The idea seems directly related to the Bogomil concept that the world of matter was constructed by the evil deity, and the world of the spirit was God's domain.[18] This has led to both the Bogomils and Cathars being considered as Neo-Manichaeans, even if the specifics of their beliefs were more solidly Christian than those of Mani and his followers. Certainly, Andrew Philip Smith sees this as clear evidence of an ongoing tradition right back to the first Gnostics, and speculates on an initiatory aspect to the *perfecti* who constituted a more informed circle of believers, in line with other Gnostic groups:

> 'It seems that only Perfects were fully initiated into the dualist teaching and mythology and into the inner meaning of their scriptures and practices. This is another indication that the Cathars might have been genuinely Gnostic: knowledge of the situation of mankind in the universe was essential to salvation.'[19]

The autonomous Bogomil churches differed in their dualist positions and other doctrinal aspects, and also sent various bishops to the West. It is notable that the Cathars appear to have subscribed to a more moderate dualism until the Byzantine Bogomil bishop Nicetas came to the West in the late twelfth century and convinced the main part of their church to subscribe to 'absolute dualism'. The Cathars in Lombardy had a bishop named Marc, who was under the authority of the Bulgarian church, whereas Nicetas/Niquinta was part of the 'Ecclesia Dugunthiae' in Constantinople.[20] The Bulgarian church were moderate dualists, holding that Lucifer – the Demiurge – was subordinate to God, whilst the Dugunthiae were absolute dualists, for whom the good and evil Creators were eternally matched. Obolensky considers that when Nicetas moved most Cathars towards absolute dualism, any remaining doctrinal links with western Catholicism were severed and 'The seeds of the Albigensian Crusade were well and truly sown at the Council of St-Félix-de-Caraman'.[21] Although doubt has been raised about the authenticity of this Council – the only description of it comes from a dubious seventeenth-century transcription of an unknown medieval document – scholarly opinion holds that if the original existed, it was at least partly correct in attributing absolute dualism to Nicetas, who is also attested in other genuine documents.[22]

Dualism, then, was the fulcrum about which the rest of Cathar beliefs turned, informing their eschatology (they did not, it seems, subscribe to an apocalyptic Day of Judgment because they did not believe in the resurrection of the body[23]); and also their understanding of the transmigration of souls. This belief in reincarnation likely derived from Neo-Platonism and the ancient Greek philosophy of metempsychosis. The transmigration of souls was specifically opposed in Christianity but became a central tenet of Catharism, and the ascension that they aimed for was a liberation from the constant cycle of death and rebirth, rather similar to Buddhist beliefs. This also brings Cathar theology close to Manichaeism.

> 'If the *Liber de duobus principiis* is at all indicative, the philosophical framework invoked by the Cathari to rationalize dualism is highly deterministic and reflects contact with Neoplatonism – perhaps through al-Kindi and Avicebron. The Cathari argued, for example, that the principle of divine immutability in itself precludes a creation in time: souls, they explained, must necessarily emanate eternally from God 'like sunlight from the sun'. Since souls are not created *de novo*, they must be reincarnated from generation to generation.'[24]

Alexander Alexakis examines the survival of ideas about reincarnation in Byzantium, and while they occasionally surfaced in the form of Neo-Platonic concepts, in the writings of Origen (who was anathematised for this reason) or with the Manichaeans, they did not become widespread. Even the assumption that they were followed by the Paulicians and Bogomils is based more on the authorities' insistence that these were 'Manichaeans'. One of the most interesting references, though, is in the works of the late medieval Byzantine philosopher Gemistos Plethon, who discussed such Platonic concepts as the transmigration of souls with his protégé, Cardinal Bessarion, who contributed much Platonic and Hermetic philosophy to the emerging Italian Renaissance. Although condemned as a heretic after the fall of Constantinople in 1453, Plethon's wide-ranging influence on the Renaissance thus included an interest in reincarnation as part of ancient Greek thought.[25]

The Appeal of Antiquity

As inheritors of Gnostic, Greek and Manichaean thinking, through whatever channels this occurred, the Cathars had links to the lost world of Classical Antiquity that the Roman Church had done so much to suppress. They could be seen as part of the ongoing synthesis that Mani achieved between the religions to which he was exposed in his childhood: Christian Gnosticism, Zoroastrianism and Buddhism.[26] Part of the appeal of Gnosticism was its willingness to acknowledge and incorporate pagan, monotheist, dualist and even Buddhist thought, fusing it into a new worldview that still reflected its combined Hellenistic and Judaic heritage.

The syncretism of Gnosticism also means it could pervade different cultures across a broad area, both geographically and temporally. The 'Book of Giants' was discovered at Qumran with the earliest-known fragments of Old Testament books assembled by the Essenes; yet the same text emerged at Turfan on the Silk Road in a Manichaean settlement, centuries later in a wholly different religious context.[27] Clearly some continuity existed between the monastic Jewish sect and the followers of Mani, and whatever currents took the text from Judea to Central Asia might also have brought concepts from the Buddhist heartland to first-century AD Palestine. There has been persistent speculation about a Buddhist influence on Jesus, and the Silk Road enabled two-way traffic between the centres of Buddhist thought and the Roman Empire.[28]

Although mainstream (Catholic and Orthodox) Christianity fixed upon

Jerusalem, and later Rome and Constantinople, as its spiritual heartland, the Gnostics were heirs to the thought of Babylon, Egypt, Persia, Greece and beyond. In our multi-faceted and pluralistic society, itself a product of empire-building and globalised trade, this cultural complexity suddenly becomes more relevant. The interchange of thoughts in Gnostic texts prefigures aspects of our own world, and in the litanies of gods and spirits we sense a coming together of the ancient world's mythologies.

Artists and writers responded to this sense of a vanished world in the Gnostic and Manichaean texts because it looked back beyond the end of Antiquity, to a period when a multiplicity of sects flourished and there was no single interpretation of the revealed word, nor a state-backed Church to enforce it. The break with the Classical world is symbolised by the destruction of the Library at Alexandria, and the lists of books forbidden to their worshippers by the hierarchies of various churches since the time of Constantine. With its emphasis on knowledge and self-discovery, Gnosticism stands apart from the mob-mentality of those early Christians who stormed temples and smashed the statues only to institute a Church that sanctioned its own statues and icons, and built temples of its own.

The Appeal of Authenticity

Ever since the non-canonical Gospels became known to a wide audience, some have thought that Gnostic sects might have preserved more authentic texts than the mainstream Christian churches. Even students of orthodox Christianity now acknowledge there is much of value to the study of the early Church to be found in the non-canonical texts.

However, there is more to this idea of 'authenticity' in Christian terms. All the challenges to the authority of the medieval Catholic church came from individuals or groups who believed it was irrevocably corrupt, and that they could return to the pure practice of Apostolic Christianity. Obviously they were not all Cathars, or even dualists; many were highly orthodox in their approach. Yet their insistence on standing up to clerical power saw them branded as heretics: even groups like the Spiritual Franciscans (as distinct from the Friars Minor), who fell in and out of approval because they encouraged radical ideas like equality and itinerant preaching.[29]

Austerity and asceticism, a strong dislike for religious imagery and the pomp of church architecture, a commitment to working with all classes of society, and translating the Bible into local languages, were seen as dangerously subversive by a Church that was heavily involved in the exercise of secular power and commanded large amounts of wealth. In a religious system where priests were the interpreters of God's Word, the prospect of laymen comprehending the Bible for themselves was revolutionary. Combined with a decentralised organisation, like that of the later Cathars in the fourteenth century, and travelling scholars like the Lollards who brought the latest ideas from university debates into the heart of the countryside, the Church authorities saw a great threat in these notions of a return to the early days of Christianity.[30]

It is evident that a major appeal of Catharism was the stark contrast between its adherents, especially the *perfecti*, and the local Catholic hierarchy. There was a growing sense that the Church was distanced from the needs of its people, that it served materialist ends and was intent on acting as an international power that politicked its way towards greater wealth and influence.[31] The simplicity of the Cathar faith and its strong local roots in the locale of the Languedoc impressed many across all social classes. Moreover it had a strong intellectual element – as evidenced by the *Book of Two Principles* – that must have attracted scholars and the literate. Finally, the powerful nobility realised that here was a faith that depended on their protection and could be nurtured as a viable alternative to the over-mighty Church that tried to dictate to them from Rome.

Did Catharism represent the survival of an early branch of Christianity – perhaps with more legitimacy – in Languedoc? Anne Bradford Townsend sees the Cathars in this light, linking it with their belief that Jesus and Mary Magdalene were married, which she finds in current among some researchers long before THE HOLY BLOOD AND THE HOLY GRAIL popularised the idea. She notes that two primary sources – the manuscript likely by Ermengaud of Béziers and the account of Peter de Vaux-de-Cernay – mention that the Cathars believed Mary Magdalene was the Concubine of Christ.

She also relates the interesting fact that Mary Magdalene became the patron saint of the Dominican inquisitors, and St Bernard of Clairvaux developed a mystical commentary around the *Song of Songs*. In early Christian commentaries, the Bride of the *Song of Songs* became associated with Mary Magdalene, who had also been linked with the Gnostic Sophia in the *Gospel of Philip*, the *Pistis Sophia* and the *Gospel of Mary*.

Thus there were already tendencies both in the orthodox Church and in Gnosticism that might have influenced Cathar thinking on this subject, quite apart from the tradition in the *Golden Legend* that Mary Magdalene fled to the South of France and brought Christianity with her. Indeed, Townsend concludes that the tradition of the divine feminine was also influenced by Cabalistic doctrine, encountered by Cathars in the communities of Jews in the Languedoc and Spain, contributing to the eventual rise of Marian worship – though centred on the Virgin Mary – that developed later in medieval Catholicism.

Townsend also notes the central importance of the *Vision of Isaiah* as a text about the ascension of the prophet to seek the divine and:

'answer questions about death, the afterlife, injustice in the world and to reassure the righteous of their place in heaven. This ascension text would help the Cathars to explain their central sacrament of salvation [because it] describes the place in the seventh heaven for the righteous dead.'[34]

She considers the popularity of Cathars in the Languedoc not merely due to the asceticism and spirituality of the *perfecti* but also their particular vision of the afterlife, and the hoped-for liberation from the cycle of reincarnation – which is an aspect of Cathar belief that often gets passed over.

'What is clearly revealed in this ascension text is that the journey to heaven is the path to salvation and there is a place for the righteous in the seventh heaven. This practice was a part of the Judaic tradition and was passed on to early Christianity.'[35]

Townsend also quotes Martha Himmelfarb, who avers that:

'The standard assessment of the apocalypses as dualistic, pessimistic, and despairing of this world needs to be revised in light of the value the ascent apocalypses place on human beings. The examples of the heroes of the ascent apocalypses teach their readers to live the life of this world with awareness of the possibility of transcendence.'[36]

This makes Townsend more certain that the pessimistic worldview ascribed to the Cathars should be rethought because they were offering a living message of ascension; it was not a case of fasting to effect a suicidal escape from the material world, but rather receiving the *consolamentum* at the right moment before death took them. Hence the importance of this rite and its continuance up to the final days of the Cathars in the fourteenth century. Later, she notes that the survival of the Cathar *Rituel* in Provençal demonstrates the Cathars were forward-thinking in their use of

vernacular texts as a means of educating the local population; they translated what had originally been a Bogomil Ritual in a Slavic language.[37]

However, this in itself preserved elements of early Syrian and Greek
Christian practices, not least parts of the *consolamentum* itself, and this
combined with other factors leads Townsend to see the Cathars as primarily a group of early Christians who continued ancient forms of the faith,
even though it was dualist. It also established a relationship of the individual with God that was entirely missing from Catholicism, with its insistence
on the hierarchy, and this as much as anything antagonised the Church.

> The Cathars' idea of an individual path to God, enriched by the ascent
> practice and outside the confines of a religious institution, became
> party of the more radical sects of the Reformation and continues to
> flourish in society in our time.[38]

When groups like the Waldenses, the Hussites and other proto-Protestants made their stand against Catholicism, they often appealed to authenticity and the uncomplicated, unadorned worship of the first followers of Christ. They did not of course develop such a radically different
theology as the Cathars, but the absorption of former Cathars into the
Waldenses, and the continuation of a tradition of wandering lay preachers
translating the Bible for their audiences, is suggestive of some influence.
Northern Italy proved a fertile ground for these later movements and the
Waldenses continued to be persecuted into the late seventeenth century.
The Hussites of course succeeded in establishing a separate church in
Bohemia but after participating in the Reformation this was brutally rein-
corporated into Catholicism, with small numbers of Moravians escaping
into the Protestant countries.

As the inheritor of the radical Protestant tradition, William Blake
would not only integrate the mysticism of Jakob Boehme and Immanuel
Swedenborg, but return to something like the Cathar dualism in his radical rewriting of Christianity in his epic poetry. Of course it derived from a
variety of sources including Platonism and Hermetic doctrines, but at the
heart of it was a desire to establish an antinomian, original Christianity
freed from the strictures (and structures) of established churches:

> 'Blake's vision is then [a] total integration of mysticism and proph-
> ecy, a return to apocalyptic faith which arises from an intuitive pro-
> test against Christianity's estrangement from its own eschatological
> ground. Blake saw official Christendom as a narrowing of vision, a

foreclosure of experience and of future expansion, a locking-up and securing of the doors of perception. He substituted for it a Christianity of openness, of total vision, a faith which dialectically embraces both extremes [...]'[39]

The Appeal of the Secret Tradition

Gnosis implies a revelation that is not available to everyone, and this forms one of the main routes of attack by orthodox thinkers (of all kinds) upon the various Gnostic sects, even in the present day. There is clearly something abhorrent to these commentators about a secret revelation, or one that is only available through initiation, because this seems to fly in the face of the egalitarian credo of Christianity. Many of these commentators are apologists for the hierarchical churches – especially Catholicism – and if not priests themselves are usually defenders of the priestly system. This is surely the hidden appeal of the Secret Tradition: although exclusive in one sense, it is also circumvents the Church in favour of a personal revelation through initiation, even though it divides believers into 'Hearers' and the 'Elect', a division observed by the Cathars, Manichaeans and many others.[40]

If the Cathars inherited a secret tradition from the early Christians, a significant part of its doctrine was its insistence that we all contain sparks of the divine and can liberate ourselves from the illusory world. According to Grimstad and others, this 'radical optimism' underpinned the interest in Gnosticism by Theosophists and others in the twentieth century.

One of the main writers influenced by this concept was the science fiction author Philip K Dick. He had a revelatory experience in March 1974, when over several days he received a stream of information from an external source that he rationalised as an ancient alien satellite called VALIS (Vast Active Living Intelligence System). Dick had a longstanding interest in early Christianity and the Gnostics in particular (he was influenced by Hans Jonas) but after 1974 he sought to understand the nature of his revelation, not only in his fiction but in a huge multi-volume spiritual diary that he titled Exegesis. He also had flashbacks to the time of the Apostles, hearing phrases in koine Greek and Aramaic, and theorised that time had not advanced since the last Apostles died, but rather kept on recapitulating, so that 1970s America was in fact the Roman Empire in a new guise. 'The Empire never ended' was a favourite saying of his.

'I, in my stories and novels, often write about counterfeit worlds, semi-real worlds, as well as deranged private worlds inhabited, often, by just one person, while, meantime, the other characters either remain in their own worlds throughout or are somehow drawn into one of the peculiar ones.'

Clearly Dick was drawn to the explicatory power of the concept that the world was illusory, that the divine power was immanent, though not of this world, and that a small group of original Christians had received a direct revelation from Christ that enabled them to transcend the material illusion. Dick elucidated the principles he felt underpinned his understanding of Gnosticism. Some of the key tenets he expounded in the *Exegesis* were:

- Each of us has a divine counterpart unfallen who can reach a hand down to us to awaken us. This other personality is the authentic waking self; the one we have now is asleep and minor. We are in fact asleep, and in the hands of a dangerous magician disguised as a good god, the deranged creator deity. The bleakness, the evil and pain in this world, the fact that it is a deterministic prison controlled by the demented creator causes us willingly to split with the reality principle early in life, and so to speak willingly fall asleep in delusion.

- You can pass from the delusional prison world into the peaceful kingdom if the True Good God places you under His grace and allows you to see reality through His eyes.

- Christ gave, rather than received, revelation; he taught his followers how to enter the kingdom while still alive [...] He causes it to come here, and is the living agency to the Sole Good God (i.e. the Logos).[43]

Undoubtedly, Dick's experience of divine immanence in his mundane phenomenal world enabled him to intuitively trust the Gnostic viewpoint, and seek ways to update it. For instance, he often spoke of the flow of knowledge as information, and wondered whether the entity that had contacted him was in fact a type of computer or an artificial construct. He was also never entirely certain of his interpretation: the Exegesis shows the shifting of his opinions as he subjected his worldview to his own scepticism. Although some commentators point to his lack of philosophical training, labelling him a 'garage philosopher' at best, and others question his mental state in the years leading up to his early death in 1982, Dick clearly tried to comprehend a highly personal and unusual spiritual experience using a framework that resonated with him, and also gave a strong direction to his imaginative writings.

The Appeal of Heterodoxy

The readers of this volume will by and large define themselves in contra-distinction to the mainstream systems of our times. Likewise, the Cathars defined themselves against their contemporary System, the Catholic Church and its clerics. They, and not the Church, possessed the truth and were willing to die for it. Moreover they developed an evolving set of concepts and practices around this core belief, and moved nimbly between the Languedoc, the Pyrenees, the Alps and Lombardy, taking their message with them.

Though the authorities eventually extirpated most of them, something of their spirit survived and the antiauthoritarian aspects of modern-day spirituality and the arts, though diverse in form, share a common mistrust of established orthodoxies whether in religion, culture or science. There is an undeniable excitement in the prospect of heterodox thinkers taking on the medieval Church at its apogee and getting away with it – at least for a time. If there is a continuing skein through the art and literature of modern times, it is surely this rejoinder to authoritarianism in human life, in whatever forms it is expressed.

It is very instructive to observe Catholic reactions to Philip Pullman's HIS DARK MATERIALS and see orthodox thinking at work. Pullman inserted a subversive, and highly Gnostic, message into his book: that the Authority posing as God in his fictional universe was in fact an impostor, and a whole misguided church had arisen to worship this false deity. The final book ends with the storming of Heaven itself by the protagonists, intent on liberating themselves from this ossified and fraudulent faith.

One sees in the suppression of the Cathars a disquieting episode instigated by a religion that demanded conformity and imposed it with the ultimate sanction. From our more favourable historical and geographical standpoint, we can hope that such things have passed, but then we read of modern blasphemy trials and the rise of new dogmatists and would-be Inquisitors. One wonders exactly how far we have come from the days of Bernard of Gui and Pope Lucius III. A range of groups, some political and some religious, have declared the Enlightenment to be their enemy and seek to overturn its legacy. If their project ever achieves success, the corpse of dogmatism will rise once again to threaten all those who value free thought and a free spirit. This time, however, we should learn from the Cathar legacy and not allow the Authority to extinguish the good men and good women.

Notes:

¹ C.G. Jung, *Seven Sermons to the Dead*, 1916, tr H. G. Baynes: http://gnosis.org/library/7Sermons.htm

² p48, 'How Jung Became a Gnostic', Review by: Gilles Quispel *The San Francisco Jung Institute Library Journal*, Vol. 13, No. 2 (Summer 1994), pp. 47-50

³ Christopher Loring Knowles, 'Our Cyberpunk Reality, or Escaping the Prison Planet' http://secretsun.blogspot.co.uk/2011/09/our-cyberpunk-reality-or-escaping.html

⁴ Christopher Loring Knowles, 'AstroGnostic: Hymn of the Pearl Revisited', http://secretsun.blogspot.co.uk/2012/09/astrognostic-hymn-of-pearl-revisited.html

⁵ p21, THE MEDIEVAL MANICHEE, Steven Runciman, (New York, 1961)

⁶ 'The Vision of Isaiah', http://www.gnosis.org/library/Cathar-Vision-Isaiah.htm

⁷ 'Philip Pullman's neo-Gnostic faith', Dec 6th 2007, http://insightscoop. typepad.com/2004/2007/12/philip-pullmans.html

⁸ p4, Kirsten Grimstad, 'Introduction: Thomas Mann and Gnosticism in the Cultural Matrix of His Time' from THE MODERN REVIVAL OF GNOSTICISM AND THOMAS MANN'S DOKTOR FAUSTUS (New York, 2002)

⁹ Grimstad, ibid, p. 23

¹⁰ Grimstad, ibid, p. 3

¹¹ p191, 'On Cathars, Albigenses, and good men of Languedoc', Mark Gregory Pegg, *Journal of Medieval History* 27 (2001) 181–195

¹² p514: [An explanation of A Compend] from HERESIES OF THE HIGH MIDDLE AGES, Walter Leggett Wakefield and Austin Patterson Evans, Columbia University Press, 1969

¹³ 'Manichaeism in the Early Sassanian Empire', Manfred Hutter, *Numen*, Vol. 40, No. 1 (Jan 1993), p6

¹⁴ 'In search of a missing link: The Bogomils and Zoroastrianism', Eva Weiling-Feldthusen, *KONTUR* nr. 14 – 2006, p4

¹⁵ p100, 'The Book of Urizen', Chapter 1, verse 1, WILLIAM BLAKE: SELECTED POETRY, ed. W.H. Stevenson (London, 1988)

¹⁶ Weiling-Feldthusen, ibid, p9

¹⁷ p3, THE BOGOMILS: A STUDY IN BALKAN NEO-MANICHAEISM

¹⁸ Chp 9, THE GNOSTICS: HISTORY, TRADITION, SCRIPTURES, INFLUENCE, Andrew Philip Smith

¹⁹ p491, 'Papas Nicetas: A Byzantine Dualist in the Land of the Cathars'. Dimitri Obolensky , *Harvard Ukrainian Studies*, Vol. 7, OKEANOS: ESSAYS PRESENTED TO IHOR ŠEVCENKO ON HIS SIXTIETH BIRTHDAY BY HIS COLLEAGUES AND STUDENTS (1983), pp. 489-500

²⁰ Weiling-Feldthusen, ibid, p5

²¹ Obolensky, ibid, p500

[22] L'histoire du catharisme en discussion: Le "Concile" de Saint-Félix (1167) by Monique Zerner, reviewed by: Fredric L. Cheyette, Speculum, Vol. 79, No. 1 (Jan., 2004), pp. 288-290

[23] p104: 'The Problem of Cathar Apocalypticism', Raymond. A. Powell, Koinonia XIV (2004) 101–117

[24] 'The Catholics, the Cathars, and the Concept of Infinity in the Thirteenth Century', Anne A. Davenport, Isis, Vol. 88, No. 2 (Jun., 1997), pp. 263-295

[25] 'Was There Life beyond the Life beyond? Byzantine Ideas on Reincarnation and Final Restoration', Alexander Alexakis. Dumbarton Oaks Papers, Vol. 55 (2001), pp. 155-177

[26] p227, 'Jesus' Entry into Parinirvna: Manichaean Identity in Buddhist Central Asia', Hans-J. Klimkeit, Numen, Vol. 33, Fasc. 2 (Dec., 1986), pp. 225-240

[27] p113 'Utnapishtim in the Book of Giants?', John C. Reeves, Journal of Biblical Literature Vol. 112, No. 1, Spring, 1993

[28] Runciman, ibid, p172

[29] p188, THE OTHER GOD, Yuri Stoyanov (Yale, 2000)

[30] p193, Stoyanov, ibid

[31] E.g. see pp234-5. 'An Exposure of the Albigensian and Waldensian Heresies', likely by Ermengaud of Béziers, reproduced in Wakefield and Evans, ibid.

[32] p146, Anne Bradford Townsend, PhD thesis – 'The Cathars of Languedoc as Heretics: From the Perspectives of Five Contemporary Scholars' submitted July 2007 at Union Institute and University, Cincinnati, Ohio

[33] Townsend, ibid, p144

[34] p152, Townsend ibid

[35] p157, Townsend ibid

[36] Townsend, ibid, p158, quoting Himmelfarb from ASCENT TO HEAVEN IN JEWISH AND CHRISTIAN APOCALYPSES (New York & Oxford, OUP, 1993)

[37] p169, Townsend ibid

[38] Townsend, ibid, p185.

[39] p676, 'Blake and the New Theology.' Review of The New Apocalypse: The Radical Christian Vision of William Blake by Thomas J. J. Altizer by:Thomas Merton The Sewanee Review, Vol. 76, No. 4 (Autumn, 1968), pp. 673-682

[40] p15, Runciman ibid

[41] 'Philip K. Dick, Sci-Fi Philosopher' Simon Critchley, 'The Stone', New York Times, 21st May 2012 http://opinionator.blogs.nytimes.com/2012/05/21/philip-k-dick-sci-fi-philosopher-part-2/

[42] 'If You Find This World Bad, You Should See Some of the Others', delivered as a speech by Dick at the second Festival International de la Science-Fiction de Metz, France, in September 1977. Reproduced in THE SHIFTING REALITIES OF PHILIP K DICK, ed. Lawrence Sutin, (New York, 1995), p240

[43] Sutin, ibid, p333

III : 2

AN INTRODUCTION TO BOGOMILISM

DIMITAR MULUSHEV

The Bogomils are frequently mentioned as possibly progenitors of Catharism, but in western Europe at least they are much less well known. This chapter is intended to fill out some of the uncertainties with factual information.

AT THE beginning of the eleventh century, in the area of the Greek Orthodox Church, a new religious movement grew up, known as the Bogomils. 'Bogomils' means 'those who love God' or 'God's friends'. It is also suggested that the founder of the sect was a man named 'Bogomil' ('God-dear'). Other authors believe that the founder of the doctrine of the Bogomils was Boyan Magus, otherwise Beneamin, who actually studied in the School of Magnaura.[1] He and Peter the First were both sons of Simeon the Great. Pope Bogomil was a priest, and he helped to spread the teaching and to organize the spiritual movement, in Bulgaria and abroad.

The teaching of the Bogomils arises from the dualistic doctrine of the Manichaeans and the Paulicians, and was brought by Syrian and Armenian immigrants to the Balkans in the eighth Century. It contains many elements of Bulgarian and Slavic folk beliefs. Unlike the Paulicians, the Bogomils did not assert radical dualism, but a middle ground between orthodox Christian views (in which the one God is an almighty and merciful God) and the Paulicians, who believed in two gods, the good God and the evil God. The teaching of the Bogomils was monarchian, which means that they had the good God as the Creator of the world, and Satan as a fallen angel (created from the good God) who would be ultimately defeated by the good God. The teaching of the Bogomils is the result of a combination of old Syrian

Dimitar Mulushev has a Bachelor's degree from the University of Plovdiv, Bulgaria, and a Master's from the University of Sofia and has also studied in France and Germany. He has worked for Bulgarian National Radio and lives in Sofia.

Gnosticism with the teachings of Messalians or Euchites.

In this account, the world was created by God the Father. Later, his older son Satanael, or Satan, fell, along with other subordinate spirits, and his place was taken by the younger son Jesus Christ. Nevertheless Satanael kept the divine power, and so he was able to organize the Earth, which was not yet formed, and give it the form in which the first humans found it. They were created by him, but their spirit came from God. Satanael eventually agreed that he would possess only the body of the man, while God would protect their souls. But Satanael did not hold to this agreement, and coveted the soul of the people. He seduced Eve and joined with her in the form of a serpent, and thus engendered Cain and his twin sister Kalomene. Out of jealousy Adam united with Eve too, and engendered Abel, whom Cain killed instantly.

Some time between 925 and 950 AD, a village priest named Bogomil became prominent in the Balkans, probably in the mountains of Macedonia. He said something like: 'Let us flee the evil world and lead the quiet, pious life of monks. All the power of the state and all wealth (such as the Orthodox Church possessed) are vain and empty. All the glory of the churches, all the splendour of the golden icons, all the pompous celebrations of marriages and baptisms do not mean anything. Let us rather live by simple food, wear simple dress and lead a modest life in prayer and contemplation.'

That message found approval from the squirearchy, the lower priests and the peasants because times were hard and uncertain. Bogomil and his followers, the 'Bogomils', began life as wandering mendicants.

As mendicants, the Bogomil missionaries came to Bulgaria and found followers there. The Bogomils practised renunciation in the context of physical life, since everything material was creation of the evil spirit; their main goal was the slow rejection and annihilation of the body – the source of all sin. They lived solely from plant foods, although fish was allowed. Wine was not. They wore a black monk's habit, including a rope, which they received at their ordination. They are described as gentle, courageous, calm and taciturn people with a pale look: people who did not talk much, never laughed and always walked with their head down. They worked, but only as much as necessary in order to eke out a meagre life. They rejected marriage, and were against children inasmuch as they resulted from marriage. Marriage was approved only when necessary, but it could be easily dissolved.

Bogomils sharply criticized the church hierarchy and the priests. They rejected all sacraments except baptism, and also the symbol of the cross, because this was the tool with which Christ was tortured and killed. They rejected the worship of saints, images of saints, icons and relics in the Orthodox Church and condemned the churches as dwellings of the devil, along with all kind of liturgies and religious worship rituals. One of their contemporaries said that the Bogomils instructed their members to refuse to obey the state authority, to revile the rich, to hate the Tsar, to berate officials and to blame the nobles. Every service and every relationship based on domination was scorned as a creation of the devil. Courts and punishments were not admitted. Consequently, Bogomils were in constant conflict with the Church and with the state, and secretly formed their own communities with their unique organisation, reminiscent of the order of the first Christian communities.

The Bogomils had no rituals or liturgical ceremonies. They wanted to build Christian life based not on tradition, but on spiritual experience. They met at a ceremonial table fellowship modelled on the early Christian 'love feast'. They had no hierarchy of priests, but merely a subdivision of their followers into 'perfect,' 'believer' and 'auditors'. The latter are better described as 'sympathizers'; the 'believers' were full members of the Bogomil communities. The 'perfect' was characterized by abstemious living, but above all by a natural authority that was based on his or her internal development, on the 'extent of the inner light, which he had brought to light'. To become a 'perfect', 'baptism in the Spirit' was needed: the only sacrament the Bogomils accepted.

The Bulgarian 'Friends of God' – that is, most of the 'perfects' and the 'believers' under them, were vegetarian and non-violent. They did not want to kill the divine that lives in everything. They saw it as their duty not only to themselves to unfold with the help of the inner light of Christ, but also to redeem the evil in the world gradually through their example and their love.

Thus they wanted to prepare for the oncoming 'Kingdom of the Holy Spirit'. They believed in the possibility of reincarnation of the soul, but not in eternal damnation. They rejected the veneration of the physical cross, but left behind a wealth of non-physical crosses of light and life.

The Bogomils' beliefs were that Evil came from heaven because of the fall of Satanael, who was a son of God. The result of this 'Fall of the Angel' were matter and the planet Earth. But because Satanael could not breathe life into the people, God gave every man a 'spirit or spark' which was a part of His own light. Hence the inner duality of man: from the outside he belongs to matter, and from within to God.

It was assumed until recently about the Bogomils that they believed only in a virtual existence of Jesus of Nazareth on the earth and in a 'pretend' crucifixion (the belief known as 'Docetism'), but this is actually based on a misunderstanding: they believed that the inner core of the personality of Jesus of Nazareth, which they called the Christ, was not from this world, and therefore could not be killed.

Because in the Old Testament there were a lot of statements that they could not reconcile with a loving God, they rejected it to a great extent, and recognized only the Psalms and the books of six prophets as given by God – but not, for example, the books of Moses, which they regarded as inspired by the devil. The possibility that these books, like so many others, had been corrupted by the former priest caste is no longer so attractive to us, but the church had a tradition of textual criticism going back many centuries.

After cruel persecution in Bulgaria and the Byzantine Empire, the Bogomils' teaching became widespread in the Balkans, and also in Serbia, Bosnia, Italy, France, Germany, England and Russia. It had different names in different countries – Bulgars, Cathars, Albigensians, Patareni, and also Kudugeri, Torbeschi and Babuni.[2] Essentially it remained the same. In Bosnia, Bogomilism acquired followers and was made a state religion. The relation between the Bogomil Church in Bulgaria and the communities of the Cathars in southern France is particularly close. Many banned books and apocryphas came to Langeudoc, or Occitania. The connection was very close, and the danger to the church and the state's power was immense.

Soon these itinerant preachers were present throughout much of Europe, preaching the way of abstinence, and denouncing the dissolute life of the Catholic clergy. The heretical voice became ever louder, and fell on more and more fertile ground.

The Catholic Church resorted to a crusade against the Cathars or Albigensians (named after the town of Albi) and burned or otherwise killed thousands of heretics. With 'fire and sword' they set themselves to root out the heresy and misbelief. Whole villages of the heretics were destroyed, but to no avail. The Cathars (or pure ones) were content to die for their high ideals. And behind them there came yet more followers and other leaders of the movement, which spread across the whole of Europe. Next there arose the Catholic Inquisition, responsible for the deaths of millions....

The Cathars have set an example: that it is possible to stand up for a heavenly ideal, even if it seems to be outwardly hopeless; that it pays not just to believe in the good, but also to testify it by the way we live; that it makes sense to fight for the light and to bring illumination in a peaceful manner. That the spiritual energy of this sacrifice at the human level was not wasted is reflected in the continuation of history – in not only religious, but also political terms. The Enlightenment of the eighteenth century would not have been able to take the shape it did without the Cathars.

The movement of the Bogomils and their principles thus strongly influenced European history and culture.

Even the church guessed that the spirit of early Christianity, which was resurrected in Bogomilism, cannot be extinguished. Pope Pius II (1458-64) had to admit that the Church was hardly ever challenged with such a robust movement and with such force. Nevertheless, the efforts of the church against these 'bad people' who call themselves 'good Christians', were ultimately unsuccessful. In fact, long before the end of the Bogomils in the Balkans, the doctrine had spread throughout Europe. Fleeing Bogomils moved from Albania to Italy. Others found their new home in Ukraine and in Russia. The famous Orthodox monastery on Mount Athos in Greece was for a long time – until the fourteenth century – a bastion of Bogomilism. Great figures of Western history, such as the Roman heretic-revolutionary Arnold of Brescia, the Calabrian abbot Joachim of Fiore, and the poet Dante Alighieri may have been influenced by the echoes of this movement. Even Francis of Assisi, who was called 'Holy' by the Catholic Church, showed in his love of nature and simplicity rather Bogomil traits – finally, against his will, there was founded 'his' Franciscan Order, and hundreds of his most faithful disciples (called Spirituals) were later burned at the stake by the Inquisition. But above all, it is clear that there were strong links between the Bogomils of the Balkans and the Cathars of southern France and Italy, and the 'Friends of God' of the Rhineland. Later came the Renaissance, the Reformation and the Enlightenment, and in this manner the ideals of Bogomilism, which cannot be wiped out, come through to us today.

Notes
[1] In Constantinople.
[2] The last three names in this list are local to the Balkans.

FROM THE CATHARS TO THE REFORMATION

ROGER SHORTER

The author looks at the Cathars in the context of Biblical translation into the vernacular from earliest times to the time of the King James Bible – and considers some of the royal intermediaries who were involved in the process.

C AN THE activities of the Cathars be linked to what happened during the Reformation?

In both cases, what was shared was an interest in the Bible, and a desire by the translators that ordinary people should be encouraged to read it in a language they could understand, and not just in Latin – which only the educated could comprehend.

So how can the work of individual biblical translators in England and northern Europe during the sixteenth and early seventeenth centuries be connected to what happened in the south-west of present-day France many hundreds of years earlier?

The task of biblical translation as a crucial part of the Reformation is usually thought to have started in a comprehensive way with John Wycliffe, sometimes described as the morning star of the Reformation in the mid-to-late fourteenth century,[1] but translation work started long before he was active in Yorkshire and at Oxford University. Some of it was undertaken by and with the encouragement of Royalty and members of the aristocracy, as will be described in more detail later, and especially those who had links with the land now known as France.

The activities of the Cathars, sometimes known as the 'pure ones', or the 'Albigensians' (because they were thought to have been associated with the town of Albi) and their enthusiasm for certain biblical writings, especially

Roger Shorter has had articles on lifestyle published by the Joint Church Press and has reviewed books for the *Methodist Recorder*.

St John's Gospel, which they encouraged the general population in their region to read and learn, may be rather unfamiliar to many people today, even
those whose special area of interest is the Reformation. But there is a bridge
through history which links the work and ideals of many individuals and
groups in this enterprise of translation, despite the setbacks and opposition
from Church authorities with which they were often faced. Not all these translators and those who supported them had links with France (or Gaul, in the
early times of the spread of the Gospels), but a surprisingly large number did.[2]

Perhaps the best way to explore how this chain of interconnected activity developed, not least for the benefit of those who know little about
the Cathars, is to start with what may be regarded as the outcome – the
end of the story, when the Reformation had become established – com-
mencing with more familiar historical figures who are nearer to our own
time. And then to work back, in broad terms – though inevitably there
will be gaps – to the time when those we know today as the Cathars were
most active, inspired by the biblical teachings that were so crucial to them.
Also, not least, to cast some light on why the Gospel of John might have
featured so strongly, as did some of the letters of St Paul.

As this chapter is being written just after the well-publicised Diamond
Jubilee celebrations of Queen Elizabeth II, a start may be made by referring
to the better-known figures associated with her namesake during a period
in history when the Reformation had become established. For it was after
Elizabeth I (1533–1603) became Queen in 1558 that England became the
people of a book, and that book was the Bible. It was the one book then
familiar to every English person. It was read in churches, and at home.[3]

Elizabeth, born at Greenwich Palace, was the daughter of Henry VIII
(1497–1547), and the Reformation is linked to the latter part of his reign
when he became involved with Anne Boleyn (c. 1507–36). Earlier, though,
the German Protestant reformer, Martin Luther (1482–1546), had protested against the sale of indulgences by the Catholic Church in 1517. He was
supported by the local population as well as by noblemen including the
Elector of Saxony.[4] In a section on Lutheranism in one reference book, the
Albigensians are mentioned together with the 'Waldenses'.[5] These were
the Waldensians, founded by Peter Waldo, a preacher from Lyon (c. 1170)
in the southern part of France. Though their views differed from those of
the Cathars, they too emphasised the importance of returning to a life of
Apostolic simplicity, based on reading the Bible in their own language.[6]

Though Henry VIII was an enthusiastic, serious, and literal-minded reader of the Bible, it was Anne Boleyn, Henry's second wife and mother to Elizabeth, who became the catalyst for the Reformation. The reform process began when she gave Henry a then controversial treatise by William Tyndale (c. 1494–c. 1536), whose work of biblical translation into English became the basis for the King James Bible, first published in 1611.

Like Tyndale the Cathars too were keen to see biblical works translated into the vernacular, so that the general population could read them, and Anne had personal experience of courtly activities that were particularly associated with the Cathars. Though she was from Kent, her father, Thomas Boleyn (1477–1539), was a widely experienced diplomat who spoke French well. His career took him and the rest of the family, including Anne, to the Valois Court of the wife of the future Francis I (1494–1547), who was from Angoulême, north–east of Bordeaux.[7] He was King of France from 1515. This Court put particular emphasis on the concept of courtly love[8] – an idealised form of love as advocated in the New Testament (Romans 12 : 10, for example),[9] and also in the songs of the troubadours, both of which were emphasised in aristocratic circles, and especially in those areas linked to the Cathars, and certainly when their renown was at its height in the twelfth and thirteenth centuries.

At that time the risks involved in passing on this work of Tyndale's were considerable – and not just for Anne. For example, when Henry was aged eighteen, Cardinal Wolsey was still said to be persecuting anyone reading Tyndale's New Bible (translation) in English.

Tyndale, in turn, had been inspired by a very much earlier generation of Royalty, namely King Athelstan (c. 895–c. 939) who was crowned in Kingston-on-Thames in 925[10] and 'had some of the scriptures translated into English'.[11] In this he was following the example of one of his ancestors who had helped to translate some books of the Bible into English and who, together with his father, had not only visited France, but continued on to Rome. If in doing so they had passed through lands where Albigensian influence was strong, this may have encouraged the work of translation, following Cathar tradition.[12]

The main work of translating the Bible into English before Tyndale, however, was undertaken by those studying with and around John Wycliffe (c. 1329–c. 1394). Born near Richmond, in Yorkshire, he seems to have commissioned the translations rather than, as others did before him, undertaken this activity himself.[13] Like Luther, he objected to the system of penances and indulgences adopted by the then established Church, and asserted the right of everyone to read the Bible for themselves – a very Cathar belief.

Wycliffe's supporters, or those who thought along similar lines, came to be known as 'Lollards' – a word meaning 'mumblers'. But, given the level of persecution of those who translated the Bible into the language of the common people at that time, it is perhaps not surprising that they had a reputation for 'mumbling', rather than speaking out more clearly. Their activities preceded the initiatives undertaken by Calvin as well as Luther. Most of those in Government may have had to wait until the time of Elizabeth I for their Reformation, but the people of England and much of Western Europe of the fourteenth and fifteenth centuries had theirs in the Lollard movement, though for those who lived in lands where the Cathars had influence, this came even earlier.

In England, great efforts were made by the Church authorities to eradicate Wycliffe's teaching and to vilify his reputation. After his death, even his body was dug up and burned by the ecclesiastical authorities so that his ashes could, more anonymously, be disposed of in a river.[14] Yet despite all these threats and efforts to intimidate during his life and beyond, Wycliffe had some aristocratic and Royal support from those who had geographical connections to areas in, or close to, Cathar country.

Richard II (1367–1400), born when Wycliffe was probably in his forties, came from Bordeaux in the south-west of France, not far from the lands most associated with the Cathars, and the region that had gained such a reputation for culture.[15] It was not perhaps surprising then that Richard himself gained a reputation for encouraging literature and the arts, following his accession as King of England at the age of ten. He was said to have ruled as a moderate Constitutional Monarch for some eight years and, unlike his successors, Henry IV (1366–1413) and Henry V (1387–1422), did not persecute the Lollards, until political and Church pressures seemed to have forced him to take a harder line against Wycliffe. In this early period, a number of influential people in Richard's Court were said to have been sympathetic to Wycliffe and his translation work. This support is likely to have been encouraged as the result of Richard's marriage, at the age of sixteen, to Anne of Bohemia.

At this time, the Kingdom of Bohemia had a substantial portion of the population who were proto-Protestants or Eastern Orthodox Christians more open to the idea of being able to read the Bible for themselves, and especially in Prague at the time of Jan Hus – sometimes spelled Huss – whose ideas of reform had, in turn, been taken from the works of Wycliffe and his followers. The connection was made because a number of scholars accompanied Anne in her journey to England, as part of her wedding party, and they took Wycliffe's writings back home with them when they left the country. These writings were put in a library to which Hus had access as Rector of Prague University, and it was he who helped to ensure that Wycliffe's Translation and reform work survived.[16]

Had Richard II, despite perhaps being influenced by what survived of Cathar culture, not married Anne of Bohemia, the process of reform and the emphasis on translating the Bible into the language that ordinary people could understand (thus leading to the Reformation) might have suffered an irreversible setback.

However, Richard, being very young, not only when he acceded to the throne, but also when he married – younger even than Henry VIII had been at the time of his first marriage – would have needed support in terms of developing policy. So who supported him during his early, reform-minded period? John of Gaunt (1340–1399), Duke of Lancaster, was not only Richard's uncle, but very influential in the Royal Court. A strong supporter of Wycliffe, he controlled the Government when his nephew was young, and in due course was made Duke of Aquitaine – Cathar country – by the King. John of Gaunt also had developed a link by family to lands that lay to the south of Cathar country when, in his second marriage, he found a wife in Constance, the daughter of Pedro, the King of Castile (1334–69).[17]

Despite the Duke of Lancaster's support for Wycliffe, though, it has been said that were it not for Hus, Wycliffe's teaching would have been forgotten.[18] So had not John of Gaunt helped to arrange, as he probably did, his nephew's marriage to Anne of Bohemia, the development of the Reformation, including biblical translation, would not have taken place as it did.

Two centuries earlier, another very influential Royal family with strong links to France came to power at a time when the Cathars were approaching the height of their fame and influence. Henry II (1133–89), King of England, born at Le Mans in western France, came to control an Empire that extended all the way to the Pyrenees. He, like his descendant Henry VIII, was an intellectual who, though he was undoubtedly energetic and brave, preferred to seek success through negotiation rather than as the result of battle.

Henry II married Eleanor of Aquitaine (c. 1122–c. 1204), following the annulment of her marriage to Louis VII of France in 1152. She was, in her own right, a Duchess of the largest Duchy in the land now known as France, stretching from Poitou to the Pyrenees. She held this title for sixty-seven years (1137–c. 1204) because she was the daughter of William X (1099–1137), Duke of Aquitaine – the same title that came to be given to John of Gaunt by King Richard II of England.

William X had been born in Toulouse, and another Royal family link with this city that was so sympathetic to the Cathar cause was created when one of the children of Henry and Eleanor, Joanne, known as Joan of England, married Raymond, Count of Toulouse. He acknowledged the Cathars to be virtuous.[19]

There is more that could be written about connections between France and several earlier Kings of England and Wessex, together with the translation work that they encouraged. A longer article or short book is feasible in view of the amount of material available, including a reference to one Saxon King who can be linked to a Black Madonna statue; how the daughter of an English King was given to a Cathar community to be looked after; and how one early translation into the vernacular had its entire focus on the Gospel of St John.

Interestingly, a number of the English Royal family associated with France and who either protected Cathar sympathisers or who helped to protect biblical translators, were also called John. One was King John; another was John of Gaunt. Yet another was Richard II, or Richard of Bordeaux, as Shakespeare describes him.[20] But he was not baptised Richard. This was the name he took as Sovereign. His baptismal name was 'John'.

Certainly the Gospel of John was very important to the Cathars, just as it was to the Apostles who fled to the lands and islands to the north and west, following their persecution.[21] Over a period of time, a number were said to have reached the western Mediterranean and Gaul, and continued on to Britain, and Glastonbury in particular.[22]. At that time – before the year 43 – the British Isles were outside the Roman Empire, and thus a safe haven.

The notion that they could have brought with them a version – perhaps an early draft – of the Gospel of John, is entirely plausible. After all, there are reports that each gospel went through several versions, perhaps as many as five.[23]

Of the Gospels, 'John's is the first fruits of the four', according to a report of the writings of one of the greatest thinkers and theologians of early Christianity, Origen of Alexandria (c. 185–c. 254).[24] Perhaps even more importantly, this gospel is regarded as an eye-witness account.[25]

What then more likely than that the Cathars, including those who may have been their first-century precursors, would have studied this gospel, and encouraged their followers and others who were in sympathy with their lifestyle and ethos to do so also? They were aided in this activity by translating biblical texts into the vernacular in the first centuries of the Christian era. This work of translation continued in succeeding centuries, culminating in the Reformation.

The Albigensians considered that understanding, and reading scripture, and sharing this understanding with the local population, was indeed very important.

This, certainly, was the Cathar view.

References and Notes:

[1] Edwin Robertson, WYCLIFFE. Marshalls Paperbacks, 1984, p. 8.

[2] Hereafter, whenever the word 'France' is used this refers to the land currently known as France, though parts were formerly known as Gaul up to the sixth and early seventh centuries.

[3] H.G.G.Herklotts, HOW THE BIBLE CAME TO US. Pelican Books, 1959, p. 14

[4] PEARS CYCLOPAEDIA. Book Club Associates with Pelham Books Ltd, 1988, B39

[5] Ibid., J30

[6] Ibid., J54

[7] N.M.Paul, TRUE STORIES FROM FRENCH HISTORY, Griffith Farran Browne & Co., 1890, p. 27.

[8] Simon Schama, A HISTORY OF BRITAIN, vol. 1; BBC Worldwide Ltd, 2000, p. 245.

[9] 'Love one another with brotherly affection; outdo one another in showing honour' (taken from The Revised Standard Version of the Bible, a revision of the King James Version, published in 1611; Collins)

[10] Neil Grant; Consultant, Alison Plowden: KINGS AND QUEENS; The Book People Ltd, 2003; first published in 1996 by Collins, p. 79.

[11] Melvyn Bragg, BOOK OF BOOKS. Hodder & Stoughton, 2011, p. 12.

[12] Christopher Brooke, THE SAXON AND NORMAN KINGS. Collins Fontana, 1967, p. 106.

[13] Edwin Robertson, p. 8

[14] Ibid.

[15] See entry for Richard II in CHAMBERS BIOGRAPHICAL DICTIONARY; Harrap Publishers Ltd, 2011

[16] Adrian Gilbert, THE NEW JERUSALEM, Bantam Press, Transworld Publishers & Random House Group, 2002, p. 73.

[17] CHAMBERS BIOGRAPHICAL DICTIONARY.

[18] John Harvey, THE PLANTAGENETS, Fontana Books & William Collins & Co Ltd., 1967 p. 756 (first published by B.T.Batsford Ltd, 1948)

[19] Jacques Madaule (translated by Barbara Wall), THE ALBIGENSIAN CRUSADE. Burns & Oates Ltd, 1967, p. 10.

[20] *King Richard II*; a final description by Sir Pierce of Exton; Act V, Scene VI

[21] e.g., Acts of the Apostles 11 : 19: 'Now those who were scattered because of the persecution that arose over Stephen travelled as far as Phoenicia and Cyprus.'

[22] Professor R. F. Treharne, THE GLASTONBURY LEGENDS; Sphere Books Ltd, Abacus edition (first published in 1971), p. 5.

[23] Introduction to 'The Gospel according to John', Canongate Books Ltd, 1998, p. ix.

[24] The Revd Professor Roberts and James Donaldson, translators, ORIGEN: COMMENTARIES ON THE GOSPEL OF ST JOHN; Red Pill Press, 2006, p. 23 (text taken from 'The Ante-Nicene Christian Library')

[25] E. V. Rieu (Editor, translating from the Greek): THE FOUR GOSPELS, Penguin Books, 1952, p. xxvii. See also John 21 : 24: 'This is the disciple who is bearing witness to these things, and who has written these things; and we know that his testimony is true'.

IV. LEGEND : 1

BOGOMILS – CATHARS:
ONE SOURCE AND ONE PURPOSE

HRISTO MADJAROV

*The author seeks to show continuity between Thracian Orphism,
Jesus' ministry, the Essenes, the Bogomils and the Cathars, and suggests
that the tradition is carried on today by the White Brotherhood of Peter
Deunov (Beinsa Douno).*

Some Basic Concepts

THE TEACHING of the Bogomils and the Cathars has been continuous for more than a thousand years. It is evolutionary, otherwise we would have had no motivation to consider it. I believe that in order to comprehend information about the Bogomils and Cathars correctly we have to understand the meaning of several esoteric concepts such as evolution, the White Brotherhood, the Cosmic Plan, mystic centres and spiritual schools, teachers, spiritual impulses, and the path of the disciple.[1]

Contrary to accepted science, which holds that evolution is a mechanical law, esotericism teaches that it is programmed to develop or cease according to the level of consciousness. The growth of the consciousness is

Hristo Madjarov is an esoteric writer, an Academician at the International Academy for Bulgarian Studies, Innovations and Culture, and a member of the All-Bulgarian Parliament at the Organization of United Bulgarians.
Note: for the photographs that accompany this article, see colour section, p. 6.

led by Creative Hierarchies who have completed their human evolution in past cosmic epochs.

Their combination represents the White Brotherhood. It is not something visible, is neither a sect, nor a church. It is an invisible brotherhood, a fulfilled idea and not an external organization. Its aim is perfection, its instrument is goodness. All religions are methods of the White Brotherhood, for the realization of this evolution is the aim that people will become co-workers with God. Christ shows this aim with the words: 'Be perfect as your heavenly Father is perfect'.[2]

Throughout all the centuries of the past, out of the mystical centre, there radiate spiritual impulses for the realization of a Cosmic Plan for universal evolution.

At the forefront of such impulses there are placed great spiritual teachers, creating visible schools with members who prepare themselves for an entry on to the path of a disciple. The teachers are supreme spiritual beings who enter into human bodies for the fulfilment of spiritual missions on a physical plane. 'The Teachers are not born', says the teaching. They never identify themselves with their material carriers.

The school is a living, conscious structure planned by a higher mind. For a definite number of willing and ready individuals another existence is being devised (a living stereotype); new cognition/knowledge is delivered, superior abilities are revealed, and higher consciousness is developed – causing an evolutionary change. As long as there is violence on earth, the schools remain occult (hidden) or esoteric.

The first spiritual impulse in Bulgaria was given by the mystery school of the patriarch of divination, the teacher Orpheus. Some of the most enchanting myths and legends of the Thracians came from there. For example, one of them is the eternal story of Orpheus, the sage, singer and teacher of the mystery Thracian faith, which is that the sons of the Sun and the Earth will continue their lives beyond.[6] The Thracians lived in today's Bulgaria, Romania, Greece and Turkey from around 4000 BC. As the twentieth-century Bulgarian teacher, Peter Deunov, stated: 'Initially there lived here the Bulgarian Thracians, calling themselves 'gentle people' or 'blagari'. From them the Bulgarians have taken the disposition towards the mystic, spiritual….'[5]

The Thracians are the first bearers of the torch of Divine Love; they prepare the world for the teaching of Christ. From precisely here, the spiritual impulses spread all over the world. The Thracians' spirituality is a contribution to European culture.[4]

The second spiritual impulse introduces the Christianity to the world. Jesus is not Judaean. He comes from the 'pagans'' Galilee and brings the teaching of love among the indoctrinated Jewish hearts. Many reject it, but the Cosmic Plan includes this sacrifice in order that his teaching may be carried into the wider world.[4]

The Thracians are the first to take it up – through the Apostles Andrew, Paul, and Erm (see Romans 16:14). From the Thracian lands comes the first initiated Christian in Europe – the Etnarch Urfil, born in the town of Nicopol by the river Yantra during the fourth century AD. He is the one who designed a new alphabet, translated the Bible into Gothic and baptized the Visigoths who in the following centuries, through the Vandals, Langobards, Burgundians and Franks would build Christian Europe.[1]

The third spiritual impulse brings the School of Boyan the Magus, the creator of the teaching of the Bogomils (the 'dear ones of God') during the tenth century AD. It is an esoteric Christianity – a synthesis of Christ's Love with the Ancient Wisdom.

Spiritually pure and devotional, the Bogomils rejected the corruption of the Church and introduced to the West the Christian virtues, sanctified by divine wisdom. The Bogomil movement has formed a valuable bridge between the coded teachings of the Essene tradition, the Druidic legacy as it merged with the Celtic Christian Goddess, and the subsequent activities of the Cathars or Albigenses in France and Northern Italy.

Bulgaria was a doorway for the Gnostic teaching, in Europe. For some centuries, the golden age reigns in the Balkans. From the ninth to the fourteenth centuries groups of people known as Bogomils teach people of different levels of society a quite special Christianity and the liberation power of the Gnosis.[19]

Let us now explore the connection with the Cathars.

Bogomils – Cathars

The biggest Bogomil influence was on the Cathars of southern France. The beliefs of the Cathars were far too similar to those of the Bogomils for this to be merely coincidence. The Cathars and Bogomils had very similar initiatory prayer-ceremonies and shared a number of doctrines, including an exclusive preference for the Lord's Prayer, the disavowal of marriage, a rejection of the doctrine of the physical Incarnation, an emphasis on asceticism, opposition to the instituted church, and belief in the Devil as a son of God who is the unjust ruler of this world. These are but a few of the common points.[7]

Some scholars have traced the Cathars' origins to Bogomil missionaries, who are believed to have passed through the Dalmatian coast and northern Italy to reach France in the tenth and eleventh centuries. Most researchers support the view that Catharism is a direct legacy of the Bogomils, though a smaller camp contends that the Cathars were formed independently by long-established Manichaean schools in France, and then linked up with the Bogomils at the end of the eleventh century.

The Bogomils' counterparts in the West, the Cathars, encountered from the Catholic Church a different response from the one the Bogomils felt from the Eastern Church. From an etymological perspective, the difference between the Catholic and 'Catharic' Christianity is in the difference between the word-elements *ol* and *ar* or *ari*. *Ol* means all. All is the whole. It speaks to the desire of the Cath-ol-ic Church to be the universal religion. This is the Broad Way.

Ari is as in 'Aryan', meaning noble, cultured, high-born or pure. Hence, the *ari* element of the word Catharic. It meant they carried the noble wise blood of the God race. More importantly, they knew how to create it within themselves. This is the Narrow Way.

The Cathars called themselves Pure Ones after the Goddess known as the Pure One, their term for the Great Mother Mari (meaning 'love').[8]

Persecutions and Migrations

The supreme leader of the Bogomils, Vasili Vrach (the Healer) was arrested in 1111 and was burnt. For his execution a huge pyre was built in the Hippodrome in Constantinople. This was the beginning of the Persecutions. The reason the Church resorted to the mass murder of hundreds of thousands of Cathars most certainly had to do with their alternative views about Jesus. The Catholics said that Jesus was a God. The Gnostics said he stood between God and man.

Rome assimilated a pantheon of ancient gods into a composite Devil. Lucifer became the catchall term for the Devil. In reality, said the Bogomils and the Cathars, the Church was the Devil, the Fallen, who had destroyed Jesus' true teachings in the most underhanded and diabolical manner, by substituting a false Christ for the real one. The Catharic was the true teaching. Like the ancient Gnostics before them, they believed that the godly 'spark,' or spirit, of man has been trapped in this evil world.

They claimed to possess a secret Book of Love (Mari). This mysterious manuscript is attributed to Jesus, who is said to have given it to John the Divine. It was transmitted through the centuries until the Knights Templar and the Cathars adopted it.[8]

The Book of Love was the foundation of the Cathar Church of Love or Amor (the reverse of Roma). The existence of this lost (or hidden) gospel was revealed when the Catholic Church subjected the Cathars and Templar to torture.

The Church, and later the Nazis, believed they must wrest these mystery teachings from those who possess them. Hitler sought to create a super race through eugenics. The Cathars' blood secrets were pure gold to him.

From 1208–1244, something akin to genocide was conducted in Europe. The Church of Rome savagely attacked the Cathars, the peaceful heretics of the Languedoc of Southern France, with a viciousness and detestable arrogance paralleled only by the Nazi atrocities during World War II.[8] Pope Innocent III proclaimed a crusade against them in 1208, and by 1244 (according to one authority),[7] more than one million Cathars had been brutally slaughtered in France. In 1209, for example, the Catholic bishop of Citeaux ordered the entire population of Béziers, a city of 20,000, put to death and their city destroyed. A minority of Catholics also perished alongside the many Cathars because the papal legate is said to have told his soldiers, 'Kill them all; God will know his own.'[7]

Together with that of their wider spiritual tradition – Cathars and Patarenes – the teaching of the Bogomils gets across to Italy, England and France. All Europe flares up because of the Bulgarian heresy. The church brings them up on stakes, burns up their holy books, relics, temples. That way it performs the first holocaust in Europe.[1]

In 1244 the soldiers destroyed the castle at Montségur. 217 men and women, taken hand by hand, perished at the stake. A legend tells the prediction of a bard, that seven centuries later, over the ashes of the martyr, laurels will be full-blown again. In 1944 Antonin Gadal was there to witness the seven centuries' completion, along with seven witnesses.[9]

Despite all the persecution, the truth survived. Bogomils and Cathars burnt like torches that awaken the spirit of Europe, asleep in ecclesiastical darkness. That way truth won its own Renaissance and prepared the souls for the following spiritual wave.[20]

The fourth major spiritual impulse for Bulgaria starts with the coming of the Master Beinsa Douno. The first three, as we saw, came through the Master Orpheus, the Etnarch Urfil and Boyan the Magus. Beinsa Douno reveals that all the three impulses are historical manifestations of the White Brotherhood and fit into the fourth one.

The Master Beinsa Douno

In the twentieth century, Beinsa Douno founds the Bulgarian White Brotherhood or the Fellowship of the Light, as a fourth spiritual impulse of the Great Universal Brotherhood. It contains the first three and brings something new as well.

The White Brotherhood, Beinsa Douno explains, is a Fellowship of Divine Love, Divine Wisdom and Divine Truth, and is responsible for all the new spiritual impulses given to the Earth. This great community is in direct contact with God.

Some of the Purposes of the fourth wave are:[1]

1. Developing new senses – particularly the 'sixth sense';

2. Setting a new paradigm, unifying matter, energy, information, time, space, life in unity;

3. Accepting life as a school for the new person, whereby he/she:

–   Improves him or herself and overcomes life's problems;

–   Steps on the path of the disciple, serves Life for the Whole;

–   Builds new culture, after synthesizing all past cultures;

–   Prepares the world for the coming of the sixth root race…

No matter how much is said about Beinsa Douno, it will never be enough. We only understand that which is below our level of consciousness. Every person is at a certain level of consciousness and has boundaries in his or her outlook. For this reason it is impossible for any disciple to evaluate objectively the work of the Master, and as for external biographers that is completely ruled out.

The bodies Teachers enter are of course not random. They are genetically prepared for a period of several generations.[10] The time of the Master has not passed: it has not yet started. His disciples are the first snowdrops of the New Spring.

Beinsa Douno and the Bogomils

A hundred years ago (1912) the Master Beinsa Douno personally invited sixty-two of his disciples to Veliko Turnovo for a special meeting.[11] There he reminded them how, at the same place, seven centuries ago, as Bogomils, the disciples of the School were cruelly persecuted from the Church and the Throne. At this time the Bulgarian Tsar Boril (1207 – 1218) had usurped the throne. He detested the Bogomils and sought to persecute them. Anti-heretical laws were issued and carried out in 1211, making this effort more or less simultaneous with the Crusade against the Cathars in the West. Boril sent men to gather the heretics from around the land, and then convened a council to try them. Details of this trial, which took place on February 11, 1211, were recorded in a church manuscript called the Synodic of the Tsar Boril. Boril himself conducted the interrogations. Most of the Bogomils who refused to join the Orthodox Church during these trials were sent to prison.[7]

And now (1912), on this same place, seven centuries later, the Master declares a new act of this world drama: 'The Testament of the Colour Rays'. Now we understood, that the bard's legend tells for all the Bogomils, not only for these of Montségur.

Ten years later (1922), when he opened his Divine School, he said to his spiritual students: 'You can say, that we are Bogomils'.[12]

The disciples around the Master have information about reincarnation. Some of them have memory and visions from the past. So Peter Deunov remembers the Bogomils' medicine and becomes 'the healer of Bulgaria'. Despite persecutions, he performs iridology and cures using herbs. His daughter – the artist Lilly Dimkova – paints a picture of Bogomil. I am using some of them in this book. And the writer Nicholay Raynov has revealed the Bogomils' legacy by names and facts, memories of the past. He found the holy Bogomil Scriptures in the island of Malta and wrote a book, not yet published. Peter Deunov's great disciple is the French spiritual teacher, Omraam Mikhaël Aïvanhov.

In 1937, the thousandth anniversary of Bogomilism in Bulgaria, a disciple asks the Master about the Bogomils and their relationship to other spiritual movements.[3] Here is such an exchange.

Disciple: 'In France documents have been found showing that the Bogomils knew about reincarnation.'

Master: 'Reincarnation is a method for self-perfection. Without reincarnation there cannot be self-perfection.... It's time to speak more openly
about the Bogomils.'[3]

And he reveals a secret plan for the education of humanity.

The Master explained that there were three branches of the Bogomil
School.[14]

In a few words they are:[15]

The Teaching of Hermes, the first branch from Egypt migrated to Thrace
via Persia and Babylon. It reappeared with Orpheus... Orpheus, in turn, was
the source from which flowed the Pythagorean and Platonic schools; both
these taught a doctrine of transmigration and purification of the soul....

The Essene Teaching. The second branch operated in Palestine. The Essenes integrated a healthy lifestyle with systematic spiritual practice and an
emphasis on purity. In the Christian epoch this branch extends to Rome,
England, Germany and so on to movements such as the Quakers.

The Bogomil Teaching (dear ones of God). They are the third branch,
who arose in Bulgaria of the tenth century.... 'The Rosicrucian Fellowship is from this Bogomil branch. They have an aim preparing for the New
Culture.'[3]

The founder of Bogomilism was Boyan, referred to by the people as
'Boyan the Magus'. He was the youngest son of Tsar Simeon and brother of
Tsar Peter. Extremely well-educated and unusually gifted, Boyan received
an excellent education and was well acquainted with the ancient cultures
and mystic societies. In the Byzantine annals it is written about Boyan the
Magus that he wore his Bulgarian national costume to Constantinople.[14]

The Bogomils opposed violence in any form; they opposed war, the
death penalty and slavery. As well as the Reformation Bogomilism brought
with it freedom of the individual, political equality and international solidarity. For this reason Bogomilism was the herald of all the great European reformers of whom civilization is so proud today. Eminent Bulgarian
scholars with an international reputation and foreign experts as well have
written about the meaning and history of Bogomilism.[14]

The Bogomils' inner spiritual knowledge or *gnosis* represents a stage
beyond external acceptance of the Church's faith, pointing to an esoteric

dimension of Christianity which has usually been consigned to heretic fringes. But the difference between esoteric gnosis and Church's faith is like the difference between essence and form.[8]

'The Bulgarians were under Turkish bondage for five hundred years as punishment for the persecution of the Bogomils', according to the Master. They were unsuccessful in Bulgaria because of cruel persecutions, but have had a powerful impact on European culture. Bogomilism, however, was of a typically Bulgarian character because the Proto-Bulgars were the bearers of ancient culture and knowledge.[7]

'The wave of Bogomilism and its Brotherhood branches in Europe carried out an enormous task, the effects of which manifested them in the West as well. In the darkness of the Middle Ages, Bogomilism paved the way for the Renaissance. It was the radiant herald of the liberation of the human spirit and personality.'[14]

'The Bogomils are between the present disciples of the White Brotherhood' (said the Master). If somebody wants to study the life of the Bogomils, let them see the life of our Brotherhood. The Bogomils and the Cathars have similar features to our stream, because both the movement comes from the One and the same great Centre of the White Brotherhood.[2]

'We will introduce the facts. Somebody will say: 'Prove this historically!'
We will answer: 'Disprove it historically!'
This is the Law: 'Wherever water sprung, will spring again.'
'Whoever's been rich will end up rich again.'
'Now the Bogomils are coming again!'[3]

References and Notes:

[1] He was announced to the world by Peter Deunov (later Master Beinsa Douno) during his studies in the USA. See Hristo Madjarov, THE FOURTH WAVE OF THE WHITE RACE, WHY THE TEACHING OF BEINSA DOUNO IS NEW. Varna: Alfyola Publishing Company, 2012

[2] The Master Peter Deunov, 'The Wellspring of Good', Compiled by Boyan Boev and Boris Nikolov, see: The Universal White Brotherhood, Bulgaria Kibea Publishing Company, 2002

[3] M. Constantinov et al., 'The Master. Conversations at the Seven Rila Lakes', chapter: The Universal White Brotherhood, Sofia, 2012

[4] Hr. Madjarov, A COSMIC PLAN FROM 5500 YEARS AGO. Varna: Alfyola, 1993, 1996, in English 2012

[5] M. Constantinov, Hr. Madjarov, THE NEW CULTURE DURING THE EPOCH OF

AQUARIUS, vol. 3, chapter: 'Why the Master chose Bulgaria'. Varna: Alfyola (vol. 1, 2, 3) 1991-94, new edition 2012.

[6] THE BULGARIANS, Atlas, Sofia, 2001, p.66

[7] Paul Tise, 'The Bogomils: Gnostics of Old Bulgaria', in *Gnosis, A Journal of the Western Inner Traditions*, San Francisco, CA 94114

[8] William Henry, 'Secrets of the Cathars, Why was the Church of the Dark Ages so Determined to destroy Them?' in *Atlantis Rising*, 36, 2002

[9] Pentagram, June/2012 Lectorium Rosicrucianum Internationale School van het Golden Rozenkruis Bakenessergracht 11-15 NL-2011 JS Haarlem The Netherlands

[10] Svetlozar Nyagolov, BRIGHT BEAM TO HUMAN SOULS (in Bulgarian). Sofia: Videlina, 1998

[11] Beinsa Douno, EXPLANATIONS AND DIRECTIONS FOR THE USE OF THE BOOK, 'THE TESTAMENT OF THE COLOUR RAYS OF LIGHT, Vsemir, 1995

[12] The Master Beinsa Douno, 'The New Life', Assemblies Talks, 19 August 1922 (in Bulgarian)

[13] Paul Roland, REINCARNATION, Arcturus Publishing Limited, 2008

[14] The Bogomils, in THE GRAIN OF WHEAT, THE WORD OF THE MASTER. Beinsa Douno, Izgrev, 1990. Chippenham: Antony Rove Ltd.

[15] David Lorimer, PROPHET FOR OUR TIMES: THE LIFE AND TEACHINGS OF PETER DEUNOV. Rockport, Mass.: Element Books, 1991, p. 4.

[16] Georg Feuerstein, THE MYSTERY OF LIGHT: THE LIFE AND TEACHING OF OMRAAM MIKHAËL AÏVANHOV. Sandy, Utah: Passage Press, 1994, ms. pp. 318,334.

[17] Omraam Mikhaël Aïvanhov, THE SECOND BIRTH: HIDDEN PRINCIPLES OF SPIRITUAL LIFE (Los Angeles: Prosveta, 1976), p.164

[18] Bishop Simeon (Nicolay Raynov), BOGOMILISM AND BOGOMILS.

[19] Pentagram, 5/2006 Lectorium Rosicrucianum Internationale School van het Golden Rozenkruis Bakenessergracht 11-15 NL-2011 JS Haarlem, The Netherlands

[20] Hr. Madjarov, THE RETURN OF THE BOGOMILS (in Bulgarian). Varna: Alfyola, 1997

...ow: John Merrill at
...ségur (*John Merrill*).
...le row: the Hermit's
... at Ornolac (*Colum
...vard*); inside the château
...ontségur, in snow (*Deirdre
...*); John Merrill's final camp,
...e Canal du Midi (*John
...ill*). Bottom: a White Eagle
...e party camps inside
...château at Lordat, 1990s
...um Hayward*), plus Phoenix
...etop (*Dave Patrick*)

page, clockwise from top left: The 'Cathar Bible' (Déodat Roché Museum, Arques. Rituel Cathare de Lyon, Bibliothéque [L]yon); Grail of light, Lanquedoc church altar; St John with cup and green snake, St Catherine's Church, Westford, MA; [J]ohn with cup, snake and eagle, Lestelle-Betharram Chapel; Lady and Unicorn tapestry, Château de Puivert; Château [Cr]oix; Henry Lincoln with Déodat Roché (Roché Museum, Arques (*all photos Ani Williams*). Top centre: Christian Koenig [play]s Pan pipes in the cave (*photo Jeanne D'Août*). **This page, above**: Ani's harp at Puivert; in the cave at Ussat; Adam & [Eve] with snake (St-Nazaire church, Carcassonne); editor and publisher at Dolmen de Sem (*all Ani Williams*). **Below**: view [of] Château de Lordat; the Montagne de Tabe, or Pic de St-Barthélémy, Ariège (*Colum Hayward*)

This page, clockwise: Memorial stele at Montségur, with red candle; Béziers; 'Église' cave, Ussat-les-Bains, 'filled with energy'; Carcassonne; Memorial in the form of a dove at Minerve (*all Jaap Rameijer*). **Right hand page**: Château de Montségur (*Jaap Rameijer*); Montségur in the snow (*Deirdre Ryan*)

Clockwise, above: Etnarch Urfil; Orpheus, by Lilly Dimkova; Boyan the Magus, by Lilly Dimkova; the Master Beinsa Douno (Peter Deunov); Burning at the stake of the Bulgarian Bogomil Vassili Vrach (the Healer) in Constantinople (*photos Hristo Madjarov*)
Below: Bogomil graves at the village of Asparuhovo (Chenge) in Bulgaria (*photos Hristo Madjarov*)

** above**: the 'Holy Mountain' which contains the caves of Ussat and Ornolac (*Jaap Rameijer*); editor and friends at the Gadal house and museum, May 2012, Ussat-les-Bains; publisher leaves the 'Hermit's' cave (*both Jeanne D'Août*). **Below**, from the May 2012 trip: negotiating a cave passage (*Jeanne D'Août*); approaching the caves (*Colum Hayward*)

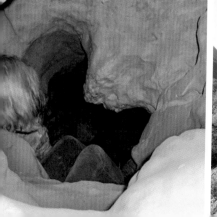

Left: supposed Cathar graveyard at Lordat, Ariège (*Colum Hayward*)
Right: Pentagon—Cathar Cross, Gadal Museum, Ussat-les-Bains (*Ani Williams*)

Above left: view from the 'Pog' of Montségur in the snow (Deirdre Ryan); **right**: Stone Stele, Déodat Roché Museum, Arques (Ani Williams).
Below left: editor and publisher with Henry Lincoln at the Jardin de Marie, Rennes-le-Château; **right**: Descent of the Holy Spirit, an image from Lourdes (Ani Williams)

AN ALTERNATIVE HISTORY

VAL WINEYARD

Among many different theories and ideas which have affected our vision of the Cathars, one thing that stands out is the deliberate suppression of any reference to the role of women in the early Church. This is just one of the things that inform Val's 'alternative history'.

THE RELIGIOUS climate after the Revolution of 1789 in France was anti-clerical – that is, it was against the Roman church which had exploited people for so long. Other ideologies and mythologies rushed to fill the gap. The rise in mysticism in Paris spread to the Languedoc, where many 'secret societies' were formed. This triggered a renewed interest in the Cathars in Languedoc.

In 1870 an anti-clerical liberal called Napoléon Peyrat wrote an account of the Cathars, in which the Cathars hoarded an immense spiritual and material treasure at Montségur that they had taken away and hidden in the foothills of the Pyrenees. In this account the fortress of Montségur became a Cathar Cathedral. Esclarmonde de Foix was portrayed as a virginal high priestess. She changed into a dove as she died, and her spirit flew to freedom. At spirit-raising sessions in Paris she started to appear to believers.

(But Esclarmonde's name is on the Inquisition's list of those who were burnt alive on that fateful day of March 16th, 1244.)

Joséphin Péladan, an Languedocian occultist, declared Peyrat's 'immense treasure' was a cache of secret ancient knowledge. Péladan was

Val Wineyard moved to the Languedoc after a career as a freelance writer and part-time editor under contract. She reads and speaks French, so can study original sources, and has recently written several books about the region of Languedoc. These include MARY, JESUS AND THE CHARISMATIC PRIEST, LOOKING FOR MARY M and THE SACRED RIVER OF RENNES-LES-BAINS, and are available directly from the author on her web-site, which carries many alternative articles: http://writingaboutrenneslechateau.blog4ever.com. Alternatively, write to Val Wineyard, 4 place de l'Eglise, 11200 Canet, France the first to point out that the holy mountain of Parsival, Montsalvat, was Montségur, and the Cathar treasure was the Holy Grail itself, hidden in the mountains between France and Spain.

From the 1930s English and German-speaking people came to find out for themselves. After the First World War they descended on Montségur, where French occultists were finding out more about the Cathars.

Déodat Roché, a notary from Arques, near Rennes-les-Bains, was a disciple of Rudolf Steiner, the founder of Anthroposophy, which promised immediate contact with the spiritual world. Déodat studied Druids and Gnostics. He was the man largely responsible for identifying Catharism as dualist and Gnostic; he was often referred to as the Cathar Bishop, or even, the Cathar Pope.

Déodat Roché wrote about and studied the religious ideas of the Cathars as truly dualist. What he discovered seemed to be some sort of echo from within himself. In short, some think he was reincarnated from one of the Cathars, probably Pierre Authié. Déodat's home town of Arques had a strong connection here. Déodat found an image of Pierre Authié who stayed in a safe house there in the early fourteenth century, and indeed the two looked alike.

Déodat Roché had studied esotericism since the age of 14, and in 1896 affiliated himself with a group run by the magician Papus. Then he joined a 'Gnostic' church and became the bishop of it at Carcassonne. He was a friend of Prosper Estieu, a *félibré* or Occitan poet, who founded a magazine called 'Montségur.' The two had met in June 1900 at Rennes-le-Château, not far from Arques, where Prosper was a supply teacher. Déodat Roché and his society, 'Société du souvenir et des études cathares', placed the stele written in Occitan at the foot of Montségur in 1961, to mark the place where the Cathars died. He himself died in 1978, aged 101.

Another great name of these times was Antonin Gadal, born in Tarascon, Ariège in 1877. Gadal grew up in a house next to the Tarasconian historian, Adolphe Garrigou, who specialised in the history of the Cathars and, seeing a kindred spirit in the young man, took him under his wing as an inheritor of his knowledge. Gadal's fascination with the Cathars led him to the caves he believed were hiding places and sites of worship for the Cathars. Through his investigations he developed a detailed picture of what he believed were the inner mysteries of Cathar faith.

In the 1930s Antonin Gadal attracted a circle of adherents, who also believed the ideas of René Nelli and Déodat Roché. They formed the 'Société du souvenir de Montségur et du Graal' to promote the hidden history of Catharism, linking it to the Holy Grail. The concept of neo-Catharism came into being. Dualism was all. Good and evil, light and dark, sun and moon, male and female. Mary Magdalene represented the feminine side of the divine duality. Her marriage to Jesus now became the sacred marriage of male and female, equal and opposite.

Déodat's ideas were taken up by Maurice Magre, a talented and prolific writer who took opium and wrote two novels about the Cathars. In Paris, he met and was interviewed by the German, Otto Rahn. Otto was passionate about the Holy Grail and was investigating the connections between the German Holy Grail stories, especially the medieval Parsival of Wolfram von Eschenbach, and decided that he agreed with Péladan. Eschenbach's grail castle, Montsalvat, was actually Montségur.

Otto Rahn came to Montségur in the 1930s, assembled all the Pyrenean Grail stories and compared them to the old German stories. Montsalvat was Montségur and the guardian of the Grail was Esclarmonde de Foix, she who was seen ascending into heaven like a dove. The Grail was a sacred stone that had fallen from Heaven and she hid it in the mountains before the taking of Montségur. Her stone was later taken to Bavaria and buried under a glacier in the Alps.

Was Otto Rahn 'taking over French culture'? He persuaded Antonin Gadal to take him on a tour of the various Cathar caves. He wrote a book called CRUSADE AGAINST THE GRAIL: not the Crusade against the Cathars, but against the Grail, the sacred Holy Grail. The brutal armies of the Pope and the King of France were not attacking an alternative religion, the Cathars: they were attacking the Holy Grail itself. Heady stuff.

Otto Rahn's Cathars were also troubadours. The royal courts of France were entertained by minstrels secretly trying to convert people to Catharism and the Holy Grail, he declared.

Suddenly Cathars were at the centre of all the Holy Grail stories, and they were also the pure race of Nordic Germans. This was strange, as the people of Languedoc traditionally hate 'the men from the north' and there is a Germanic 'scent' to the whole story of the Grail.

However, the mysterious Countess Miryanne Pujol-Murat adopted, or patronised, Otto Rahn, lending him her car and chauffeur to do his research. She owned the castle of Lordat, a Cathar retreat never attacked, and Otto joined an archeological dig there organised by the Polaires, another mystic research group. They were expecting to find Cathar treasure, a Gnostic Gospel of St John, or the grave of Christian Rosenkreutz, the founder of the Rosicrucians.[1] But they didn't.

The Countess claimed to be reincarnated from Esclarmonde de Foix, she whose spirit escaped in the form of a dove, one of the most esteemed Cathar *parfaites* and held responsible for the rise of Montségur as the 'Cathar Vatican.' It was more than a place of refuge, it was a cathedral, a temple – a solar temple, no less![2] The Countess was hoping to discover the lost treasure of the Cathars. The Countess believed this treasure was hidden at Montségur by Esclarmonde herself, who then threw herself off the mountain to escape the Papal troops.

Some people believe, as Rahn apparently did, that Esclarmonde had found an actual physical artefact, like a cup, which was the Holy Grail, which was then spirited out of Montségur.

Otto was then obliged to join the SS and returned to the Ariège and Montségur in 1937 to write THE COURT OF LUCIFER. His superiors expected him to prove definitively the German Parsival story, and reveal the actual physical Holy Grail – for Germany. This led to the legends of Germans visiting the region to find the Holy Grail and take it back to Germany; they seemed to think it belonged to them. Otto was obliged to return empty-handed; to his death.

In France the writings of Déodat and Magre led to serious archeological studies at Montségur which gave interesting insights to medieval life but never found anything holy. They found everyday things like buttons, small coins, a set of dice, a pair of scissors, all moving rather than dramatic. Then Fernand Niel researched Montségur as a solar temple. This led to the idea that all Cathar castles were solar temples ... and the Cathars were sun-worshippers....

In 1945 the Gnostic Gospels were discovered and added to other Gnostic fragments found earlier, making a body of knowledge that completely changed ideas of Christ and his teachings. These gospels were hidden by monks to save them around 380AD, because of the purges against heresy made by the Roman Emperor Theodosius. The Gospels that mention Mary Magdalene turned traditional Christianity on its head; these are the *Gospel of Mary* and *Pistis Sophia*.

The *Gospel of Mary* was dated to the second century and could not have been written by Mary Magdalene; the name reflected the style of the times, and today we would call it the 'Gospel about Mary'. The Gnostics who wrote it, recounting events around the time of the Crucifixion, obviously knew of Jesus and Mary Magdalene and their circle. For the first time, it was clear how close to Jesus Mary Magdalene was.

Only seven pages survive and we believe over half is lost, maybe for ever, although one never knows. Various fragments in either Greek or Coptic have been found in quite different places, evidence that it was widely circulated in the fifth and sixth centuries.

The Gospel opens, says writer Karen King, 'in a scene set after the resurrection. Jesus commissions them to go out and preach, then leaves. But they are frightened that the same fate as Jesus awaits them. Mary Magdalene reassures them. But they wept greatly, saying, How shall we go to the Gentiles and preach the Gospel of the Kingdom of the Son of Man? If they did not spare Him, how will they spare us? Then Mary stood up and said to her brethren, Do not weep and do not grieve nor be irresolute, for His grace will be entirely with you and will protect you.'

The Gospel makes it quite clear that the disciples such as Peter hid during the crucifixion. 'If they did not spare him, will they spare us?' They were afraid they too would be crucified. And Mary, as the one closest to Jesus, was the one they came to for answers.

The other Gospel mentioning Mary Magdalene, *Pistis Sophia*, was dated even later, about 250 AD. Sophia means wisdom. This Gospel uses the editorial device of setting an idyllic scene where the evangelists and Jesus debated dogma by a Socratic question-and-answer method. Mary Magdalene played a large role in this, more than Peter, more than John. It makes it quite clear that the early Christians, that is, contemporary followers of Jesus, accepted women initiates who could freely enter or even orchestrate discussions. But Mary fought hard for this. In *Pistis Sophia*, she had to defend her position against Peter, who thought that women should say nothing, in public life or private, never mind preach. But the other disciples supported Mary, because she had such a depth of spiritual vision they wanted to share.

In *Pistis Sophia*, Jesus returns to the disciples eleven years after his ascension into Heaven to exchange views on his teachings. The discussion took place on a mountain in Galilee and during it Jesus prepared a picnic with bread and wine for his disciples. But *Pistis Sophia* is very long, and one man could not have written it in an afternoon with a break for the picnic.

But the mention of eleven years does illuminate something else; Lawrence Gardner, in his books about the bloodline of the Holy Grail, consistently tells us that Mary Magdalene went to Marseilles in 44 AD (eleven years after 33 AD, the supposed date of the Crucifixion) and Jesus later followed her there. Laurence Gardner had been reading *Pistis Sophia*.

This does not ring true. Mary would not have gone to France and left Jesus at the mercy of the Herods, the Pharisees and the Romans. Jesus could not possibly have lived eleven years in hiding in the Holy Land with a death sentence for treason on his head. No, the two left the Holy Land together in May 33 to arrive in Languedoc in the June of that same year. That at least is the conclusion I have come to in my book, LOOKING FOR MARY MAGDALENE.[3]

Pistis Sophia, written in 250 AD, was composed to pass on the Gnostic teachings of Jesus and Mary Magdalene, rather than define history. It was completely natural to them that Mary and Jesus loved each other and she was his closest disciple. That was the Gnostic belief when the book was written, over two hundred years after Jesus was crucified and he and Mary Magdalene fled to France.

I have a copy of *Pistis Sophia*, and it can be read online or downloaded, e.g. at earlychristianwritings.com. I advise all spiritually-minded people to read it, for the spiritual concepts in it are incredibly deep, and relate strongly to the beliefs and practices of spiritual people today.

Back to Modern Days

In the 1960s the British psychiatrist, Arthur Guirdham, found that several of his patients in Bath seemed to have reincarnated from Cathars, and even named them – he himself was Guilabert of Castres. A second book proved they had also 'group-reincarnated' in Napoleonic times. Cressida of Roman times, for example, became Trubellia of the Celtic Church, who became Esclarmonde, who became Pierre in Napoleonic times and is now an English lady called Clare Mills. Descriptions of meetings between these people, and recognitions of their past lives are so vivid one can almost believe it.

In 1969 the Roman Catholic Church, perhaps because of the new evidence of the Gnostic Gospels, after hundreds of years of labelling Mary Magdalene as a sinner, relented and, rather quietly, canonised her. There was a sudden sea-change, and interest and mystic belief in Mary Magdalene grew steadily.

The book HOLY BLOOD, HOLY GRAIL (1982) brought a new surprise; the Holy Grail was the bloodline of Mary Magdalene and Jesus, who had been, according to the Cathars, married; their children lived in Arcadia of Greece and founded the Merovingian bloodline of France; this was pure Pierre Plantard. It was also total fantasy. The book said the priest of Rennes-le-Château, Bérenger Saunière, was paid vast sums of money by the Vatican to keep this secret knowledge from his flock; this was pure Henry Lincoln.

However, this book, along with the books of Laurence Gardner, made it 'common knowledge' that there was a holy bloodline: that Mary and Jesus had given birth to children who were the distant ancestors of spiritual people alive today. That holy bloodline was also the Holy Grail.

In the 1990s there was published Margaret Starbird's book, THE WOMAN WITH THE ALABASTER JAR. Margaret is a sincere Catholic scholar; the last thing she wanted to be was controversial. Because the French word for Holy Grail, *sangraal*, had the same pronounciation as *sang réal*, which means royal blood, she felt compelled to believe that when Mary Magdalene came to the south of France after the crucifixion she was carrying Jesus's child. Her womb was a cup; Mary Magdalene herself was the Holy Grail.

The Holy Grail was the Holy Bloodline.

Interest in Mary Magdalene has expanded like a great atomic cloud. Elizabeth van Buren, who lived at Rennes-le-Château, wrote about her spiritual experiences in LORD OF THE FLAME. They included Mary Magdalene, who gave the Cathars a great treasure – the *Book of Love*, written by Mary herself. It was this book that was smuggled out of Montségur, she says – from the 'cathedral' of the Cathars where great religious secrets were held. The *Book of Love* is linked to the Gospel of St John, and is claimed to contain the great secret teachings that Jesus confided to his disciple John. These teachings were so powerful that all hatred, anger and envy would vanish from the hearts of men and women. Divine Love, like a flood, would submerge the world and indeed, lead to a New World.

At the time of writing, this is all destined to take place on December 20, 2012. Ideas about Mary Magdalene in our region today are overwhelming. You can join 'The Order of Magdalenes' and you can do trance work at spiritual centres here in Languedoc to promote Mary Magdalene's love and compassion, which will change the world. Many people are receiving 'channelled' messages (that is, through a medium) from Mary herself. The messages tell us how much Mary Magdalene loves us and, into the run-up to

20-12-2012, she was promising to change the world afterwards for the better.

The picture of Mary Magdalene is quite clear. Not only was she intensely spiritual, she was Jesus's closest companion, she was not afraid to face the most testing of real life experiences. She was a natural leader and possibly, in some ways, stronger than Jesus himself. He was a man who had thrown the final dice in the game called life; he had risked all and lost but Mary Magdalene had carried him through.

Physically in history, and now spiritually, Mary Magdalene has well arrived in Languedoc. Her link with the Cathars? Her newly-born Christian religion, based on baptism and the forgiveness of sins, with a Gnostic aspect of personal knowledge of God, was known in Languedoc and evolved to become Catharism.

Notes:

[1] Rosenkreutz's grave was to be found at Lordat in the Ariège, according to a local newspaper report about the Polaire trip there in 1931 (see Colum Hayward's article in this book, pp. 173–186); it is also supposed to be at St Salvayre near Alet-les-Bains.

[2] QUE SAIS-JE? ALBIGEOIS ET CATHARES, Fernand Niel, Press Universitaires de France, first published 1955, twelfth edition 1990. On page 115 is a diagram showing how Montségur was aligned to the winter and summer solstices, plus some text on how this descended from the *symbolisme solaire* of the Manichees.

[3] For LOOKING FOR MARY M, and Val's other books, see her own website, http://writingaboutrenneslechateau.blog4ever.com.

LOU TERRADOU

A life as Jules Azéma? See Val's other article in this book, pp. 230–8. The photos show the dedication to Azéma mentioned there, and Azéma's funeral.

CHRISTIAN ROSENKREUTZ, CATHAR?

SYLVIA FRANCKE

Sylvia Francke explores further another local tradition in the Languedoc, which is that it was from the area that Christian Rosenkreutz, the mysterious founder of the Rosicrucians, sprang.

EMBARKING on a personal investigation into the mystery of Rennes-le-Château led me to discover that the hidden mystery stream of esoteric knowledge investigated by the three authors of THE HOLY BLOOD AND THE HOLY GRAIL was a subject of central concern in Rudolf Steiner's research, a subject which I had never had time to fully investigate in the previous decades of my interest in Anthroposophy. It was then I learned that the Cathars were a link in the chain of knowledge and revelation originating in the ancient mystery schools referred to by Rudolf Steiner, who indicated that this 'underground stream' of esoteric Christianity had also passed through the Gnostics, Manicheans, Knights Templar, Rosicrucians and had finally emerged again in Anthroposophy. Steiner particularly refers to the influence of Manichaeism in relation to this stream, which he describes as:

> 'a spiritual movement which, although at first only a small sect, became a mighty spiritual current. The Albigensians, Waldenses and Cathars of the Middle Ages are a continuation of this current, to which also belong the Knights Templar ... and also – by a remarkable chain of circumstances – the Freemasons.'[1]

It appears that there were at least two different streams of Catharism – one, the ascetic stream, dying with the last vestiges of what Steiner describes as mankind's atavistic clairvoyance, and the other going willingly

---

Sylvia Francke studied for the stage and for the teaching of Drama at the Rose Bruford College in Kent. She is an Anthroposophist, being a student of the spiritual scientific research of Dr Rudolf Steiner. Sylvia has used this background of knowledge as an aid to solving the mystery of Rennes-le-Château in her book, THE TREE OF LIFE AND THE HOLY GRAIL.

to the fire knowing that the time was not yet right for what Catharism had to bring humanity. I feel that this second stream inherited the teachings of Mani or Manes, a thirdd-century Initiate who, according to Steiner, later reincarnatedas Parsifal, the central figure in the legend of the Holy Grail.

In his lectures, 'The East in the Light of the West', Steiner speaks of how a gathering took place 'in a spiritual sphere belonging to the earth in the fourth century AD.'

> 'Those who were gathered there were Skythianos, the keeper of the wisdom of Ancient Atlantis; Gautama Buddha, and the then reincarnated Zarathustra. A fourth individuality is mentioned 'behind whom something is hidden which is higher, more sublime' ... than in Skythianos, Buddha or Zarathustra: Manes, 'who is acknowledged as an exalted messenger of Christ.... Then the plan was laid down, how all the wisdom of the Bodhisattvas of the post-Atlantean times was to flow ever stronger into the future of mankind. And what was then decided upon as a plan for the spiritual development on earth was preserved and carried into those European mysteries which are the mysteries of the Rose Cross.'[2]

The besieged Cathars at Montségur were overcome by the French King's army in February 1244. They asked for a truce of fifteen days which they were granted, provided they recanted their beliefs. It seems strange that they should ask for this space of time when they knew that to recant would not be an option and so faced death with courage to the end. The final day of their reprieve, March 14th, coincided with the Spring Equinox that year, the day of 'Bema', the Manichean Easter Festival.[3] They handed themselves over on the 15th and were all dragged out and burned in the field below Montségur on the 16th.

Might it be that the ceremony performed inside the Château de Montségur on that night was also in some way dedicated to the future in keeping with the council in the spiritual world referred to above? Could it have been that preparation was being made for our present time at the turn of the twentieth and twenty-first centuries and for an even more distant future time, in which Manichaeism will be the inspiring impulse for humanity?[4] The twelfth century has been described as a time when humanity was nearly bereft of the original spiritual vision, the darkest time in evolution before a new form of consciousness could come into being. In saying this Steiner is speaking from his view of the evolving relationship of the body, the soul and the spirit.[5] The ceremony in Montségur would then mark a last possibility of establishing the esoteric Christian Stream for the future before the storm clouds of materialism engulfed the western world.

The ceremony Steiner refers to was carried out only six years before the initiation of an earlier incarnation of the 'Christian Rosenkreutz' known of in the fifteenth century, and has been described by Steiner as happening 'In a place in Europe which cannot be named yet'.[6]

A rumour went around Ariège in the early 1930s that the French esoteric group known as the Polaires, who have reason to be considered in this tradition, were in the area looking for traces of Christian Rosenkreutz, whom they believed to have passed through the area. This may or may not be true, but certainly the Polaire author Maurice Magre wrote in MAGICIENS ET ILLUMINÉS[7] that Rosenkreutz had had an incarnation in Cathar times, preparatory to his better-known one. Elsewhere in this volume Colum Hayward describes how certain French Polaires and also Grace and Ivan Cooke were at the Château de Lordat in 1931 possibly searching for a material treasure, but that both Grace and her husband emphasise the power of the spiritual discovery that she (Grace) made, and 'how her discovery may always have been planned to be unique and private to herself'. They say that in this place she had 'an experience so beautiful that it changed her life and guided all her future work'. It connected her channel of inspiration with the particular mission of St John, the 'Beloved' of Jesus. It was initiatory, and is in its own way remarkable because she had left England with almost no idea whatsoever of who the Cathars were, and certainly it is unlikely to have known how crucial to them was the Gospel of St John. Rudolf Steiner describes the previous incarnation of two successive 'Rosenkreutz' individuals as having been 'John the Divine'. Hence in the line of these incarnations Rosenkreutz is often referred to as 'the John Being'. The vision Grace Cooke had left her 'as in a dream or haze of happiness for days'.

All of this is further prompting to wonder if there was a connection between this earlier incarnation of Rosenkreutz, the ceremony held at the end of the siege and the actual identity of the 'Treasure' of Montségur: something or someone smuggled out in the moonlight down the steep cliff walls before the Cathars met their end? In other words, was the 'treasure' a young Rosenkreutz being taken to safety before his initiation in 1250? After this he only lived for a short time, and reincarnated again in 1413 – this time living to a ripe old age, once more surrounded by the circle of twelve who had previously initiated him, this time acting as their leader and Initiator.[8]

On Christmas Day 1923, at the Goetheanum in Dornach, Switzerland, Rudolf Steiner laid a spiritual Foundation Stone for the Anthroposophical Society in the hearts of its members, at the same time opening the Mysteries to all humankind.

'The seven or eight hundred members present represented the membership at large. But in a deeper sense, they represented the spiritual quest of modern mankind. They were chosen by destiny to receive the Foundation Stone into their hearts directly from Spiritual heights. But they could also feel that those not present – including perhaps those not living on the physical plane, were participating in the laying of this Foundation Stone as well. Certainly many souls in the spiritual world were listening, both the departed and those yet unborn. The Hierarchies – called upon with such great power – listened too.'[9]

It has been related that, as he did so, several of those present witnessed how 'Christian Rosenkreutz and his host marched into the Schreinerei "as the mantra was spoken"'.[10]

Montségur has sometimes been referred to as a 'Grail Castle'. In the Grail Legend it has been described how Parsifal rides from the Court of King Arthur, representing the Western Mysteries, to find the Holy Grail at the Grail Castle – which have been connected to the Eastern Mysteries. Might it be that these two ceremonies, one at Montségur in 1244, the second taking place in the Goetheanum at Christmas 1923, were linked? Maybe Rosenkreutz, who has been described as representing the Mysteries of the South, brought these together with the Mysteries of West and East at Montségur in 1244 in his third European incarnation. Then, in 1923, when he joined the assembled company at the Goetheanum, the time prepared for in the fourth century was beginning to be fulfilled. Christian Rosenkreutz, representing the Mysteries of the South, met the Mysteries of the North, Rudolf Steiner's twentieth-century Spiritual Science.[11] From that moment onwards all of mankind could benefit from the possibility of access to what was once hidden in the Ancient Mysteries.

Notes:

[1] Rudolf Steiner, 'The Temple Legend', lecture 6, p. 61. Berlin, 11th November 1904. Rudolf Steiner Press 1985

[2] Rudolf Steiner, 'The East in the Light of the West.' Munich, August 31st

1909 (at Steiner House, 35 Park Road, London W1).

[3] The day when the Manicheans commemorated the conversion of King Shapur by Mani.

[4] See Rudolf Steiner, The Temple Legend, Lecture 6, pages 70-71. Berlin, 11th November 1904. Rudolf Steiner Press 1985.

[5] Steiner describes the human 'soul' as the mediator between the physical body and the eternal spirit … the Ego which was liberated by the Fall of Lucifer. Man began as a being who had originated in a purely spiritual world, through the fall he was increasingly distanced from it. In one of his fundamental books, THEOSOPHY, Steiner describes this changing relationship between the human being and the spiritual world of his origin now mediated by the activity of the "soul".

'Through the body we belong to the physical world. With our spirit, we live in a higher world. Our soul binds the two worlds together during our lifetime…. Between the Body and the Spirit the Soul lives a life of its own. It is served by its likes and dislikes, its wishes and desires, and places thinking at its service.'

An aspect of the soul is the 'astral' body. The 'ego', or 'I' are alternative names for the Spirit. Rudolf Steiner named the different stages through which the soul developed in this gradually changing relationship between the ever more conscious activity of the human body and fading perception of the spiritual world. Each stage lasted for over a thousand years whose duration was named according to new faculties the soul was experiencing at the time. Steiner named the stages of this changing relationship as follows:

Sentient Soul 1900 B.C. orektikon
Intellectual Soul 747 B.C. kinetikon
Consciousness Soul 1413 A.D. dianoetikon.

As connection with the spiritual world faded, so human beings gained independence and began to develop individualized thinking bound to the material brain. It was because of this limitation that human beings could advance with freedom to nurture their innermost forces, which could eventually be turned outwards to grasp the spiritual in nature and by so doing begin to re-attain the spiritual origin from which they had been alienated by the Fall. This alienation has intensified through the time when the Consciousness Soul was developing, a time which has to do with the awakening activity of human individuality, the eternal spiritual core of our being, the human Ego. Since its first feeble activity began, this Ego has the task of transforming the subtle human sheaths which had been impaired by the Fall. The ultimate goal of the Consciousness Soul Age has to do with the eventual transformation of the astral body which will then become an effective tool for reversing the damaging effect of the Fall on all of the human bodies, both subtle and physical.

[6]Rudolf Steiner, 27th September 1911, Neuchâtel, in the Steiner House collection. 'In a place in Europe that cannot be named yet – though this will be possible in the not very distant future....' A note against this states: 'this place was not named later, either'.

[7] Paris, 1930, and translated into English as THE RETURN OF THE MAGI (London, 1931). For all other references in this paragraph see Colum Hayward's article, 'A Trip to Ariège in 1931', on pp. 173–86 of this book.

[8] The first European incarnation of Christian Rosenkreutz is also mythically connected with Fleur from the legend of Fleur and Blanchefleur, the two figures known historically as the grandparents of Charlemagne. (See Walter Johannes Stein: THE NINTH CENTURY IN THE LIGHT OF THE HOLY GRAIL, London: Temple Lodge Publishing, 1991, pp. 68, 76 and 86.) The birth and death dates of the second European incarnation are not known, he has been described as a youth who was initiated in 1250. The third, more widely known European incarnation of Christian Rosenkreutz was between 1378 and 1489.

[9] F. W. Zeylmans von Eimmichoven, THE FOUNDATION STONE, Rudolf Steiner Press, London, 1963, page 37.

[10] Bernard Lievgoed, MYSTERY STREAMS IN EUROPE AND THE NEW MYSTERIES, New York NY: Anthroposophic Press, 1982, p. 71. The 'Schreinerei' was the carpentry building remaining from of the original building, the Johannes Bau which had been burned by an arsonist on New Year's Eve 1922.

[11] Ibid.

V. SEARCH : 1

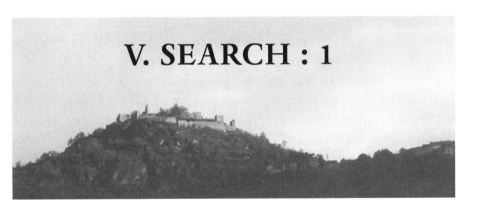

A VISION OF A CATHAR BROTHER

GRACE COOKE

*The story of Grace and Ivan Cooke's visit to the Château de Lordat in Ariège
with members of the Paris-based Groupe des Polaires is given in 'A Trip to the
Ariège in 1931', which also describes the 'Oracle' that led them, mentioned
here. This is the account she herself gave of her vision at Lordat.*

THE BULK of humanity takes little account of what might be called
'spiritual' treasure, which, as Christ said, is laid up 'where neither
moth nor rust doth corrupt, and where thieves do not break through nor
steal'. In other words, the inner light cannot be destroyed by time or death,
for, like the life of the mystical Phoenix, it can spring up again from the
burnt ashes of the past.

The enemies of the Great White Light are legion and think that they
can forcibly destroy the influence of the inner light by massacring its followers; being ignorant that invisible guardians have this ancient wisdom in their
charge, and that wherever the Light of God has been established by the lives
of saints, its power will persist, and its influence for the upliftment of man-

Grace Cooke (1892–1979) was the medium for the spirit guide White Eagle and
the co-founder of the White Eagle Lodge. She was also a notable teacher of
meditation. The extract given here is from her preface to White Eagle's commentary on the Gospel of St John, in the original edition of 1949. White Eagle's
best-known book is the volume of his sayings published as THE QUIET MIND.

kind continue. This is proved by the spiritual power which can so often be felt or 'sensed' near places recognised as sacred and hallowed, usually where saints have lived or been buried, or where once a brotherhood of the White Light or monastery has been established. I would repeat that the destruction of any group of people living in accordance with the Law of Christ, which is the Ancient Wisdom, cannot annihilate the eternal secret. It remains stamped on the surrounding ether, and is as enduring as a treasure buried in the earth. For this reason I believed that the secret left behind by these pure brothers, who, by virtue of their lives belonged to the Great White Lodge, remained to be discovered by who should follow after. In like manner Jesus was crucified and for a time abandoned by his followers, but the power of his life could not and never will be destroyed. He taught in parables and demonstrated this secret power by his miracles; and today, nearly two thousand years afterwards, the influence of his life and teaching continues. Moreover, the spiritual power left by that wonderful life is still felt by those who visit the Holy Land.

I felt assured that these people, the Albigenses, had also a mission, and were guardians of a secret which had been given to them by one of the world's great teachers of spiritual truth.

This, briefly, is the story of the place to which many centuries later we were thus guided by the Sages, in search of the hidden secret of the Albigenses. During our stay we climbed each morning to the summit of the mountain in the hope of being led to the right spot for beginning excavations, for I, for one, still thought we might find written documents containing this secret. From the beginning we were strongly impressed by the dual nature of the unseen powers around us. There were times when the dark forces were predominant. Then, immediately following the resulting confusion which afflicted some members of the party, came, like a breath of heaven, a sweet, pure, gentle loving influence like a spiritual illumination, which made us certain of the presence of the immortal brothers waiting and watching. At such times as these we felt we were under the protection of great white wings, guarded by a power which must be experienced to be believed. Although we were wandering on the top of the mountain amidst dangerous elemental forces, and in the company of unbalanced human minds, we were constantly reminded, by the whispers of the unseen – ghosts of a by-gone age – that Christ is all-love and his spirit has power to comfort and protect from all harm. This strengthened our will to proceed. Many times this wave of spiritual light and power caused the dark veil between matter and the inner world to become thin, to such a degree that we found ourselves in company with the gentle spirits of the Albigenses, who for centuries had walked this very plateau on which we stood.

The days were often warm and even at so great an altitude the atmosphere could grow hazy with heat. On the third day after our arrival, when we were idly contemplating the grand panorama of mountains under the intensely blue sky with, in the distance, the ancient castle of Montségur,[1] my attention was caught by the sudden appearance of a shining form. The word 'shining' is the only word to describe the aura of the spirit who appeared, but his manner was as normal as that of any human being might be who, while out walking, had stumbled by chance upon a stranger. He appeared simply, kindly, and treated the situation as naturally as if it were customary for discarnate people to talk to men and women. He looked like an old man at first sight; that is to say, he wore a longish white beard and his hair was silver, but, apart from this his skin was youthful and clear, as though a light shone behind the flesh, and his warm blue eyes were alight with an inner fire. He was clothed in white, in the garb of some early order of Christian Brothers and bore himself with noble meekness. 'Could this be one of the Albigenses?' I asked mentally. Yes. It was true; by sign and symbol he proved to me that he belonged to this age-old Brotherhood. Why had he appeared in this manner? In answer he pointed to what appeared the opening of a cave in the side of the mountain half a mile away across the valley....

In answer to my mental questions he replied that he had been directed by the Sages to guide us in our search. It was true, he said, that great treasure had been hidden by his people, but then these ancient sun-brothers held knowledge of much secret wealth, which was guarded until the time came for its wise and right use. The world's standard of values must change before man could be trusted rightly to employ precious metals and stones, which were however in the past regarded as symbols of spiritual wealth. Until humanity should be ready to use nature's wealth for the spiritual culture of the whole community, it could not bring happiness, but instead a heavy burden. Man must learn the correct value to the soul of both spiritual and material gifts before he can safely and happily handle either.

The messenger continued: – Only through development of this soul-knowledge and its use for the good of all, would humanity qualify to find the buried treasure. For the spiritual law is that the candidate for initiation into the mysteries of life, both human and spiritual, must proceed on his course without deviation, patiently and steadfastly discovering and uncovering within his own divine nature attributes and powers which will give him the key to wealth, both physical and spiritual. Therefore it seemed that the first step towards the locating of this treasure was to find some spiritual clue which would help us towards the completion of our task.

In the life and teaching of Jesus the Christ, our visitor continued, would be found the key to the spiritual treasure buried within man. After the resurrection and departure of his Master one of his disciples, John the Beloved, had voyaged to the West and had visited this same mountain, where he had spent long hours in spiritual communion with his Master. Then, returning to the east, John had founded the Brotherhood (which became known as the Albigenses), imparting to it the wisdom that he had learnt from his Master. Its treasure and its secret was that store of spiritual wisdom which might indeed be called the complete Gospel of St John, of which the existing gospel is but a fragment. Before his passing John had been called to the Sages in the east, where he had spent the last years of his life. Nor did John die as most men die, but passed onwards to the higher life as his Master had done before him.

Many centuries later it appears that the Brotherhood founded by John took ship and sailed to the west, subsequently settling among the mountains of France, where they became known as the Albigenses. They were in fact still the Brethren of John, the founder of their group, whose gospel was their secret and their treasure.

When our visitor had gone the writer lived as in a dream or haze of happiness for days. Not that she did not do her best to help the other members of the party, who spared neither time nor effort to find or unearth something tangible as a result of their visit....

It will be remembered that it was through the 'Oracle' that the instruction had come from the Sages which had brought us to the Pyrenees, and 'They' stated further that it would take three days for the person they had chosen to find this treasure.

On our third day on the mountains this White Brother had appeared and given his message. Now the treasure, after a lapse of years, appeared as none other than these true teachings of Divine Life; which coming in the form of messages are gathered in the book, THE LIVING WORD, setting forth the inner meaning of the life contained in the Gospel of St John. For the treasure, if received, is none other than Life itself. This is the secret of the ages which men have to find: the Christ Secret of Eternal Life. And this was the intention of the Sages, which by their particular methods, they had accomplished.

Next, a year or two after this visit to the Pyrenees, directions were received to form a group of the White Brotherhood in England, whose first task was to help suffering humanity through the 'Years of Fire'; and during those very years the contents of this book were given.

The plan thus seems to have originated with the Sages, who had produced the 'Oracle' and arranged the long series of events to precede the reception of the later messages. To me the work seems similar to the construction of a temple raised by invisible builders and composed of spiritual substance. To me each episode in the story seems like a stone gradually being shaped and perfected, until ready to be laid in its appointed place. All has been done with a skill and foresight beyond the power of man. The writer is convinced that this plan has been perfectly conceived and executed with the object of uncovering from the dust of ages a buried spiritual treasure, ancient but ever new in its power to reveal to man how to find the secret of happiness within himself and to lead man from ignorance into the Eternal Light.

Since our visit we have come to know more of the brothers of the unseen, who say that they come from the Cave of the 'Cross within the Circle' in the far east. The Albigensians had also adopted this as their symbol, which, being interpreted, means 'those who have both overcome the darkness and limitation of the lower-self or the baser nature; and by precept and practice have been admitted into the holy rites of brotherhood, i.e., who have partaken of and continue to partake holy communion with their Master throughout their earthly lives, and so live as brothers in service to mankind'. This act of continued communion through brotherly service is symbolised by the tau cross, but is incomplete without the circle of white light surrounding the cross. The whole signifies the partaking of and absorption into the heart of the cosmic essence or 'wine', sometimes referred to as Christ's 'blood'. It is the life of the Sun which gives life and substance to the grape from which wine is extracted. The Sun represents the light and life of the world, a physical representation of the light of Christ which lighteth every man. To live wisely and well man must live in constant communion with the bread and wine.

Bread represents the mortal body (or earthly life) which must be lived in brotherhood and love one towards another, and wine is the symbol of the true spirit or life-force of Christ, the Sun or Love of Christ living within the heart.

[1] See an explanatory note on p. 175 of this book.

THE CALL OF THE CATHARS

L. SHANNON ANDERSEN

*'I did not know that something, or someone was calling…. I did not know that
a voice in the night could be the mouthpiece of a memory, and that friends
could speak after seven centuries of silence…. I did not know that the Cathars
were calling.' Arthur Guirdham,* WE ARE ONE ANOTHER

WHAT MAKES anyone an expert on the Cathars? Even more important, why would anyone strive to be an expert on a group who practised a form of primitive Christianity seven hundred years ago? For me it
was an unquenchable thirst for knowledge, a magnetic pull to walk on their
paths – a call. It was the 'call of the Cathars'. And I had questions myself.
Was their message one that was shared by brotherhoods with secrets from
the time of Jesus, and if so, what was the message, and why is it still important today? Were the Cathars connected to Mary Magdalene, and if so, how?
Why are there groups and individuals having clear, documented experiences
of past lives as Cathars? Is the message of the Cathars still important?

I first discovered the Cathars after joining a White Eagle Lodge group
in Flagler Beach, Florida, facilitated by Keith and Heather Threlfall. One
evening I showed up for the regular meeting and Heather and I were alone
for the first time. Keith was in Costa Rica working on building a centre
for White Eagle. Heather and I shared our own story of awakening, after
which Heather felt it appropriate to lend me her precious copy of the book,
THE RETURN OF ARTHUR CONAN DOYLE , edited by Ivan Cooke. I had read about
the Cathars, also known as the Albigensians, in the introduction to White
Eagle's book THE LIVING WORD OF ST JOHN, but it was from the story in THE RE-
TURN OF ARTHUR CONAN DOYLE that I began to explore their significance to my

---

Shannon is the author of the very successful book THE MAGDALENE AWAKENING.
She is also a licensed counsellor, transpersonal life coach and hospice bereavement counsellor and trained in regression under Dr Brian Weiss. A popular
speaker, she lives in Florida, USA when she is not travelling internationally.

life. Arthur Conan Doyle had come back through the medium and White Eagle channel Grace Cooke to tell about what he had learned since his death. (The latest publication of the book through the White Eagle press is under a different title, ARTHUR CONAN DOYLE'S BOOK OF THE BEYOND.)

After the death of her mother when Grace Cooke was seven, her family deepened their interest in the Spiritualist movement. From then on it became normal for her to see and hear the spirits of those who had died. White Eagle, her Native American guide, had visited her at about this time. He most often came at night or waited for her to wake in the morning. He was more than a disincarnate spirit. White Eagle was the voice of the Masters, known as the Great White Brotherhood, who watch over the planet, but he always appeared to her as a Native American chief, which was one of his incarnations. As an adult she began her career as a gifted medium at a time when many were losing their loved ones to war.

Grace Cooke first met Arthur Conan Doyle's daughter in his bookstore in London. His daughter arranged for the two to meet; however, one week before their appointed meeting, Arthur Conan Doyle died. Six months later, Arthur Conan Doyle's spirit came, via an arithmetical oracle, to a group of seekers in France known as the Polaire Brotherhood. The Polaire Brothers were directed to go to London and meet with Conan Doyle's family. They were seeking an exceptional medium to accomplish their goals and they were told how to identify the right person. They found their 'clear channel' in Grace Cooke.

Arthur Conan Doyle was not only the famous author of the Sherlock Holmes mysteries, but a crusader for Spiritualism, especially after the death of both his younger brother, Innes, and his son Kingsley in the influenza epidemic after the first world war. Doyle proclaimed he had just entered the most significant mission of his life. For the rest of his life he travelled all over the world to give free lectures on life after death and Spiritualism. For this he was severely criticized, losing many of his friends. He said, 'From the moment that I had understood the overwhelming importance of this subject, and realized how utterly it must change and chasten the whole thought of the world when it is wholeheartedly accepted, I felt … that all other work which I had ever done, or could ever do, was as nothing compared to this.' His message: 'They are not dead'. The message was so important to him that he spent over a quarter of a million pounds of his own money to take it to the world (THE LIFE OF SIR ARTHUR CONAN DOYLE, John Dickson Carr).

THE RETURN OF ARTHUR CONAN DOYLE was fascinating. It recounted all that

Arthur Conan Doyle had not known while still alive on earth. There was so much more to know. The book described the journey of our souls after leaving the body, what happens after death. It resonated with what I had learned so far on my path. The book inspired me, but the epilogue changed my life forever.

When the book was completed there was another instruction given to the Polaire Brotherhood in Paris. They were told to go to the south of France to a castle at Lordat, near Montségur, where they were told they would find the hidden treasure of the Cathars. Grace Cooke trusted the Polaire Oracle, and along with a group of the Polaire Brothers, travelled to the Pyrenees Mountains in southern France to use her psychic abilities to help find the treasure. While the other members of the party dug for treasure, Grace Cooke encountered a gentle spirit, a shining brother who identified himself as a Cathar, an Albigensian, coming from the sphere of 'John' – the writer of St John's Gospel. Perhaps there was treasure in terms of gold, or manuscripts containing hidden knowledge not yet found, but the real treasure came in the message given to Grace Cooke that day.

The treasure was one of a spiritual nature. I believed the treasure was the lost message of the Cathars, and Grace Cooke was charged that day with her mission to transmit this teaching, which had been passed from Jesus to John the Beloved. She would continue the works of the great brotherhoods by bringing the teachings of the Cathars to the world through the words of White Eagle. White Eagle's message began to form the philosophy of love that has ever since helped and healed people all over the world. The teaching has become a simple revelation of mystical Christianity. It transcended religious dogma and brought together the wisdom teachings throughout the world.

Both the story and the Cathars immediately intrigued me. When Keith returned from Costa Rica, we sprawled the map of France across the table and began to look for the Languedoc, the region known in France for its Cathar heritage. We knew it was near the Pyrenees. Finally we located Montségur, the last stronghold of the Cathars. I knew, in that moment, that I had to go.

When I first began to seek information on the Cathars, the history fell short of what I intuited. They were actually branded heretics, persecuted, and eventually annihilated by the Catholic Church through the Albigensian Crusade and the Inquisition that followed. I read everything I could find on the topic, including the books of Dr Arthur Guirdham, the senior consultant psychiatrist in the area of Bath, in the west of England for well over thirty years. Dr Guirdham was an Oxford scholar, a doctor of medicine, a psychiatrist, scientist, philosopher, poet, and writer of many medical books, but was primarily known for his books on the Cathars. He uncovered a group reincarnation of Cathars and diligently spent years researching the facts through the Inquisition records. As a result he became a world authority on the Cathars and came to believe, like them, in the pre-existence of the soul and that it was possible for the soul to be united in successive human bodies. In other words, he believed in reincarnation. Dr Guirdham's experience was tangible and documented and led him to a belief in group incarnations himself. Life for him was much bigger than what could be superficially observed with the physical senses. One of his clients, remembering a lifetime as a Cathar, had been able to write poetry in Mediaeval French and the distinct language of the Languedoc.

Our perspective on the Cathars and their historical and literary records is distorted by the Inquisition and conflict with the Church destroying many of the Cathar records and literature, just as it killed off the living exponents of Catharism. What I learned about the Cathars was that they were a group of Christians who suddenly appeared in the Languedoc region of southern France during the late twelfth and early thirteenth centuries and attained prominence during that time. The teaching had origins in Bulgaria, with the Bogomils, and it spread to northern Italy and to the Languedoc.

The Cathars were simple, clean living, good people. Their 'priesthood' (it was more of a system of elders), called the *perfecti* or *parfaits*, were known by others as *les bons hommes*, the good men. They believed that Jesus was a divinely inspired teacher, and he was their spiritual master, but they did not venerate the cross. Would you worship the rope they hung your father from? They were, like those living at the time of Jesus, a small number of individuals with special gifts who healed and preached the word of God, passing their gifts on to others to continue the healing mission by a transmission known as the *consolamentum*.

They repudiated the Catholic Church's sacraments, and unlike the Catholic priesthood, theirs did not live in luxury. They lived poor, simple lives, in humble communities, teaching and preaching. Like the Essenes during the time of Jesus, broadly speaking, they were Gnostic, immersed in that which is beyond the body, and they used their inner connection to God for healing, clairvoyance and telepathy, with pure spirit as their source.

The Cathars were dualists. They believed there were two Gods. One created the evil earth and the other created the world beyond. The faithful were divided into two groups: their elders, or *perfecti*, who admitted women as well as men, and the followers or believers. The believers had no strict rules; they were expected to eat and procreate just like everybody else. The ultimate aim was for them to prepare themselves to undergo the sacrament of *consolamentum*. When one had the *consolamentum* one became a perfect. For the vast majority of believers this was administered on their deathbed, which is probably just as well, because as a perfect they had to live a very strict life, abstaining from eating meat and from performing sexual activities, and had to dedicate their lives to the service of the community of the Church. They were extremely admirable people. The churches began to empty and the Cathar faith took hold. Because of their encouragement of industry and activity, establishing papermaking and craft centres throughout their region, a level of prosperity was reached in the Languedoc. According to some historians, if the Albigensian Crusade had not frustrated it, the Renaissance would have taken place two hundred years earlier, not in Italy but in the Languedoc.

Their activities did not endear them to Rome or to popes such as Innocent III, and after the murder of one of his legates who had been sent to represent him and quell the problem, it was this Pope who decided to call a crusade. Before he did, however, he sent in a preaching ministry headed by a Spanish priest, Dominic de Guzmán, who founded a home for fallen women, which failed miserably. Dominic, along with several others, went on a vigorous preaching campaign but lost his patience and said 'preaching and entreating has failed us, now you will receive the stick'.

The Albigensian Crusade started shortly after Dominic's preaching ended. By joining the crusade, the crusader would receive forgiveness for all sins past and future. The heretic's possessions, including land, would be forfeited to anyone who could grab it. It was a licence to rape, pillage and steal. The crusade went on for over thirty years. What was worse was the Inquisition that followed. Dominic de Guzmán and the Dominicans began their brutal campaign in an attempt to stamp out the Cathars (a name given them by the Catholic Church). De Guzmán, for his pains, became St Dominic in 1234. The Holy Order of the Inquisition terrorized the area for another sixty years and then went on to terrorize Europe.

My relationship with the Cathars continued through synchronicity, travel and the past-life memories of those who entered my life. I was led to France so that I might walk in what I knew were the footsteps of the Cathars. It was before I understood exactly why. I felt propelled to continue, and during the last decade I have returned to the pays des Cathares, the Languedoc region, a total of eight times. As I walked in their footsteps and read their story, I began to unravel a truth about them, weeding out the historical reports laid down by the recorders of history that called them heretics. I heard their message in my heart, through the veil that thinned as my feet walked on their path.

My first trip to Montségur was in 2001. We left for France on May 13, the anniversary of the first day of the last battle of the thirty-year crusade against the Cathars by the Catholic Church. For some reason I was driven to be there on May 22. Why I had to be there on May 22, the two-two day as it was called in THE RETURN OF ARTHUR CONAN DOYLE, I didn't know at the time. I also didn't know at the time it was a significant day for Mary Magdalene and the gypsies in Saintes-Maries-de-la-Mer, a small town on the Mediterranean coast of France. I began to connect Mary Magdalene and the Cathars, because of the synchronicities. During that part of my journey, the three major synchroncities were between the master numbers (444, 222, 1111, etc.), Mary Magdalene, and the Cathars.

It was years before I began to contemplate a connection between Mary Magdalene and the Cathars, even though one of the early pointers was the fact that the first battle of the Albigensian Crusade, in which Arnold Amalric and his crusaders approached the gates of Béziers to ask for the citizens to turn over the 222 Cathar priests held within their walls, was on the feast day of Mary Magdalene: July 22, 1209. As with so many of my initiations on the road to awakening, I may not have understood all of the implications, but the result began the process ever so subtly to create the inner knowing and trusting. (This story I recorded in my book, THE MAGDALENE AWAKENING: SYMBOL AND SYNCHRONICITY HERALDING THE RE-EMERGENCE OF THE DIVINE FEMININE.)

During the years of studying the Cathars, I often misread, misinterpreted and misunderstood, made assumptions and had to backtrack, but I jumped into my journey to know the Cathars with my whole heart. I studied White Eagle and after many years of seeking, discovered the connections. My questions still remain unanswered. What were the connections between the other synchronicities in my life, the master numbers (222, 444), Mary Magdalene, the Cathars, even the Knights Templar? I can only speculate.

In 2002 I went to the English Lake District to follow leads I'd found in the work of Arthur Guirdham. I sat in the Pheasant Inn near Bassenwaithe Lake. I contemplated the Cathar journey and pondered its relevance. That day I sat in an overstuffed armchair and composed a letter to the deceased Dr Guirdham on the Pheasant Inn's elegant stationery. From his book, THE LAKE AND THE CASTLE, I knew he had been there many times, reading, thinking, and contemplating his mysterious experiences. Not long ago I found that letter in a stack of souvenirs from my journey. I had expressed my appreciation for his work and his guidance and offered my services to continue his work by carrying on the Cathar message.

Over one-third of my book, THE MAGDALENE AWAKENING, in some way dealt with the Cathars, their history and their presence in the past and present as their influence showed up in my life, some through the past-life memories of my clients and my friends all over the world. I remember one specific incident when I exchanged a past-life regression for a reading with a woman who channelled John the Beloved. (Around this time John seemed to be showing up in a variety of ways.) Helen Barton was living in Australia but working in Hong Kong in 'Reflections', a spiritual bookstore where I sometimes work. Ruby Ong, the owner, had encouraged the exchange, and during Helen's past-life regression she had a memory of being a Cathar. I was a part of her memory. When she arrived home from that trip, a friend knocked on her door. She handed her a book, Arthur Guirdham's THE CATHARS AND REINCARNATION. She remarked in an email message following the experience, 'the circles within circles of synchronicity continue to bring the group together'.

The first edition of my book was published in 2006, with a second edition coming out in 2008. At that time my life took a turn that pulled me away from my writing. A series of family deaths and then illnesses required my attention, not to mention my full-time job with hospice. I shelved the Cathars along with my book, so to speak, for a while, but that changed in April of 2012. I received an email from Mary Dodd. Mary asked if it would be okay for her brother to send me a letter. He had read my book and was having an experience and he hoped I could help. I agreed.

Just a month before I received the request from Mary, around March, my daughter, Melissa, asked me to join her on a trip to England and Scotland. I agreed and booked a flight but added a bit of extra time on both ends of my trip to spend on my own. I did not know the Cathars were once again about to breach the barrier of time in my life. After booking the flight, I received the letter from Mary's brother. The sixteen-page handwritten letter from Robert Ellison, called Butch by his friends and family, arrived in April. A Florida native born in Miami, he was an outdoorsman, raised hunting and fishing in the Everglades, not even computer-savvy let alone interested in spirituality. He had a basic Christian upbringing with little questioning or interest in metaphysics. In his letter he told me of an experience that started in 1983. At that time, he had a mysterious contact at a camp he'd built in the Everglades, and for many years felt himself possibly possessed. Butch was confused and frightened by the experience but became obsessed with it, bringing concern to his friends and family. A mysterious young woman appeared to him in a series of visions that began on April 4, 2004 (4/4/04!). She was sitting on a bench in front of a castle. In her lap she held a bowl and in the bowl were three lilies, one red and two white. It always happened in the same way. In the vision she placed the bowl down on the ground on her left side and then would begin to dance. She spoke with an unrecognizable accent and eventually another woman came in his visions and became her interpreter.

Both women were very real to Butch. He could actually feel the interpreter rest her head on his shoulder. With the help of the interpreter, the dancing woman began to give Butch detailed information including specific locations in and around Tipperary County, Ireland. Of these places he had no foreknowledge, and wrote the names phonetically, checking for correlation later and he drew by hand a map on the lined notebook paper for me to study. The castle he came to believe was the Rock of Cashel, in Ireland, the castle of St Patrick.

I wasn't sure what to think when I received the letter, but I knew that what he was experiencing was not uncommon in the world I lived in, so I felt I could help him at least feel sane in the midst of his experience. I called a friend, Fred – a left-brained engineer, open to right-brained ideas – and asked him for help. We then called Butch and communicated via speakerphone; our first conversation went on for over an hour while Butch told his story. We were able to give him some confirmations, some education in the subject, and we agreed to support him.

The reason Butch had sought me out was the synchronicity of the numbers 444. He had read my book, which described my experience with the master numbers, particularly 444. At the end of our conversation, when I hung up the phone, I looked at the time. It was 4:44. In the light of my long history with the angelic message of 444 I paid attention. And there was more. His vision always came at the same time, 11:44 pm. His son calculated that this time was 4:44 am in Ireland.

When Butch became more comfortable with this mystical relationship, he was given more information. The woman gave him her name and date of birth. She said she was born in southern France on May 22, 1191; her name he understood to be C.D. Muir. Among other things she said she was coming to him from 1212 and that she had been on the run for three years. She provided another clue that tied me to the story. She began to talk about a river he could never find in modern Ireland. He Googled the name along with the year 1212 and found it. Today it is called the Shannon, which is my name too.

C.D. Muir told him I could be included in their communications. She said, 'To be perfect, you must also be pure. Dispel the devil of the earth. Don't be afraid'. I was told to 'take a walk on my path'. Two words triggered a Cathar connection: the word 'perfect' and the word 'pure'—the Cathar priests were called *perfecti* and the Cathars were called the 'pure ones.'

If C.D. Muir was coming from the year 1212 and had been on the run for three years, she very well could have been fleeing the crusade that had been called against the Cathars in 1209. Here also was my link to Magdalene. C.D. Muir's birthday correlated with the gypsy ceremony in Stes-Maries-de-la-Mer, which is not far from Marseilles. (May 22 is also significant to Arthur Conan Doyle and Grace Cooke's joint mission.) It would also place her in the southern region of France during the Albigensian Crusade against the Cathars.

Through C.D. Muir, Butch was taken on a journey from the south of France to cross the English Channel, and to Wales where a ferryman took her to Ireland. She described herself as the Queen of the Gypsies and the Keeper of the Bowl. The bowl, Butch believed, was a relic guarded by her family for centuries and he believed that she was given the mission of protecting it. She also talked about the danger, claiming 'the Pope's dogs were upon her' and she ultimately revealed glimpses of her demise to Butch in his visions. He saw her body being thrown into a river in Ireland.

I have shared an abbreviated version of Butch's story. I was drawn into this tale because it was obvious I was someone who would recognize important clues in the story and its details. Many times I had been to all the places she described, including Montpellier, Béziers, Carcassonne, Toulouse, Nantes, Brest, Cornwall, and Wales. Her call for me to walk on her path in many ways, I had already followed. It appeared that what was left for me to do was to complete her walk in Ireland. I knew now what I would be doing at the beginning of my trip. I had to go to the castle, the Rock of Cashel, Tipperary County and the River Suir.

As if planned by a celestial travel agent, the details of my trip magically fell together. I wrote to a friend from the White Eagle Brotherhood, now living in London. Janet Duncan, a longtime member of the White Eagle Lodge, was an inner brother and worked with their healing circles., Along with our mutual friends Keith and Heather, she and I had visited Iona in 2002. In my email message to Janet, I had shared a little bit of my unfolding Cathar story and she agreed to join me in London.

Janet was interested in learning more about the unfolding Cathar story. She mentioned my interest in the Cathars to Colum Hayward, from the London Lodge, and the editor of ARTHUR CONAN DOYLE'S BOOK OF THE BEYOND. Colum had led a course on the Cathars at the Lodge a few months prior and he had taken a group of people to Cathar country for a visit. He was interested in my involvement with the Cathars. It happened that he would be free on the afternoon of Friday, July 13 when I was scheduled to arrive in London, and he wanted to spend some time discussing the Cathars. I told Janet that I was delighted. She would be a welcome face at Heathrow Airport on my arrival on Friday, July 13, a lucky day for me and an important day for one of my favourite brotherhoods with secrets, the Knights Templar.

I then received another really interesting email from someone I had never met. 'Hello Shannon', it read ... and was from Dave Patrick, the editor of this book. Asking me to contribute, he said he was 'amazed at the number of parallels with [his] own unfolding spiritual journey' to be found in my book THE MAGDALENE AWAKENING. He continued:

'Synchronicity indeed, especially your mention of the 444's and other numeric combinations... [the number combinations I tend to be aware of spotting, in triples, pairs and even quadruples, especially on car number plates are 22/222, 33/333, 44/444 and 77/777]. My own synchronistic spiritual experiences have led me to Sir Arthur Conan Doyle, the White Eagle Lodge, Sir Francis Bacon ... and now the Cathars!'

His invitation to contribute felt like the opportunity to continue the work of Grace Cooke and Arthur Guirdham, something I longed to do.

Janet met me at Heathrow and we took the Tube to inner London, getting off at the stop nearest the White Eagle Lodge. We arrived around noon, where we met Colum. From the start, I felt a tremendous connection to Colum. For one thing he reminded me of his mother Ylana Hayward, whom I had been honoured to meet ten years earlier. Ylana was the Mother of the Lodge following the death of her mother, Grace Cooke, who during her spiritual work became known to all as Minesta. I was very saddened by Ylana's death in September 2011. I had met Ylana on 11/11/2002 at the White Eagle Lodge in Liss, southern England. She was taking a portion of the service that day, a special day of remembrance. Having recently lost a loved one, a young man I loved like a son, I was in tears throughout. During the service I kept thinking I wanted to hug Ylana, heart to heart.

Ylana had stood at the door to greet us on the way out, and when it was my turn, she hugged me and said, 'Yes we will hug, heart to heart'. As I stood back, she looked past me and said to my amazement, 'I feel my dear mother around you'. I was thrilled. I had always felt Minesta around me and talked to her often in my mind. When I reminded Janet of that day, she asked me if I remembered what I had asked Ylana during that conversation. At the time I was in the midst of my deep work of understanding the Cathars and their connection to all that was in my world. As I was not a part of the inner brotherhood of the Lodge, I had many unanswered questions. I wondered at the depth of connection that existed within the White Eagle community and the Cathars. I asked Ylana if she had been there and if she had walked into the flames at Montségur. Janet reminded me that in her heart Ylana believed she had been there on March 16, 1244, when approximately 220 Cathar priests walked to the pyre singing.

Both Colum and I had lost parents in recent years, most recently both my in-laws of almost forty years, and I had helped care for my father-in-law. I knew the difficulty, the grief, and expressed my sincere condolences for his loss. He told me that at 95, Ylana was clear to the end and would join in singing some of her favorite songs while they sat with her. 'Hymns?' I asked. 'Yes,' he said, 'but others as well.' He then sang aloud, 'It's a long way to Tipperary, it's a long way to go....'

Janet and I looked at each other. I told Colum my next stop the very next day was Tipperary County, Ireland. He looked directly at the empty chair next to me and acknowledged what I felt as well, that his mother was with us. That day Colum officially invited me to become part of this book. I was excited and went on to enjoy a tour of the Lodge and the opportunity to sit in the room where so many beautiful messages had come through Minesta.

It is experiences such as these that White Eagle and the Cathars taught. It is the message of gnosis. It is the inner knowing and connection to God and all that God represents. As initiates mature they begin to experience meaningful coincidences with regularity and these synchronicities give credence to the mystical experiences. The spiritual path brings levels of awareness similar to the dream state while awake, using signs and symbols as its vocabulary and imagination as the tool to unravel the meaning. Life becomes a mystic adventure.

It was through a series of synchronicities I met Isaac George, a trance channel and spiritual teacher who was also being called by the master numbers. I had contacted Isaac when I learned he had moved from Scotland to Ireland. He and his wife, Lynn, were now living in Cork County only an hour and a half from the Rock of Cashel. They agreed to let me stay with them a couple of nights. Lynn had not yet visited the Rock of Cashel and wanted to join me. I was happy to have her but it wasn't by chance. She was in fact part of the story, for C.D. Muir was bringing her a message, too. Lynn was English/Scottish and her parents had moved to America. She had only visited America a few times before she married Isaac. Her parents lived in a Florida community only twenty-three miles from where I met Butch, the bringer of the message from C.D. Muir. The circle tightened, emphasizing the connections. Lynn and Isaac were a part of this Cathar story. On their first trip together they had traveled to Montségur, walking in the steps of their own past lives.

When I arrived at Kerry Airport, I picked up my rental car and started driving northeast across Ireland toward the Rock of Cashel. It had been suggested that I first go there alone. The tiny roads lined with hedges and fences framed the green fields of grazing sheep and houses with thatched roofs, which were interspersed with modern buildings. Though physically alone, not once did I feel it. I imagined the car full of my support team: Ylana, Minesta and Arthur Guirdham. I thought about the Tipperary song Colum had sung and wondered if Ylana would give me another sign. Though I felt them, as always, I wanted proof! Perhaps I would hear the song.

Several times along the way I stopped. First, I pulled over when driving through a town where I heard Irish music and saw some brightly coloured gardens and thatched-roofed houses. I wanted to walk and shoot some pictures, to take in as much as possible on my brief trip. The sun was out, which it hadn't been all summer in all of the British Isles. After enjoying a cup of coffee, taking pictures, buying some Irish soda bread, and calling home, I got back on the road.

It wasn't long before I saw a small village bustling with people. The streets were blocked and it was obvious something was going on. A long red banner spanned the street overhead and I slowed down to read it. I couldn't believe my eyes, my proof, and Ylana's message. The banner read:

IT'S A LONG WAY TO TIPPERARY FESTIVAL

I thanked my support team and immediately stopped and walked along the streets with men, women and children dressed in costume, schoolgirls dancing, bands playing and a gypsy begging. Colour, sound and the delicious tastes of sampled cakes gave me an amazing detour on the way to Rock of Cashel. Approaching the castle I had found the river Suir that Butch had described. It was late afternoon when I bought a ticket to take the tour of the Rock of Cashel. Butch had instructed me to say Muir's prayer in Cormac's chapel, the oldest room inside the walls. After the prayer, I left some rose petals that I'd carefully gathered in Florida before I left, on the altar. I returned the next day with Lynn.

The story of C.D. Muir continues, the mystery yet unsolved but unfolding. When Butch searched the genealogical records he found her. It was not, as he had interpreted, C.D. Muir, it was C. d'Muir. Her history in France was documented by a genealogical search that found a Cliona d'Muir born in Montpellier in 1191 (May 22–28?) to parents, Cliona Rosetta d'Muir born in Marseilles in 1163 and Philippe d'Augusta d'Muir, born in Marseilles/Arles. The year of his birth is unknown. According to the records, Cliona d'Muir's family spoke a language that was a combination of Latin and French, the language of Oc spoken by the Cathars in the Languedoc. The d'Muir family were coastal traders between Montpellier and Béziers. They were found to be related to the Viscount Guirdham de Minerve, who during the Albigensian Crusade in 1210 surrendered to save the village. Doing so meant sacrificing the lives of the 140 *perfecti* of the village who would not deny their faith. They were burned at the stake.[1]

Never in all the history of the Cathars had I read of a connection to Ireland, but the story Butch shared made sense. If the family did own a precious relic that had been passed down, they would have wanted to protect it by smuggling it away. And, it could have been significant enough to get the carrier of the relic killed if she actually did make it to Ireland. But once again, all of that is speculation. Lynn and I stumbled on the ruins of the oldest abbey in Ireland, an Augustinian monastery that was in existence during the years C. d'Muir would have fled the Languedoc. It was 2 km from the river Suir in the area Lynn later found was actually called the Golden Veil (an expression C. d'Muir used when communicating with Butch.)

I had another Cathar connection that showed up on the trip. A woman in Mull, Scotland, named Elisa found my Facebook group, 'Magdalenes Around the World', and introduced me to a woman doctor who lives in Yorkshire. She had worked for hospice as I do, and I learned that she had had a mystical experience that led her to start writing a book about the Cathars. We ended in Edinburgh on the same morning and were able to connect spending two amazing hours sharing stories. It is said that Mary Magdalene came to what is now the south of France by boat after the crucifixion, and that she was among the Apostles who spread Christianity to that part of the world. We both believe it was her bloodline that continued in the Cathars and the message of primitive Christianity that she taught that was left as the legacy. But here's the point of my storytelling. The message of the Cathars is that we are all a part of soul groups incarnating together. As Arthur Guirdham expresses in the title of one of his books about the Cathar incarnation, WE ARE ONE ANOTHER.

It is likely that all those who travel in and around you are part of your soul group. Edgar Cayce, the American psychic who was a contemporary of Minesta, once said in a reading that if you stood on any corner in New York City, everyone who walked by, you would have known in another life. We are not here on this planet, at this time, by accident. Each of us is here with our own significant mission, accepted or not. The stories of Minesta, Cliona d'Muir, and Arthur Guirdham's soul group give credence to a holographic universe, the paradox of the timelessness of time. The quantum physicist of today might agree. We cannot understand the reality of time through the view of the body. This life and the soul's journey are about service, the message of the Cathar religion, the Religion of Love. And during our present times, when the world has been experiencing an economic jolt, we have the opportunity to come back to the true message, the true values, those that have been espoused by good men throughout time.

I agree with Arthur Guirdham when he said that there are three major messages the Cathars are bringing us today. They are about the existence of reincarnation and the work of group incarnations, the holographic nature of time and the importance of the return to primitive Christianity. I believe the bottom line is gnosis, the inner journey, the inner experience, the journey to connect with God, the Universal God, the Native American Wakan Tanka (the Great Mystery) that transcends all religions and peoples. The Cathars did have a voice in their time, as Jesus did in his, and like Jesus, their message continues and is relevant today. It is the heritage of humankind, the continuity of people seeking. The Cathars manifested in their lives the life Jesus taught: they walked the walk, they lived the message, they demonstrated their faith in their lives—the pure ones, the good Christians, les bons hommes. They are still here, coming to us across the Golden Veil to remind us of their message.

For the most part, what the Church sold us throughout history is dogma originating from the politics of religion. It was not what Jesus taught. Jesus had two commandments: love your neighbour (brother) as yourself, and love God with all your heart. The churches took that message and slowly turned it into a licence to kill anyone who didn't agree with their dogma.[2] The message that Minesta brought through White Eagle, the message of the shining Brother (the Albigensian) who spoke to her at Lordat and continued to come through the messages of White Eagle during her lifetime and beyond teaches us to live peaceful, loving lives without fear of death. The message is about transforming our lives today so that we become better people, rest easily with our consciences, and treat each other with respect and love. The message teaches us that all people are children equal in the eyes of God. The Golden Rule is the message behind all hidden streams of spirituality that kept the truth of Jesus' teachings alive and separate from all the dogma of the Church. The message emphasized brotherhood, fraternity, self-sacrifice, and charity.

The spiritual teachings the medieval mystics like the Cathars left people of faith today, whether they are Catholic, Protestant, Buddhist, or Baptist, inspire us with the potential of great transformation. Cathar teachings remind us that spiritual thirst is universal. People today are finding that religion isn't providing all the answers. We are no longer accepting secondhand information. Like the Cathars, we are seeking within. The Cathar message is to go out and look for yourself, and all paths lead to the one true God.

When I was preparing for this project, I took THE RETURN OF ARTHUR CONAN DOYLE from the shelf to read some of the significant sections. As I was closing the book something fell onto the floor. As I reached to pick it up I saw Ylana's signature. It was on a Christmas card that had been tucked in the pages for many years. Thanks, Ylana, for your support and help in continuing the message of the Cathars. This was a true example of gnosis, synchronicity, the experience of God from within and beyond.

[1](Genealogy Database Software Program France 1000-1300 A.D.: Gedcoms Church record in towns of Provence).   [2]www.truthbeknown.com.

BACK TO THE SOURCE

JEANNE D'AOÛT

Jeanne D'Août goes back to the bees and to the Aramaic original of the Lord's Prayer for the sources of the gospel of love.

WE HAVE always felt the urge to seek the truth and to understand what it is we see around us. From studying nature to the need of rule and order, we have searched for a way to control the world around us and understand the reason why we are on this planet. While studying nature, we also lifted up our heads and studied the skies. And the moment we started to take notes, when the first texts were written down, these were written down by the rulers, the victors, the ones with the power. This resulted in two separate streams of history running parallel to one another. One, the outwardly visible or exoteric, is commonly known as 'history'; the other, hidden to all eyes but those of the initiated, is the esoteric spiritual stream which continually influences it, reacts against it and thus shapes it further.[1]

It is not easy to try and uncover the hidden history of our spiritual journey. The last two thousand years have been filled with wars and the growth of material wealth, capitalism and selfishness. So we must follow the trail of compassion, purity and love, all the way back to its source, to uncover the true path of our soul growth and find out what inspired the Cathar faith and way of life.

Jeanne D'Août – author, historical researcher and tour guide – is the author of a novel called WHITE LIE, which involves the Knights Templar, the enigma of Rennes-le-Château, the Cathars and Otto Rahn (www.jeannedaout.com). Starting her research at the age of seven, after finding a contradiction in the New Testament, Jeanne has made it her life's work to unearth the hidden and forbidden history of the first century and the history of civilization. She now lives in southern France where she works for Barinca Travel, a specialist tour operator in the region (www.barinca.fr).

Manichaeism

Among the Gnostic sects that were popular in the east (e.g. Persia and China) between the third and seventh centuries CE, was Manichaeism, which at its height was one of the most widespread religions in the world. 'It taught an elaborate cosmology describing the struggle between a good, spiritual world of light, and an evil, material world of darkness. Through an ongoing process, which takes place in human history, light is gradually removed from the world of matter, and returned to the world of light from which it came. Its beliefs, based on local Mesopotamian gnostic and religious movements, contained elements of Christianity, Zoroastrianism and Buddhism.'[2] 'One of the symbols of the Spirit that is also God – a symbol taken from Buddhism by the Cathars – was the Mani, a precious stone that illuminates the world with its flashing, and makes all earthly desire disappear.'[3] The Mani is the Light of the World. In Occitan French, *Esclarmonde*. The Great Esclarmonde is, of course, the name of the most famous Cathar *parfaite...*

The Essenes

One of the most intriguing groups of people who in their time have committed their lives to service, healing and teaching are the Essenes, a mysterious sect of humble people who, according to the Roman historian Josephus, avoided taking an oath, tried to live a life of celibacy, practised the virtues of love and holiness and inhabited many cities and villages of Judea. They lived according to common rules of simplicity and abstinence. The Essenes were called 'The Bees' by ancient writers, a term which goes back to ancient Egypt and perhaps even older civilizations. Ancient travellers described how they came upon a village of beehive shaped houses in Carmel, Israel, where industrious Essene monks lived, while their teachings were as sweet as honey. We can follow the symbol of the bee from Egypt and ancient Palestine to the Visigoths, who ruled a large part of the Iberian peninsula in the first half of the Middle Ages, and to popes, saints and the French emperor Napoleon. What is so important about the bee?

Hermetic Teachings

A bee lives in a perfectly organised society and produces honey, a substance which is known for its healing properties, and when stored, it does not spoil. Many of the Pharaohs of ancient Egypt carried the title of Lord of the Sedge (Reed) and the Bee (symbols of Upper and Lower Egypt). In many cultures, the queen bee symbolised the Mother Goddess. Bee symbolism may well have its roots in the Hermetic Teachings, which had come from India into Egypt and were introduced to the western Hellenistic world by the ancient Greek philosophers.

'In the beginning was the Word, and the Word was with God, and the Word was God' (John 1 : 1). According to Buddhism and ancient Indian teachings, the First Word was *Uhmmmmmm*, which reminds us of the buzzing of bees. In Hebrew, the name 'Deborah' means 'bee'. It is the feminine form of the word *davar*, which means 'word'. The male form, *davar*, is untouchable, invisible, and may refer to the immaterial world, the spiritual essence of God. The female form, *debora* (Bee) refers to the material, visible world, the feminine principle of God, Mother Earth. This concept of God is dualistic. Spirit and matter. Just as the sword penetrates the stone in Arthurian legend, the breath or word of God has impregnated Mother Earth and enabled life to exist on earth, and thus allowed soul growth through learning, sacrifice and love. The pillars of the Temple of Solomon were black and white, Boaz and Jachin, female and male, queen and king, in perfect balance.

A Hermetic Journey

To be able to understand dualism, we must try and understand the Hermetic Teachings. As above, so below. The number 8 returns again and again when we study mysticism. The twisted circle which became the 8 is a quiet witness to the creation of opposites. Alpha (beginning) and omega (end), birth and death, heaven and earth, body and soul, good and evil....

While the sacred teachings of the Kabbala travelled to Europe with the Jewish mystics, the Hermetic Teachings travelled to the western Mediterranean shores with the early Gnostics and Essenes, who had formed several communities in southern France and northern Spain. In the Languedoc-Roussillon, France, the remains of hundreds of beehive-shaped stone huts are scattered throughout the area. The biggest community, however, is near Rennes-le-Château, in the Aude, Languedoc. Smack bang in the middle of Cathar Country....

Mysticism had found fertile earth in these regions. Gnostics and early Christians were able to spread their teachings until the second century, when early Christians in Europe became the victims of Roman persecution. When Christianity was embraced during the reign of Constantine the Great in the fourth century, Christianity evolved from a mystical way of life into a religious system of dogmas and doctrines; ecclesiastical rules invented to control the subjects of Constantine's gigantic realm. But there were also many esoteric streams, who tried to hold on to a purer form of Christianity and ancient mysticism. And throughout the centuries, Gnostic forms of Christianity proved to be more popular, especially in southern France and northern Spain, than the imposed doctrines and dogmas of the Catholic Church. The realm of the Pyrenees, with its many tellurian 'power places', was already attractive to worshippers of ancient cults millennia before the birth of Christianity, and proved to be a fertile soil for the Hermetic and Gnostic teachings that would arrive from distant shores in the first centuries CE.

AMOR *against* ROMA

'Among the esoteric streams in the early centuries of Christianity were Gnostic cults, mainly of Greek, Egyptian or Essene origin, who were persecuted mercilessly.'[4] Among them were the Manichees, and several centuries later, the Bogomils and the Cathars. The Cathars did not only believe in dualism and reincarnation, they also believed that the material world had to have been created by an evil God which was opposite to the God of Love who created the Heavens. Trapped inside the body, they felt imprisoned, and this created the need to free themselves by perfecting their conduct and lifestyle. They rejected baptism by water and replaced it by baptism of the Spirit, the *consolamentum*. They insisted that one could communicate with God directly. If the Cathars would succeed in convincing the masses of their beliefs and way of life, the Catholic Church would become superfluous.

But the Cathars did more than spread their teachings. Disapproving of the more and more materialistic Catholic Church they started to oppose it, and formed what is effectively a church of Love, AMOR, against the church of Greed, ROMA. They remind us of the act of Jesus in the Temple, when he disapproved of the tradesmen and shouted out that this was a Temple, a house of prayer, not a den of thieves. The Catholic Church tried to confront the Cathars by sending representatives, who would then debate with them publicly, trying to persuade the masses to choose the Catholic Church instead of the Cathar church. However, the Cathars won the debates thanks to their vast knowledge and wisdom. They became more and more popular and therefore also an increasing threat. And so, in 1209, the Catholic Church turned her face towards the south of France and showed her teeth. It was Pope Innocent III who finally decided to get rid of the Cathars. One way or the other.

The Treasure of the Cathars

The Crusade against the Cathars turned out to be little less than a holocaust, a genocide which killed an unbelievably large number of people. In French history books we merely read of the 'uprising of the southern Lords', which was quickly dealt with by King Louis of France. We cannot begin to imagine what it must have been like to live in this region in the thirteenth and fourteenth centuries. It is clear that all valuable possessions such as scrolls, teachings and knowledge were quickly transported to safer destinations. Thanks to the vast banking system created by the Knights Templar, the Cathars did not have to carry all their money with them. But they would never part with what was most sacred to them. Therefore, to see what the treasure of the Cathars may have been, we need to follow the esoteric spiritual stream.

St Francis of Assisi (1181/82–1226) was born as Giovanni Francesco di Bernardone. He was the son of a wealthy cloth merchant. His mother, Pica, is said to have belonged to a noble family from Provence, France. In his young life, Francis was taught by the priests of St George's at Assisi, but it is more likely that he learned more in the school of the troubadours, who were also in Italy.[5] These popular minstrels travelled through Europe spreading their extensive knowledge, and were famous for their songs of courtly love. Around 1200, *Parsifal et Le Conte du Graal* was very popular. This was the first of several stories about chivalry and the Holy Grail, and the basis for the tales of the Knights of the Round Table.

While in the army in his youth, Francis was a captive for more than a year at Perugia, where he may have met other prisoners. Some of them Cathars, perhaps? We cannot fail to notice how Francis of Assisi tried to be different from others inside the Roman Catholic Church by preaching poverty, love, service to others and repentance, almost as if he were the reincarnation of Jesus, as if, somehow, he wanted to insert several aspects of the Cathar way of life into the then largely corrupt religious system, which stopped at nothing to control the world. Is it possible that he had talked to Cathars and was perhaps inspired by some of their points of view? In the book FRANCIS: A SAINT'S WAY by James Cowan[6] it is also suggested that his father, being a merchant, may have been exposed to Cathar teachings while travelling through France and northern Italy. Pietro di Bernardone insisted on calling his son Francesco, after his beloved France, and not, as his mother wished, Giovanni. Perhaps Francis was more Cathar than people think?

I first thought of this possibility when I found what is said to be the oldest surviving version of the Lord's Prayer, which was sung, not recited. It is in Aramaic, and this version is also kept and sung by the Franciscan order today. The original Lord's Prayer (reproduced opposite) is also said to have been one of the treasures of the Cathars. Did a scroll containing this song, along with someone who could still sing it, find its way from the Occitan south of France to northern Italy?

At the Galamus Monastery in the Languedoc-Roussillon, which once belonged to the Franciscan order, I found a beautiful Templar monument. A magic square reads: SATOR AREPO TENET OPERA ROTAS. Above it, God, with an open mouth, as if intonating The Word. The magic square reveals P.N. as well as Alpha and Omega. P.N. stands for Pater Noster, the Lord's Prayer. I have a theory about the intention of this particular monument. Maybe it refers to the possibility that three suspected treasures of the Cathars: the Hermetic Teachings (Alpha and Omega), the original Lord's Prayer (P.N.) and the Gospel of John, which starts with 'In the beginning was The Word', have survived, and were kept at Galamus until they found their way to northern Italy along with the Franciscans?

Our search for the purest form of Christianity and the Hermetic Teachings brings us to the next question: Where do we look for the original teachings of Jesus? How can we strip away two thousand years, searching through the mud of alterations and mistranslations, hoping to discover the true message of this timeless Avatar? We try to follow the esoteric stream, through ancient Gnostic Gospels, and by studying gems like the Gospel of Thomas. Gems like the original Lord's Prayer, which was, perhaps, one of the treasures of the Cathars....

'The anxiety of mankind consists in reaching the kingdom of the heavens.'[7] When we go back to the source, we find the Secret Teachings, which 'are "sacred open secrets" written in the language of nature, in the movement of the stars and the singing of the birds. The answers are there for all

ABWOEN
Abwoen d'bwasmaja, nitkadesj sjmach
Teetee malkoetach, neghwee tsevjanach
Ajkana d'bwasjmaja af b'arhah
Habwlan lachma d'soenkanan jaomana
Wasjbooklan cha-oebween
ajkanna daf chnan sj-bwokan l'chajabeen
Wela taghlan-l'nesjoena
Ela patsan min biesja
Metol dillachie malkoeta
waghajla watesjboechta
l'oghlam Almien
Ameen

All-Father-Mother
All-Father-Mother, All One
Of the All, in the All
Holy and secret are Your names
You live in activity and Light
Let Your desire be with mine
Here now and in the All
Touch me, feed me with your astonishment
To fulfil Your desire
My surrender to You, the other and the All.
Accept me, that I am not yet whole,
Not yet connected to You
Forgive me my hesitant effort
To connect myself with You
As I accept my fellow-man
His being un-whole,
His being un-healed.
Lead me away from show and ignorance
And free me of what keeps me from the Light
Because in You and from You
Is the Light, the Power and the Life
Here, now and for ever
Always

who are able to look and listen with minds unclouded by others opinions.'[8] And by using this method we also can find the Grail. In legend, the Cathars possessed and protected the true Grail. Not the Grail as we know it; the cup of Christ which, according to the Roman Catholic myth, was used at the Last Supper, and which had caught the blood of Christ during the crucifixion, but the Grail that symbolises the Spirit, the Mani or Light of the World, the soul and most of all, Love. When we go back to the source of the Hermetic Teachings in Egypt, we find that the Egyptian hieroglyph for Heart, *Ib*, is a vase…

In a way, the Cathars did possess the Grail. They preached Love in their church of AMOR, which is the foundation of Jesus' teachings. Love knows no religion, race or politics, for it rules the realm of the Heart. The Universe bends because of Love, and the Earth kneels before it, for Love is God.

Notes:

[1] Tim Wallace-Murphy, HIDDEN WISDOM: SECRETS OF THE WESTERN ESOTERIC TRADITION. New York, NY: Disinformation Company, 2010

[2] http://en.wikipedia.org/wiki/Manichaeism

[3] Otto Rahn, CRUSADE AGAINST THE GRAIL, trans. Christopher Jones. Vermont: Inner Traditions, 2006

[4] Entry on Francis of Assisi by Paschal Robinson in THE CATHOLIC ENCYCLOPAEDIA, 1913

[5] Tim Wallace-Murphy

[6] James Cowan, FRANCIS: A SAINT'S WAY. London: Hodder, 2002

[7] Otto Rahn, CRUSADE AGAINST THE GRAIL

[8] Timothy Freke and Peter Gandy, THE HERMETICA: THE LOST WISDOM OF THE PHARAOHS. New York: Tarcher, 2008

This page, clockwise from left: the memorial to Maurice Magre beneath the château of Montségur; Grace Cooke and Betty Caird Miller with two Polaires at Lordat, 1931; Grace Cooke seated within the ruins of the Château de Lordat; the copy of White Eagle's book ILLUMINATION which Walter Birks gave to Antonin Gadal along with a White Eagle Lodge prospectus from before the War. See pp. 173–86.

Overleaf, clockwise: the actual postcard of Lordat sent by Grace Cooke to her daughters in July 1931; Antonin Gadal, Grace Cooke returns to Lordat, 1956; page from Grace Cooke's photo album of the 1931 trip including Lordat excavations; Grace and Ivan Cooke take refreshment at the hotel in Ax-Les-Thermes (again see pp. 173–86).

For captions see preceding page

VI. REDISCOVERY : 1

A TRIP TO THE ARIÈGE IN 1931

COLUM HAYWARD

Much of what is called 'neo-Catharism' today began in a tide of enthusiasm in the 1930s. Here Colum Hayward picks up on a visit to the area that has often been mentioned by researchers and provides background to the 'Vision' on p. 141.

IN JULY 1931, an unusual Anglo-French party were to be found at Ax-les-Thermes in the Ariège, unusual enough to make the local newspaper.[1] Among those whose names we know on this Cathar quest were the French-Italian occultist who went by the name of Zam Bhotiva, along with the 'Chief', René Odin, of the esoteric group known as the Polaires, who followed a present-day arithmetical oracle, and which Bhotiva had been instrumental in founding in 1929. They are visible in the pictures reproduced on pp. 171 and 172. Other French Polaires were present, but the only actual name we can put forward is the Countess Pujol-Murat, who owned the château in the little mountain village of Lordat, the primary destination of the group. Among the English there were undoubtedly Grace and Ivan Cooke, both of them noted for their mediumistic abilities in Spiritualist circles in London, and a friend whose name was Betty Caird-Miller, who seems to have been linked both to the Polaires and to Lady Conan Doyle, with whom the Cookes had worked after the death of Sir Arthur in 1930. The party made archaeological excavations, apparently unsuccessful, and

---

For an author biography, see p. 11, and for pictures see the previous pages then left, whereupon historical attention naturally shifts to other visitors to the region in the early 1930s, such as the German, Otto Rahn, of whom more later, and local researchers such as Antonin Gadal (photo p. 172) and Déodat Roché.

Lordat is not one of the primary châteaux on the Cathar trail, indeed its significance is not normally enough to get it into the popular guidebooks, except that it is now occupied by an eagle sanctuary, so that tourists flood in and watch birds of prey in flight, soaring, feeding, and occasionally alarming visitors in a carefully-controlled drama of human and avial interaction. The château would attract more note if the competition were not so great; it has not the history of Montségur nor the precariousness upon its rock that Peyrepetuse has, or the size of some of the others. The geography is nonetheless a fine one. The Ariège river flows 400 metres below it through a valley with such steep sides it almost merits being called a gorge. Behind it rises the Pic de St-Barthélemy, sometimes still called by an old name which links it to the Mt Tabor of the Transfiguration, to a height of 2368 metres; it is thus snow-covered for more than half the year. Directly behind the mountain is the Cathar fortress château of Montségur, which fell to the army of the Seneschal of Carcassonne and Archbishop of Narbonne, acting for the Pope and the King of France, in 1244. Although Lordat's own outcrop above the valley is dwarfed by this mountain, it commands remarkable views down the Ariège and more particularly upriver, towards the high peaks of the Pyrenees. The road and railway far below were once main routes from Paris to Barcelona, and also to Andorra. The tiny road that leads off RN20, from the talc-factory town of Luzenac all the way up to Lordat, contains what feel like enough hairpin bends to get us up an Alpine peak.

We don't entirely have to speculate or go to printed books of period photos to experience what the area must have felt like in 1931. What happened there made such an impression upon Grace and Ivan Cooke that they wrote about it no less than four times: twice in 1946 (Ivan Cooke in a magazine article and Grace Cooke in a personal memoir entitled THE SHINING PRESENCE (hereafter 'SP'). They each wrote more in the Preface to a book, THE LIVING WORD (hereafter, 'LW'), in 1949, and they revisited Lordat twenty-five years after they first went, in late August 1956.[2] In the personal memoir, we read of a rather alarming drive with an 'erratic' chauffeur (Ivan Cooke's magazine article speaks of a heady reverse on a hairpin bend), a 'very old and quaint' village (it was probably the first time either of them had been to France, and Ivan Cooke called it 'primitive almost beyond description'), locals who first treated them with suspicion but who, respecting the Countess, became gradually friendly. We learn (taking any measurements in the quotations as rough!) of how above the village there lies the château area, evidently quite open then:

> 'The last five hundred feet had to be made on foot. The climb was a difficult one as the incline was steep and there was no road. On the crest of the mountain … was an area of some two acres. Before us lay the ruins of the old chateau and below was a magnificant view of the Pyrenees, mountain height following upon mountain height, reaching out to the horizon. On the opposite mountain the castle of Montsegur appeared almost like a celestial fortress against the snow-clad peaks. It is reputed that the treasure of the Albigenses lies buried there....' (SP, pp. 31–2).

The fifteen-year interval has slightly corrupted her memory, for Montségur is not visible from Lordat, a mistake she had already made in 1949. Otherwise, the clarity of their remembering is apparent in the letters she and Ivan Cooke wrote ten years later (1956), when at last they revisited the area with friends. At the time, 64 years of age, she was recovering from illness. Here is Ivan Cooke:

> 'Paul & the car negotiated the stoney [sic] mountain roads in grand style. Up & up we went, literally mountain high in the car until we reached Lordat village, no longer quite as degraded, unfriendly & unkempt as before. Then came the finale up the steep, dangerous path for the last 500 feet. Up & up we went, M. keeping up well, & with such zest that she reached the Castle without a rest.

He continues:

> 'Afterwards we went away, having visited the tiny chapel in Lordat village, to a hill nearly in sight of Lordat for lunch. This was at 3 p.m. so you will see we spent a long time at the chateau. All the rest of the day we were conscious of the heavenly conditions & we shall never forget yesterday   I have 16 snaps of Lordat to tell the tale.
>
> 'Ax is quite a place now, gone all towney [sic], with a winter Season for Sports & its Spas & Hotels for visitors in the summer. So it is prosperous at last, with new life & hope, hotels, garages etc every where. Despite this, it is still charming & very Spanish-French In the valley below Lordat is the biggest Face Powder factory in the world, where they grind up 20,000 tons of mountain limestone yearly into face powder. So

you may be putting a bit of Lordat on your face tomorrow morning!'

(Ivan Cooke to Joan Hodgson and Ylana Hayward and their families, Ax-les-Thermes, n.d. [marked by archivist, '27 August 1956'])

In this account, 'Paul' is a personal friend of the Cookes, the English Spiritualist Paul Beard, who organised the trip; while 'M' is Grace Cooke, probably standing for 'Mummy' but just possibly for 'Minesta', a name by which she was commonly known. As she was my own grandmother, I probably never called her by any of those names, but we will keep 'Grace Cooke' for general use in this article. At the time, she was beginning to make a name for herself as the channel for the spirit guide White Eagle, as well as for clairvoyance and other psychic gifts.

*

It is more than time to write about why the party was there. All I remember my grandmother saying in my childhood was that 'the Polaires were looking for buried treasure' and did not find any, but though she seemed to regard the trip as having been very special she never made it remotely clear, and may not have known, what treasure they really expected to find. I had the impression she wasn't sure that they knew either. Here is what she wrote on the issue in 1946:

> 'According to instructions we were to commence our investigations from the old chateau on Mount Lordat and to search for an entrance which led to the famous cave in the neighbourhood of the castle which had been the meeting place and final refuge of the simple White Brothers.' (SP, p. 32)

I think there is a little confusion here, since Lordat is high above the gorge and some ten kilometres from Ornolac, where there are indeed caves; she shortly mentions as the final Cathar hideaway, and though she mentions the cave at Lombrives, the one Napoléon Peyrat identified as the one where Cathars were 'walled up' and left to die, it is the other side of the valley from Ornolac. We know that Maurice Magre, among the Polaires, took Peyrat's account at face value, which the whole party seem to have done; it has never been substantiated. Of some interest, though, is the reference to buried treasure in the memoir, but with reference to Montségur: 'It is reputed that the treasure of the Albigenses lies buried there'. In short, she seems to distance herself from treasure-seeking: they are at the wrong castle for physical treasure. Interestingly, when she mentions her instructions a few pages earlier, there is no mention of treasure:

'A special piece of work was to be accomplished in the French Pyrenees at an old castle which had once been a mystical centre, or place of worship, of a sect known as the Albigenses.... Our subsequent visit ... was all part of the plan to link us up with the medieval French Brotherhood.' (SP, pp. 29–30)

The 1949 account by contrast stresses that the French group at least were seeking some treasure. It reminds us, though, that the château at Lordat is of later date than the Cathar period and that the treasure would not be found there but somewhere deep below, maybe via a tunnel. It describes several abortive digs, each one meeting solid rock, and describes how the English group began to wonder if the treasure was documents rather than objects, and if so how they could have survived.

How do we resolve these seeming contradictions, other than on grounds of poor memory? The spiritual instructions, we know from Grace Cooke's memoir, came directly from the Oracle the Polaires followed, although White Eagle, as well as Ivan Cooke's spirit guide The Friend, were consulted for corroboration (SP, p. 29). In the instructions quoted in that 1946 source, there is nothing mentioned about treasure, and as we have seen, Grace Cooke speaks of it being associated with Montségur not Lordat. Yet in 1949, alluding to the same instructions, Ivan Cooke states that the Oracle told the group that treasure was to be found (LW, p. 3).

The two writers have different purposes, I think. Grace Cooke is writing about how experience marked the inception of an inner work of brotherhood, five years later to become the White Eagle Lodge in England. Ivan Cooke is writing, with literary licence, in a way that points up the supreme quality of his wife's personal experience: he needs the contrast with the shallow search for treasure to suggest the power of the spiritual discovery she made, of which more shortly. He reminds us how her discovery may always have been planned to be unique and private to herself: 'Note that it was said that the person would find the treasure; and nothing about the party as a whole finding it' (LW, p. 4). To bolster the contrast between the party as a whole and the power of her vision he also stresses how far the trip was outwardly a failure. Her only reference to failure is a brief acknowledgment that at the material level, this has to be conceded, but only at that level (LW, p. 15).

My own reconstruction would be this. I think the Oracle, and the spirit guides, wanted the deep spiritual link to be made. If they mentioned the treasure, it was perhaps something of a lure to get the party there. Having studied the Polaires in some depth,[3] I would personally surmise that the 'core' group knew this very clearly, but that there were others among them who could not resist the hint of a treasure to be found. That they did so gave Ivan Cooke help with literary framework, but my grandmother's earlier account is probably the more reliable. It also explains some of the divisions that arose – which we have yet to hear about.

With the benefit of hindsight, many writers have believed they know what the treasure supposedly sought might have been. Variously, this could be the legendary material treasure of Montségur (which Inquisition records tell us was removed around Christmas 1243), lost manuscripts from the Cathar period (the most likely answer, but Cathar studies were somewhat in their infancy, so it's unlikely the group knew what to expect), the Holy Grail (whatever form it might be regarded as having), the secret of the bloodline of Jesus (though no one suggested that as early as 1931), or some trace of Christian Rosenkreutz.

The last is not outlandish: the Polaire writer Maurice Magre wrote at some length about Rosenkreutz's 'Cathar indication', but there is nothing in his book THE RETURN OF THE MAGI to suggest a connection with Lordat specifically, though writers at the time and since have kept to the story. In 1946, in his article, Ivan Cooke alluded to Cathars who escaped as possibly having 'founded the Rosicrucian Brotherhood'. One might expect the Cookes, while there to have met the local authority on the Cathars, Antonin Gadal, but I can find no reference to this. It may have gone unrecorded, but we shall see that six or seven years later an English protégé of theirs was referring to him as though there had been no contact between them, and indeed presented a White Eagle book to him, as though introducing him (reproduced on p. 171). They were probably in the region just too early to meet the other great Cathar authority of the time, Déodat Roché.[4]

The supposed treasure of the Cathars haunts writers and readers to this day. My grandmother's belief, reprinted in this book (pp. 141–5), is a far from traditional comment on it. Nonetheless she felt she had, in an extraordinary way, found it when she had an experience so beautiful that it changed her life and guided all her future work. It connected her channel of inspiration with the particular mission of St John, the 'Beloved' of Jesus. It was initiatory, and it is in its own way remarkable because I believe she left England with almost no idea whatsoever who the Cathars were, and certainly is unlikely to have known how crucial to them was the Gospel of St John, since its importance has become more and more recognised as Cathar studies have progressed, in the eighty years since. Yet for all that, the vision she had left her 'as in a dream or haze of happiness for days' (LW, p. 13), there was more to it than that. In THE SHINING PRESENCE she wrote:

> 'I believe we were taken to Lordat, not so much to receive a spectacular visitation of a holy and blessed personality, but to receive the vision of truth and so to absorb it that we had no choice but to forge ahead with the work....'

The memoir makes it absolutely clear that 'the work' was the promotion of the teaching of 'the White Brotherhood' on earth. 'The purpose of this work is to provide the conditions necessary for the outworking of the principles of the Christ life through as many groups of the White Brotherhood as can be formed on earth' (both quotations p. 36). That was not just for the sake of growth, as she explained a few pages earlier: 'The Sages had stated that if mankind would make an effort to live according to the laws of the ancient brotherhood, the catastrophe towards which the world was moving might be averted'. (p. 30)

Although the deep inner rapport she felt with the Cathars was the overriding thing that came out of her trip to France, it is just worth remembering that it also included her initiation, in Paris, as a Polaire, along with her husband Ivan. Thus the three elements – Polaire, White Eagle and Cathar – came together in July 1931.

*

So who were the Polaires? Although 'Les Polaires' or 'Le Groupe des Polaires' included some quite well-known names on the Parisian intellectual scene, they have dropped back into history's shadows. In 1931, however, they were quite newly-formed, having emerged publicly in 1929. From May 1930 they had a monthly journal or *Bulletin*, the first issue of which served as something of a manifesto, and from the year of their inception, they could also offer a book with the Latin title ASIA MYSTERIOSA. It described the source of their wisdom, an arithmetical oracle which gave them contact with spiritual masters in the Himalaya.[6] Among them at least four members seem to have been held by the spell of the Cathars or Albigenses, and maybe Bhotiva and Odin (already mentioned) were fascinated to a lesser extent than Otto Rahn, who was their associate, and Maurice Magre, some of whose writing on the Cathars is reproduced in this book. He also wrote on them in MAGICIENS ET ILLUMINÉS (Paris, 1930) translated into English the

following year as THE RETURN OF THE MAGI, and in two novels, LE SANG DE TOU-
LOUSE (1931) and LE TRÉSOR DES ALBIGEOIS (1938). It is assumed that Magre introduced Rahn to the subject in depth, although we know that Rahn, born
in Michelstadt in 1904, heard of them from his professor at the Univerisyt
of Giessen and began a dissertation on the poet Kyot, the putative source
for Wolfram von Eschenbach's *Parzifal*. A plaque in memory of Magre has
been placed high up the pog, or peak, of Montségur (see photo, p. 171).

It would be perfectly reasonable to say, from what we know, that the
Oracle that guided the Polaires took them to the Pyrenees, and it is certainly
true that both Bhotiva and the operator of the Oracle, Mario Fille, were strikingly obedient to instructions from their masters – as was my grandmother,
although there's no reason to believe White Eagle sent them all south. Bhotiva's was nonetheless an adventurous spirit,[7] and the very fact that the trip
seems to have 'gone wrong' might imply that he was doing more than was
instructed. This calamity was much more than failure to find the treasure:
something happened among the Polaire visitors and it manifested as one of
the party losing his mind and threatening the others with a knife.

How the English visitors perceived the calamity is of interest. First,
the spirit guides had warned of the danger they faced by visiting the area,
and Ivan Cooke's guide, Friend, had performed a ritual of protection upon
them (*Angelus*, 1946, p. 202; SP also). They give slightly different theories
for the source of the danger. Ivan Cooke speaks of Druidic magic invoked
by the original Cathars for their own protection, still lingering (LW, p. 5),
while Grace Cooke speaks of mischievous elementals and adds:

'We were able to watch the result of these influences upon members
of the French group and see each one in turn – without exception –
succumb sooner or later to forces which affected him, if not physically,
then mentally or even spiritually.' (SP, p. 33)

Even Grace Cooke herself was briefly afflicted with a strange and painful inflammation, until The Friend gave her healing. The Polaire who attacked the others was carried off to an asylum, but only after several days
(SP, pp. 33-4; LW, p. 6). Just how real my grandmother saw that threat to be
is evidenced by the presence, in the White Eagle Lodge archives, of a scrib-
bled Will she made on the spot. For all that, he seemed to respect her calling
upon the Christ and would say to her 'White Eagle is good. I am not afraid
of him. He is beautiful and he will take care of me'. I have no knowledge of
the identity of this Polaire.[8] After she came home, there is no indication of

contact between her and the Polaires until 1934. Ivan Cooke, writing in the White Eagle Lodge magazine *Angelus*, later said that it took her ten years to realise what had really transpired at Lordat – in other words, after White Eagle had given through her most of the messages that form his commentary on St John's Gospel, the basis of THE LIVING WORD.

I have already mentioned the presence in the region of the German researcher, Otto Rahn, who, it is reliably reported, spent time there in July or August 1930, and came to Ussat-les-Bains to live in November 1931. There was anti-German feeling prompted by his visit, leading to a misleading newspaper report. His researches led to the publication, in 1933, of an eloquent but highly personal view of the Cathars, CRUSADE AGAINST THE GRAIL, first in German and then in French, and ultimately to LUCIFER'S COURT (1937), although in writing the latter he may have been under a lot of pressure from his German masters, who even seem to have had antisemitic passages added to his text. Much has been written on Rahn, a lot of it speculative. One thing that no one can possibly deny is Rahn's love of the area, which is sometimes called the Sabarthès. He once wrote:

'In this valley cut by giants, it is enough just to look around to be transformed, and above all, to understand what happened. Everything is written here. The Sabarthes is a great book, the most beautiful book in the world.' (Letter to Antonin Gadal)[9]

*

The next notable visitors to the area (so far as concerns my story) were an English family with the surname Birks. They were apparently sent there by the suggestion of my grandmother's spirit guide, White Eagle. According to the book their son, Walter, wrote with R. A. Gilbert half a century later, White Eagle's words were these:

'The purpose is for you to make contact, with Walter, [with] certain places in France which hold the Light Ray. You have to learn to discriminate, to look beneath the material substance and read or absorb the beauty of the atmosphere. There are places, and in the French Pyrenees there is the ancient home of a brotherhood … the Albigenses.'

Walter was either to continue in the Languedoc or return there, and White Eagle added to the family:

'The point of your going is for him to contact the Inner Planes.'

(Sitting of 5 July 1937, quoted in Birks and
Gilbert, THE TREASURE OF MONTSÉGUR, p. 21)

It is interesting how close is the language of these instructions to Grace Cooke's view of her own purpose in going to the area (which, we must remember, she set out nine years later).

Unlike the earlier party, Birks met and became very familiar with Antonin Gadal, and either he or his colleague R. A. Gilbert wrote the whole story up and published it exactly fifty years after White Eagle spoke his words. The story is not completely accurate, and in the interests of scholarship I need to correct a couple of points. First, Birks and Gilbert chastise my grandparents and White Eagle himself for not telling Walter that Ivan Cooke returned to the Ariège in 1932, a year after the visit I have been detailing. This story has been repeated many times by subsequent writers, but as one who knows my grandparents' papers very well, and knew them as an almost inseparable couple, not only were they far too busy setting up their first healing retreat centre (Burstow Manor, near Horley, Surrey) and releasing its ghost, Mary, in 1932, the likelihood of Ivan Cooke travelling without my grandmother in 1932 is almost zero. And why would he? It was not in the nature of either of them to be so disingenuous as to conceal the fact from Birks and his family. Moreover, there is no particular reason to doubt that the correspondence between M. Bhotiva and my grandparents, in the White Eagle archives and augmented by the Conan Doyle papers in the library of the University of Texas,[10] is seriously incomplete, and if he went with the Polaires (he had no French whatsoever) there would surely be reference there. Lastly, he quite accurately referred to the 1931 visit in 1956 as being twenty-five years previous; if he had gone in 1932 on his own would there not have been some reference to it in the private letter I quoted at the beginning of this article?

The long and the short of it is that somewhere Walter Birks' notes must surely be confused, or maybe they got confused when he passed them to R. A. Gilbert, as he apparently did. It is a pity, because subsequent researchers have built on the Birks-Gilbert story, and I am glad to have this opportunity to correct the account.

The second point is that Birks and Gilbert accuse White Eagle of insisting on 'selfishness' in being less than frank with Antonin Gadal about what he felt or found in the supposed Cathar caves of Ariège. What White Eagle actually said from the start was that Birks' real purpose was to find something at the inner level, not at the outer – maybe just as my grandmother, going there in 1931, had not found material treasure but something she could 'treasure in her heart', to borrow a phrase from another feminine revelation. In short, he did not want Birks to be distracted, and Gadal certainly had plenty of ideas with which to distract him. In my own opinion Birks failed to appreciate the distinction made between the inner plane and the outer. He actually warned Birks, interestingly, that in Gadal there were, as in everyone, 'these two aspects in every human soul': the higher and the lower. Gilbert (I assume) calls this a devious ploy, but I think that White Eagle was absolutely consistent in what he seems to have said to Birks.[11]

Consistent, and categorical too. On September 29th he warned, in another sitting, 'You will hear of buried secret treasure. Treasure lies in wisdom and love, remember' (Birks and Gilbert, p. 22). Did Birks hear him? I wonder. Gadal, who as White Eagle had already intimated had anticipated Birks' coming and looked upon him as his successor, handed the job of hotel and spa manager in Ussat-les-Bains to Birks in 1939 to support him, and initiated him as his successor in September 1939 – again as predicted by the spirit guide. So all appeared to have been set, even at the outbreak of the war; but with the German occupation of France in May 1940 Birks left the area, to return after 1945. By this time tourist revenues had collapsed with the war and Birks became more and more disenchanted.

As a wartime Intelligence Officer in Syria, not distracted by the clues on the outer plane, Birks had nonetheless had an experience around the Cathars and the Grail that led him to a deeper understanding of what the Cathar treasure might have been than he maybe ever expected. His very beautiful account of this discovery is reprinted in this book on pp. 191–6.

*

One final question about the little Anglo-French party of 1931 remains. 'Did they visit the crown jewel of Cathar tourism, Montségur?'. Given Montségur's significance, it's highly unlikely that they passed it by, yet there is no record among my grandparents' papers of their having done so. Twice, as we have seen, (above, p. 145, 175), my grandmother's memory was hazy enough for her to forget that the Pic de St-Barthélémy hides Montségur from Lordat, and if they went it is odd they forgot what would have been quite a long drive on 1931 roads. The question has some significance because there has been speculation about excavations taking place at Montségur as well as Lordat, and items in the form of 'wooden books' being found there; I can say with reasonable confidence that my grandmother was not involved in any 'dig' other than at Lordat; the trip was simply too short for that. As for the Polaires, M. Bhotiva would have participated in my grandparents' initiation into the Polaire 'brotherhood' in Paris earlier in July, and then would almost certainly have escorted them down on the train, given that neither of them spoke French. Some of the Polaires may of course have stayed, but if so that is another story.

The Internet is full of both information and disinformation, and I have seen it stated that the Polaire dig went on for forty days. Grace Cooke is clear that her own trip lasted just ten, and if there were further Polaire excavations, I think they took place on a different occasion.

The dark presences they had felt around the château in 1931, and the terrifying memory of the knife attack, seemed to have dispersed in 1956. Indeed, they seem to have been forgotten in exchange for a sense of something wonderful having happened. This time we turn to my grandmother's own letter:

'It was simply grand (the view & the spiritual atmosphere) We were surrounded by white brothers & angels. It seemed as though we had been levitated up there. I shall never forget the experience. We remained up there for some hours, before we descended & found a lovely shady resting place in the valley, where we had lunch. Bread & tartex or cheese & tomatoes topped with peaches & grapes, then a short sleep on the grass. It was so so lovely....'

Grace Cooke to her family, from the Hotel Grillon, Ax-les-Thermes
'Sunday morn.' [marked by archivist, '= 26 August 1956']

Nothing but happy memories there. And here is Ivan Cooke, no less content:

'Everything was just the same, except that the ground was very scrubby owing to the absence of rabbits. We circled the ruins, noting where the Polaires had dug. How it all came back! & how wonderful it seemed to be back there again after 25 years. There was wonderful power & presences with us, of which even the Beards were aware. The whole place was heavenly with bright bright sunlight from a cloudless sky with a vista of mountains everywhere. We formed a little group & had a message after sitting in meditation – not a trance message – which I wrote down more or less accurately. The condition was more important even than the message, you understand.'

(Ivan Cooke to Joan Hodgson and Ylana Hayward and their families,
Ax-les-Thermes, n.d. [marked by archivist, '27 August 1956'])

We will leave them in their happiness. In 1931 they had visited the Ariège at an exciting time in their own lives, but with storm clouds already gathering in Europe, loyalties becoming strained by politics, and fears and thoughts of dark forces surrounding them, enemies of the light. It must have been good to go back with what White Eagle (picking up on a Polaire phrase) called 'the years of fire' apparently over. Even with the degree of hindsight she had acquired by 1946, she could see in the whole trip a remarkable degree of planning by the brotherhood in spirit.

'It must be remembered that the initiates, the wise men and the masters of all ages, are not limited by our conception of time and they work, not for the immediate future, but for the gradual spiritual evolution of the whole race. Days, months and years are nothing to them. They will work through incalculable time to obtain the object of aspiration. Their vision is very very wide and stupendously grand; they count nothing wasted if out of it can be born ultimate perfection of life and happiness for mankind.' (SP, p. 36)

In this respect, it is not we who have rediscovered the Cathars, but they who made ready our spiritual processes of today.

Notes:

[1] Reported by Joscelyn Godwin, in ARKTOS: THE POLAR MYTH (Kempton, IL: Adventures Unlimited Press, 1996), p. 90, but see also note 4.

[2] These sources are, first, the monthly White Eagle magazine *Angelus*, volume ix, pp. 200–4 and 238–42; second, THE SHINING PRESENCE (London: White Eagle Lodge, 1946); third, THE LIVING WORD (London: White Eagle Lodge, 1949; later editions carry a much shorter preface, and all quotation here is from that edition); and, lastly, uncatalogued letters in the White Eagle Lodge archive, with the dates shown.

[3] See my two extended prefaces, first to ARTHUR CONAN DOYLE'S BOOK OF THE BEYOND (Liss, White Eagle Publishing Trust, second edition 2003, updated 2006; the core of the book was first published as THY KINGDOM COME in December 1933) which tells the full story of the Conan Doyle / Polaire / White Eagle Lodge connection; and secondly, my preface to the Polaires' book about their Oracle, ASIA MYSERIOSA, by Zam Bhotiva (first English translation, London: Polair, 2012).

[4] The English protégé was Walter Birks. See below, pp. 181–4 and 191–6. His copy of White Eagle's book ILLUMINATION, given to Gadal with an inscription, is in the Gadal museum at Ussat and reproduced on p. 171 (I am grateful to Christian Koenig for sight of this). Birks, or his co-author R. A. Gilbert, later mentioned the story about Christian Rosenkreutz in THE TREASURE OF MONTSÉGUR,

p. 21, but it is extremely difficult to discover the origin of this. As I have said, the local press bore a brief story about the excavations, and Joscelyn Godwin, in ARKTOS, states that the paper announced the Polaires as having found traces of Rosenkreutz through the area, but gives a reference in Christian Bernadac's book about Otto Rahn which is incorrect. Birks and Gilbert's mention of the story offers no source, and it is not clear whether we are hearing Birks's memory or Gilbert's research here. The story has also been linked to the name of Joseph Mandement, a local tourist chief and rival of Gadal who sparred with Otto Rahn over his archaeological findings. For Ivan Cooke's mention of the Rosicrucians see *Angelus,* 1946, p. 202. For Bernadac see LE MYSTÈRE OTTO RAHN (Paris: France-Empire, 1978).

⁶ It was published in French in 1929 (Paris: Dorbon-Ainé). For an English edition, see above, note 3.

⁷ For obedience to the Oracle, see ASIA MYSTERIOSA, pp. 34–5 , and for Bhotiva's taste for adventure see there and also René Thimmy (actually Maurice Magre), LA MAGIE À PARIS, Paris 1934, pp. 164, 176–8)

⁸ White Eagle Lodge archives, at Liss, in Hampshire, England, Conan Doyle correspondence. For the rest, again see THE SHINING PRESENCE, p. 33.

⁹ KREUZZUG GEGEN DEN GRAAL. DIE GESCHICHTE DER ALBIGENSER was first published in 1933, and in French as CROISADE CONTRE LE GRAAL the next year. An English translation, by Christopher Jones, waited until 2006 (Vermont: Inner Traditions). Rahn is a highly controversial figure upon whom it would be most unwise to pronounce outside the context of a deep understanding of the climate of the 1930s. Here is not the place for that. Although he was wild in his idealism, Nazi ideology ran totally counter to the apolitical and gentle unifying ideals of the Polaires, with whom he is associated, and he seems to have died a broken man, in the Bavarian mountains, in March 1939. The coincidence of his death with the anniversary of the fall of Montségur has been noted, and there is little doubt that his abiding ethic was one inherited from Catharism – one that placed the values of the life beyond a long way ahead of anything the earth could offer. For the passages added to LUCIFER'S COURT by the Nazis, the source is his friend Paul Ladame. For the dates of his arrival in the area, actually from a police report of 1938 (which indicates how strong national feelings were) see Bernadac, pp. 22–3; for the letter to Gadal, see http://www.gadal-catharisme. org/study-circle_3_12_en.htm.

¹⁰ They are in the Conan Doyle papers in the Harry Ransom Center at the University of Texas, Austin.

¹¹ For the text of the sittings, the quotations in the book are the only source; for reasons of confidentiality, records of private sittings with White Eagle would almost never have been kept at White Eagle Lodge.

CONSIDERATIONS ON THE CATHARS AND THEIR DOCTRINES

MAURICE MAGRE

This early twentieth-century author stresses the unity of thought that lies behind Catharism; he is noted for linking Cathar, Buddhist and Hindu beliefs to each other, or to some common original.

EVERY CONCEPT is *one*: all ways of seeing things come from the same source – and a morality, a religion, an organization all logically grow from this parent dogma.

The parent dogma of Catharism is the exile of man on the Earth; he is the captive of matter, which is his tomb. The Cathars could say with Plato: 'The flesh is fatal'. There, in all its beautiful simplicity, is the whole of Cathar morality.

Catharism is essentially a purification, and an aspiration to the heavenly life.

From this principle there arise three consequences, of an immense range:

1. *Poverty*. The true Cathar should not own anything in the world – not fields, not home, not money. If he set himself to the service of work on the earth, it was to relieve those brothers who are less fortunate, beset by

---

Maurice Magre (1877–1941) was a playwright and novelist well celebrated in his own day – and a passionate student of the Cathars before scholarship had given us the fuller picture of Cathar life and belief we have today. In this article, reproduced from the *Bulletin des Polaires* of 9 July 1931, he shows a pleasing modesty and does not claim that his understanding is complete. It is true that sources such as the Inquisition records and discoveries of the words of their rituals have increased our picture of the Cathars, yet what Magre does is to make the Cathars familiar to our hearts and sympathies in a way scholarship rarely can. The article is signed 'P.M.' in the Bulletin, but there is little doubt as to the authorship. It is in the style of Magre's MAGICIENS ET ILLUMINÉS (1930, translated as THE RETURN OF THE MAGI, 1931).

their tremendous burdens. And before such dedication, the poor and the miserable peasantry remained struck with wonder. These men, of such charity, were known as 'the good men'. Such was the opinion of the ordinary people; to tell the truth, was their voice not God's voice too?

As for hospitality, they were provided with lodging; as for charity, they received food.

Not only did they possess nothing – they did not even possess themselves. They belonged to the Cathar community.

2. *Abstinence.* The Cathars abstained from all flesh: from eggs, which carry with them a seed of the mortal flesh; from milk, an animal fluid. However, no matter what St Augustine says, they ate fish in Egypt, and they drank wine in the West. They fed almost exclusively on plants – and the less substantial the better: fruits such as melons and figs, whose flesh and whose syrup appeared to them like frozen sunlight. In addition to their continual abstinence, the Cathars observed three fasts during the year, each of forty days. These 'quadragesimas' corresponded to the three major holidays: Christmas, Easter and Pentecost. They were identifiable by their leanness, to the point almost of transparency, 'as thin as air'. The phrase used was: 'pale as a Manichee'.

3. *Absolute Continence.* Their ideal condition was virginity. Celibacy was held to be a very holy state. Widowhood was to be venerated. However, it was an exceptional state. And marriage was the rule among the faithful, so it was not an imperfection. In fact, we see in St John's Gospel Christ holding marriage sacred at the wedding of Cana, and taking on himself the mystical name of the Bridegroom. Did he not give the name of Bride to the Church and Holy Jerusalem? So that is Christ's own wisdom. The Cathar Perfects were therefore an exception, and could be compared to these 'voluntary eunuchs of the Kingdom of Heaven' referred to by the Saviour.

Did not Christ glorify the family right up to the one in Heaven, giving to God the title of the Father, to himself the name of Son, and uniting in the Spirit their love, mutual and perpetual?

The Albigensian houses therefore buzzed with the sound of small children.

The inspiration behind Catharism came from India. Like the Brahmin who only after giving the day to his large family – his crown and his glory – the Albigensian gave the end of his life to chastity, when he was preparing for a venerable end.

No people has known as well how to express conjugal and paternal feelings like the Brahmins. 'Listen, the voice of my divine legislators', said the Indian poet. Remember that in their immortal songs, they said of the woman, the modest companion of the man – the one who, in the son that she gives him, prolongs his existence by letting him live through another. It is to this son that he hands on the issue of the souls of his ancestors.

We can therefore believe that among the Cathars as among the Brahmins marriage was sanctified as a means for the transmigration of souls into new bodies; transmigration which had the result of their gradual purification and their final delivery. The joy that they experienced to see the souls of their ancestors live again in the personalities of their children, finding inspiration in this touching phrase: 'Beside the sounds of the new-born child, even the song of the birds is charmless.'

But when their body approached to the time of death, when their family was complete, old people separated themselves from their children, untied their conjugal union, and by a voluntary widowhood prepared themselves in solitude, by prayer, fasting, charity and contemplation, for the return to God. After the life of the world and of the Earth came apprenticeship to the angelic life. Thus they prepared for the life of Heaven.

This is what we have been able to gather on the Cathar Doctrine, from a number of impartial authors.

The Cathars did not engage in monastic customs. However, sometimes they adopted the pace of life of the anchorites in caves and wild forests. They were poor, gentle, peaceful, and pure of heart.

They had several degrees of initiation. First, there were those who completely observed the three vows; they were called by the Greeks 'the perfect' and by the Romans: 'the elect'. The elect were the teachers: they taught the multitude. And the novices, living in the world, and who had the right only to listen to them in silence were for this reason all called: 'auditors'. They were the 'postulants' of the primitive Church – not of the Apostolic Church, which, especially that of Saint Paul, was essentially free, popular, and exoteric – but from the esoteric Church of the second age which, hiding itself from the daylight and the crowd, sought the shadows of the catacombs, and enveloped itself behind the veil of the Oracle of Eleusis and the mysteries of Egypt.

Therefore, the secular lived the normal life of the laity; they married, had possessions, acquired, sold, ploughed and reaped, drank wine, ate meat, hunted, waged war, mounted their horses for battle, and dressed themselves in armour.

The Perfects, by contrast, were only seen in battle in order to prevent bloodshed, heal the wounds of warriors, and to offer the *consolamentum* to the dying. Following the example of their Saviour, they were doctors at the same time as preachers, and tended the infirmities of the soul as well as those of the body. They knew the stars as well as the plants, following the example of the Magi from the East. They had the reputation of being able to command the elements, calm the waves, and divert the storms.

Legends and traditions of their supernormal powers still exist in the Ariège: the waters of one of the lakes of Mont St-Barthélémy smokes and seethes sometimes, announcing that an event is about to occur, and the smoke is changed into a cloud. This is only legend – but it also proves the faith that the people attached to everything that came from the Cathars.

A PERSONAL REMINISCENCE

WALTER BIRKS

An extract from a study first published in 1987, and possibly written earlier.
It brings Catharism into a very different Middle Eastern context, and draws
particular attention to the symbolism of the Grail.

FROM THE Lebanon northwards to the Turkish border stretches a range of mountains known as the Jebel Ansariya or Alawite mountains which has been for over a thousand years the home of the Nosairi sect, named Alawites since the French occupation. In this region, extending for approximately one hundred miles along the Syrian coast and some thirty miles inland, the Nosairis form the overwhelming majority of the rural population, while the Sunni Moslems and Christians are concentrated in the small townships on the sea coast.

The Nosairis practise a secret initiatory religion whose real tenets are known only to the adepts and which it is death to disclose to the profane. No proselytism is ever practised, and in order to divert or discourage inquisitiveness it is permissible to pretend adherence to the outward forms of the prevailing religion, such outward forms being but the garment which conceals the true faith.

In its historical origins Nosairism is considered to be a branch of the Shia heresy and to have arisen in the general anarchy of the Qarmatian period. When the power of the Abbassid caliphs was declining a movement arose within Islam to throw off Arab political domination and to infuse a more mystical element into the Moslem religion. This movement had its origin in Persia, and in the political sphere it ultimately gave rise to the

---

Walter Birks (1912–99) left his career as a school teacher to pursue a study of the Cathars and was designated by Antonin Gadal as his successor in carrying forward the esoteric tradition in the Ariège. After the Second World War he became progressively disillusioned by the occult, but fascinated by the connections he found in wartime Syria, told in this chapter. His study of Catharism, THE TREASURE OF MONTSÉGUR (with R. A. Gilbert) was published in 1987, and it is from this book that the above extract is taken, with permission.

Fatimite caliphate, while on the doctrinal side it left its traces in the gholat, the secret, initiatory sects, such as the Druze, the Ismailis, and the Nosairis. Of these the Nosairis are the most extreme and the farthest removed from the Dar-al-Islam. They share the general characteristics of the Shia sects, the exaltation of Ali, the practice of secrecy and dissimulation with regard to their beliefs, and the allegorical interpretation of the Koran. In the case of the Nosairis, however, these characteristics are pushed to such an extreme as to remove them altogether from the general community of Islam. Moreover, the presence of Christian and pagan elements among their beliefs has been remarked upon by all scholars who have studied their religion – such practices as the sacramental use of wine in their ceremonies, together with candles, incense and odoriferous plants, the observance of Christmas, Epiphany, and Whitsuntide, and the veneration of Christian saints such as St George and St Matthew. Pagan survivals are even more evident in the practice, particularly among the *Amma* (the uninitiated) as distinct from the *Khassa*, the chosen), of congregating for worship at the qubbas, characteristic white-domed shrines which are built upon the 'high places' and surrounded always by a sacred grove of evergreen oaks. Here incense is burned and invocations made to the *genius loci*.

A number of scholars, notably Massignon,[1] have contended that the Nosairis are really Christians who have been obliged to cloak their faith under a semblance of Moslem heterodoxy in order to escape persecution. This theory proved particularly attractive to the French for political reasons, and an attempt has been made to trace their origin to the Ghassaniya, a Christian-Arab feudatory kingdom which, until the Moslem invasion, held the southern frontiers of the Byzantine Empire against the Bedouin of Arabia. It is suggested that when the Moslem conquest of Syria took place the Ghassaniya migrated to the Jebel Ansariya and continued to nourish their Christian faith in a secret and disguised form among these inaccessible mountains, deriving fresh strength from the period of Crusader rule in the twelfth and thirteenth centuries. During the mandatory period the French set up the Alawite area as an autonomous territory and there were plans to separate it entirely from Syria in the same way as the then largely Christian Lebanon.

Dussaud[2] considers that the Nosairis were established in the area long before any Ghassaniya migration. He cites the references in Pliny and Jerome to Nazarenes in the area and says there is some evidence that they were also called Galileans.[3] Dussaud, however, considers that the core of

their religion is pagan and that they have successively adopted a protective covering, first of Christianity and then of Islam. Toynbee[4] summarizes
Dussaud's view: 'The Nosairis have travestied the Ismaili Shi'ism which
forced an entry to their mountain fastnesses in the age of the Crusades by
deifying Ali – but this is only an accretion – the core of their religion is a local worship more ancient than Islam or Christianity and perhaps even pri-
or to that impact of Hellenism on the Syriac world in which Christianity
and Islam originated.' The Nosairis themselves claim to derive their name
from a certain ibn Nosair, an obscure partisan of one of the Shi'ite Imams.
This is probably a good example of their genius for protective covering.

During the Second World War I served with the British Security Mission
in Syria and for three years I was Head of Mission in Lattakia, the capital
of the Alawite territory. My responsibility was Intelligence throughout the
territory and particularly in the sensitive area of the Turkish frontier. This
gave me a unique opportunity to study the Nosairi religion at close quarters
and to establish personal relationships with its leading exponents. Like all
the aspects of religious expression we have examined in this book, the Nosairi religion is a product of its history and the impact upon it of a variety
of ideologies. The remoteness and inaccessibility of much of the area has
meant that ancient beliefs and ceremonies have lingered on there. Over the
centuries governments have tended to ignore the mountain districts, unless
the inhabitants gave trouble, in which case repression was usually brutal,
especially in Ottoman times. The Nosairis therefore have learned to 'keep
their heads down' and to dissimulate. Their religion is characterized by the
use of allegory and symbolism in bewildering complexity, all devised to
conceal esoteric inner meanings which must not be reveaied to the profane.
This enables them to pretend that beneath whatever traditional practices
or beliefs the 'powers that be' find objectionable, their 'real' faith is whatever those powers approve of. Under these conditions it is hardly surprising
that the French were able to contend that the Nosairis, whom they called
Alawites, were really Christians and to plan to set them up in a state separate from Moslem Syria. Today, when the Alawites have become the ruling
group in Syria (thanks to the French having created a largely Alawite army),
they are of course good Moslems! It is the tragedy of the Middle East that
one's politics are always held to be determined by one's religion. For this
reason I found it convenient to let it be known that I was a Buddhist. This
was given some plausibility by the presence of Gurkha troops in the area at

the time and had the advantage, not only of enabling me to assume political impartiality, but also to decline the more rebarbative aspects of traditional Arab hospitality without giving offence. Moreover, no Nosairi had any motive for pretending to me that their religion was really Christian.

The Nosairis are divided into two main groups which we may, for convenience, call Northern and Southern. The Southern group is the preponderant one in the territory today, many of the Northerners having been taken out of Syria when the region round Antioch (Antakya) was ceded to Turkey in 1939. The Southern group more readily accepts the designation Alawite since this emphasizes their adherence to the Shia (Shi'at Ali) branch of Islam. The Northerners are noticeably less 'Islamic', and, in view of their cross-border relationships with their co-religionists in Turkey, it was with them that I was principally concerned from a security intelligence point of view. I made it my business to get to know their leaders as intimately as possible and, in particular, one of them who was said to be regarded as a manifestation of deity. I established such a close personal relationship with him that, when the war was over, he invited me to stay as a guest in his house. There, sitting on his verandah, which commanded a stupendous view of the mountains, we discussed religion in every aspect, and it was there that I received the enlightenment which had eluded me in the Pyrenees.

The two most important symbols in Nosairi religion (at least in its 'Northern' form) are Light, and the cup or chalice which contains rthe-sacramental wine, in drinking which the worshipper says, 'I drink to the Light'. This symbolism of the cup led me to tell my host the legend of the Holy Grail. When I had finished he said,'I am going to reveal to you the greatest secret of our religion, but you must never disclose that it was I who told you. This Grail you speak of is a symbol and it stands for the doctrine which Christ taught to John the Beloved alone. We have it still.'

It is now forty years since my friend 'took the Way of the stars' and I feel that though I still may not name him, it is important that this revelation should be made known. The Nosairi obsession with secrecy was in the past essential to their survival, but I cannot believe that today such a revelation need be concealed. Of course, it is totally unsupported by any evidence other than my assertion. The reader must judge by what follows whether to think it credible. For me this was the final link which completed the chain I had been trying to reconstruct from the Cathars back to Christ, the culminating proof that my quest had not been in vain. Here surely, preserved like a fossil in this mountain fastness, is a precious relic of what I have called the Alternative Tradition. The Nosairis, and especially the Ghaibiya sect, which is the one I was able to study most closely, have preserved all the characteristics there listed: the idea of a divine spirit dwelling in man, of Christ as the man who realized his divinity, the potential in others to follow his example, the distinction between the hearers (*Amma*) and the elect (*Khassa*); and, finally, the putting on of a girdle which marks the Nosairi initiate as it did the Essene, the Paulician, and the Cathar.

The Northerners are themselves divided into sects and the one whose symbolism was revealed to me is known as Ghaibiya. This word is derived from the Arabic for absence and it means that God is absent or concealed from men. But although He is invisible He is yet omnipresent. It is the very Light that is His symbol which veils His presence, for the man who can raise his consciousness towards the apprehension of Godhead finds himself blinded by excess of Light. The heavenly wine is indeed offered, but he cannot take his communion unless he can find a vessel, a cup in which to receive it. A conception of God in whatever form is a vessel which can hold some portion of the Divine Light. This vessel may be anything from a material image to the most abstract of spiritual conceptions. These differ only in degree, in their capacity for holding the Light. The more closely the vessel corresponds to the divine the better it can serve as its vehicle or embodiment. Christ is more than the best of vessels: He is a living Grail. But other men can become Light-filled vessels too, according to their capacity to hold the divine essence. Christ was one who realized his Godhead in full consciousness. But he was still a man. He became God, but only in so far as a man can become God. He could not hold more of the Infinite than the greatest and holiest of vessels can hold. In him God was manifest to the world in the form of a man, reduced to the measure and stature of a man.

This doctrine solves a problem which had baffled me in my study of the Cathars. How was it that they held St John's Gospel, and especially its preface, in such reverence when their view of Christ was Adoptionist? The Word is the expression, not of a transcendent Person but of a transcendent quality in the universe. The ultimate reality, the Absolute, is not personal in its own nature but by personifying it we create a vehicle through which it can be expressed. This is what the Ghaibiya symbolism conveys in the idea of the 'absence' of God and of the cup in which God can be made manifest.

Because he had realized his Godhead in full consciousness Christ also realized that the individual cannot become wholly divine until all have attained that realization. He must return 'to seek and to save that which is lost'. From the very threshold of the Holy of Holies he must turn back and give himself utterly, even to the Cross. He can do no other, for he is God and that is the nature of God. God eternally gives Himself, pouring out His life that the world may be – and that again is the meaning of His 'absence'. The world's suffering is His suffering, and the world's joy is His joy. Suffering and loss is the universal law of loving creation. All creation, all activity, all motion, all progress, can spring only from selection. Selection implies rejection, and rejection implies suffering and loss. But without that suffering and loss there can be no love and no joy, and those who suffer most love most. God suffers infinitely and His love is infinite.

So we are brought back to the Cross, no longer a gibbet on which a sinless being atoned for man's iniquity, but a symbol of the Love that is Divine.

I told my host about the Cathars. He had never heard of them but he was, of course, immensely interested and we discussed at length the similarities and the differences in their respective beliefs and practices. One striking common feature is the idea of the fall of the soul condemned to wear a human body. By degrees the soul purifies itself and rises again towards God. There is a Nosairi prayer, 'Deliver us from these human forms and reclothe us in light among the stars'.

There is a mystical element in Languedocian Catharism which does not seem to owe anything to Bogomils or Paulicians. It is apparent in this imagery of Light and the Stars, which is also such a notable feature of Nosairi imagery. Could it be that some Languedocian crusader or pilgrim to the Holy Land encountered, as I did, a Light-filled vessel? Could this be, perhaps, where the idea of the Holy Grail originated? At all events, it was there, high in the Nosairi mountains, under the clear stars, in intimate converse with such a one, that I finally shed the fantasies of occultism and realized the true nature of the Cathar treasure.

Notes:

[1] ENCYCLOPAEDIA OF ISLAM (1936)

[2] The best published account of the Nosairi religion is by René Dussaud, HISTOIRE ET RELIGION DES NOSAIRIS (Paris: Bouillon, 1900). No satisfactory account has been published in English [at the time Birks wrote].

[3] The Arabic for Christians is Nasrani. Ansariyah is the Arabic plural of Nosairi.

[4] STUDY OF HISTORY, vol. 2, p. 56

VII. MEMORY : 1

MONTSÉGUR

ANNA HAYWARD

A memory that threatened but in fact brought about a spiritual awakening.

THE STORY I'm about to relate was revealed to me over a period of years through direct experience and in meditation, and gradually it has become a more or less coherent picture of part of a past life. Many of the direct experiences were evidential to the extent that a far memory of a past life was for me the only way to understand what happened.

The story begins when I was staying in Toulouse in the 1970s, with friends. In those days I was an extremely shy person, which is relevant to the unfolding events, and up to that point I had not so much as come across the words 'Cathar' or 'Albigenses'.

My friends decided to take a trip by car to Montségur, the last stronghold of the Cathar movement, but they didn't talk to me about what had

Anna has been exploring the inner worlds for over forty years. She is an experienced practitioner and teacher of meditation, firstly with TM, then as a Theravadin Buddhist and for many years and currently as a minister of the White Eagle Lodge. As well as meditation, and discovery through the arts, Anna has been a counsellor since 1982, during which time she has been privileged to witness to the psyches and the personal spiritual worlds of people from many walks of life. This experience formed the basis for her published book IN A NEW LIGHT (Polair, 2011) which is an original look at psychology.

happened there and I had no idea where we were going. We took a long time to find our way out of Toulouse, but eventually were free of the suburbs. I remember it being a beautiful day, until I began to panic. I had never had panic attacks before, so the severity of the feeling was shocking, and became worse the further we travelled, so much so that, despite my lack of confidence, I asked to stop and eventually was taken back to our apartment in Toulouse, feeling dreadful. My friends then went off again, ostensibly to Montségur, but as it turned out they changed their minds and went to Andorra instead.

The panic subsided somewhat on my return to Toulouse, and a few days later, when my friends again decided to visit Montségur, I went with them. I had no reason to suppose that it was the proximity to that area which was causing the fear, but, yet again and at roughly the same distance away, I began to panic. This time I was far too embarrassed to ask to stop, so we continued down towards the mountains.

Anyone who has suffered panic attacks will know how I must have been feeling. By the time we arrived I was shaking and cold, trying to hide how I felt from my kind friends, and as we began to climb the hill towards the castle, it was hard to tell whether my racing heartbeat was due to the climb or the fear. As soon as we entered the castle environs, however, something changed radically, and strangely. With a sense of abandonment and even joy, I raced through and up the steps to the battlements (they were not roped off then as they are now) and sat, feet over the edge, looking up to the mountains and listening to the cowbells and cicadas in the valley below with a sense of deep, joyous peace. The poem opposite, written some time later, may convey some of the feeling.

I did not want to leave, much to the annoyance of my friends! I still had no real idea what the castle represented, what history had been enacted there, or who the Cathars were.

On returning to England the panics resumed; so much so that, from the position of being a slightly cynical intellectual, I nevertheless began to look for a way to control my mind, and came upon Transcendental Meditation. This opening to a more spiritual understanding was the beginning of a journey for me, which continued until I found the White Eagle Lodge, which is now my spiritual home. In between, I became a Theravadin Buddhist but finally I was drawn towards spiritual healing (which is another story, this time involving Egypt). I became involved with the work of the

MONTSÉGUR

Climbing the pinnacle of rock the light spreads,
As flames once leapt in pyres, so we spiral
Round the dark earth face,
Leaving the valley floor, where cowbells and cicadas
Weave the air into a spell of sound.
We move beyond these temporal things
Into the world of mountains.

For a while the drum of the heartbeat pervades,
Adrenalin rising like panic, and the way steep with stones,
The boulders of life; our pain singing,
And then the castle grows out of the rocks around us
And I do not wish to stop,
Drawn on a timeless, rushing wave
I climb the ramparts to the south
And sit, legs dangling, before the silent peaks.
And oh, what stillness forms around me!
Fear falls beneath my feet, and the eternal peace,
Beyond all understanding, grows in my heart.

I am there still,

Though distance separates the senses
And other journeys intervene,
The smoke has cleared and tears
Of love now heal the pastures.
Nothing has ended:
The spirit lives in every pebble on the hillside;
In every moment of the stillness,
Or breath of wind across my cheek,
Conferred by the touch of death
Consolamentum est.

Anna Hayward

Lodge. I began to realise that one of the reasons for the panics was that it was a way of forcing me to look at life again. It was the re-finding of my spiritual path. As a result, besides study, I learned to meditate and began to have inner experiences which elucidated what had happened to me at Montségur in that past life.

For those unfamiliar with deep sensory meditation, it is worth saying that there are often two phases. The first is when you deliberately focus on something, or create a scene in your mind, often as a way to gain calm. In fact what happens is you are opening a door. I have studied perception, and, put simply, the brain experiences a lot more through the senses than it allows us to see. The brain needs permission to allow to the forefront of the consciousness things which are not part of the survival of everyday in a material world. Creative visualisation in a meditative environment gives that permission to the brain.

The next stage, however, is where the inner senses (visual, auditory etc.) begin to recognise people, events, things, which you have not deliberately created. You might think this could be simply something like word-association operating, but in fact the things experienced are often quite unusual, even unrecognised at first. They are not what you might expect with the frontal mind.

It was in such times of deep meditation that I began to piece together, over the years, what happened to me at Montségur—sometimes in glimpses, but also in extremely vivid moments of clarity, lasting for longer than simply a flash. What it led me to realise is that, far from going 'singing into death', which many people say the Cathars did, there were those of us who were, at the end, afraid. All my life I have struggled with fear on many different levels, indeed the shyness was a fear of getting things wrong, of not being good enough. Life has presented me with a number of fear-inducing situations, and now it does not surprise me that fear would have been the deepest feeling for me in those moments at the end of that Cathar life. What follows is the story of what happened as it has come together in my mind and been revealed to me.

My first far memory was of standing on the battlements in the castle of Montségur, not far from where I had sat in this day of life. I was dressed simply, and I remember, in the meditation, looking down at my arms and seeing sun-browned skin, with large pores and coarse dark hairs, very different from how I look now. I was a woman of peasant stock.

The sergeant-at-arms came up the steps towards me and said: 'Madame, le Parfait, ils sont arrivés.' This is how my modern ear heard the words, but of course he would have spoken to me in the mediaeval, Occitan, tongue and this odd phrase is how it has come across for me to understand it. 'Ils sont arrivés' means 'they have arrived.' What I was not aware of then, but have found out since, is that there was a short hiatus at the end of the siege, after the castle fell, when a small garrison was allowed to stay, along with the Cathars, while the pyres in the valley below were being prepared. The sergeant had come to tell me that they had finally come to take us down.

Instead of funeral pyres and flames, curiously, the next clear memory I have is of being in a dark cave, on one side against the cold wall, and gradually feeling enormously afraid, along with deep shame at this weakness. I was a *parfait*. I, of all people, should have been able to lead people in acceptance, even joy, at being once more united with God, but my body-self would not be calmed and I passed into death gasping for breath—for life!

In this current lifetime, all through the years, I have had fears about not being able to breathe. There have been no physical symptoms, except heavy catarrh, particularly at night, and problems with finding my voice, but in a variety of circumstances, fears of that confining, suffocating moment when you struggle to take in the life-force have resurfaced strongly. It is not surprising to me therefore, that as I've come to understand the lesson Montségur held for me, so those fears have abated as well.

So what was the purpose of these far memories? I believe it was to help me understand the need to experience fear and the way out of it. But it was also to heal the shame of that death, because the next experiences that came to me in meditation were of what actually happened on the other side of death at that time. There were two of these experiences. In the first, the memory was of relief and shame, so that even though there was an atmosphere of love, I was still hooked into that feeling of failure, of letting people down. In the second, I was immediately surrounded by all those who had died with me in that cave, and the feeling was of their absolute forgiveness and understanding, which, finally, I could accept. This released me from the sense of guilt. It was an extremely powerful and humbling moment when I allowed into my being their love and continued respect, which I felt I had lost.

I work nowadays as a minister in the White Eagle Lodge, and thus in a somewhat similar position of responsibility to what I held in those days in Montségur, and I am sure that these far memories and the healing that has taken place have also been ways to enable me once again to be in this position. Hopefully I have come with deeper understanding, with more compassion in times when our physical, earthly weakness overcomes our spiritual strength. The experience has also helped me truly to believe that a position of responsibility does not mean or confer greater ability on any level—we all have our struggles and our triumphs. Perhaps it has also helped me better to understand one of White Eagle's wise instructions, 'Do not expect too much of your brother' – not because he is sinful, but because if we weren't all learning we wouldn't be here. No matter who we are, learning involves mistakes and what we think of as failures. One of the most loving assertions White Eagle has made is this: 'Failure is good ... through failure we may mount the hill of vision'.

I should like to finish with another White Eagle passage which touches my heart, and just why will become obvious in the reading of it.

'We beg you to gain a more comprehensive view of the process of spiritual growth in men and women, remembering always that God's plan is to bring beauty—I will not say perfection, not in the limited sense in which the word is understood. To us there is no standing still; even with God, we do not see a perfected Being, completely finished and there for ever.... We wonder at and worship a God ever growing more beautiful, ever sending forth greater waves of life and light, expressing Him–Herself not only in this universe, but in universes yet unborn. As this growth of the divine spirit takes place, so also does development in each one of the individual life spirits of which you are one—there is growth of creative powers within you and increasing harmony and attunement of each individual spirit to the Father–Mother God.'

HELEN'S STORY

SYLVIA FRANCKE

*Four lives that after death became united in their desire to help
others and are linked by memories of Cathar times.*

THERE ARE several threads to the story I have to tell. First, there are
those above the surface, telling of a family who experienced Helen's
death from cancer at the age of eleven, and how they faced this. Then
there are the unexpected events that followed, and an undercurrent which
these began to reveal, which is yet another story, whose symbols gradually
organised themselves into a recognisable pattern. This pattern has continued to emerge since Helen's death in 1982 after which another, wider, family has increasingly gathered, taking their places in an unfolding twentieth
and twenty-first century story which appears to continue events begun
eight hundred years ago.

My husband is from Turkey, where Islam was adapted to a more Western perspective in the 1920s by Turkey's great leader Kemal Ataturk. As the
years passed, the differences in culture blended, but I was still anxious to
keep a balance between Christianity and Islam in the family atmosphere.
My background was the modern esoteric Christian path of Rudolf Steiner's Spiritual Science or Anthroposophy, which recognises the place of all
the world's great religions in the spiritual development of humankind.
Steiner has described Anthroposophy as the present-day re-surfacing of an
'underground stream' of knowledge which began in the ancient Mystery
Centres and continued through the beliefs of the Cathars, Templars and
Rosicrucians. I believe that the Templars and Rosicrucians worked towards
a synthesis of Christianity, Judaism and Islam. In the twentieth and twenty-
first centuries Anthroposophy is in a position to look back further to the
great contribution given to humanity by earlier beliefs such as Hinduism.

For Sylvia Francke's biography see p. 135

The spiritual perspective given by this modern update of Mystery Wisdom provides an extension of information that has been applied to many of the practical avenues of modern life: education, farming, medicine, art, and the care of people with special needs, among many other activities instigated by Dr Steiner.

Before Helen was taken ill I had never heard of the Cathars. During the months preceding her illness, she and I had begun to escape from the rest of the family to watch quite serious programmes on television. She was very musical, so it began with the Master Class series on BBC2. On one occasion Owen Brannigan presented 'The Great Roles in Opera'; on another there was a lesson in playing the harp. Then two old friends came to tea one Sunday and told me that the second of a very fascinating series on the mystery of an ancient French village would be shown that night in BBC 2's 'Chronicle' programme.[1] We watched it together and, for me, that was the beginning of an interest in Rennes-le-Château and the subject material of HOLY BLOOD, HOLY GRAIL by Michael Baigent, Richard Leigh and Henry Lincoln – an interest which later led me to the Cathars.

During August in 1980 my family and I spent a lazy day out at sea in the South of France on an aptly-named boat: 'Endless Summer'. Enter a new character, Alice. I had first met Alice that morning when she arrived at the quayside carrying a picnic for us all. She was wearing a white chiffon dress with navy spots, and I, a navy chiffon dress with white spots! After the picnic, we were all lazing about on deck in our swimming-suits, reading books or sleeping in the sun. Helen, my third child, had discovered that Alice was adept at reading palms. After scanning Helen's palm for a few minutes, Alice said, 'You will possibly break an arm or a leg next year, and the year after you will have a very serious illness.' Helen was delighted with the prospective drama and immediately leapt to her feet, dancing around the deck excitedly singing: 'I'm going to break my arm, my leg, my arm, my leg!' The following year Helen was knocked over on a pedestrian crossing on her way to school. She broke her leg.

After our day out at sea, we all dined together in the beautiful medieval town of Eze, high in the hills above Nice. Alice and I had slipped off to the cloakroom. Through the cloakroom window we could see the tower of a castle from which a banner was floating in the bright moonlit sky 'Do you think we once lived together in a castle like that?' mused Alice. We both laughed, but the first note of a new theme had been sounded.

Two years on, the year after Helen broke her leg and just after her eleventh birthday, she came home for Sunday lunch having spent a morning at the local swimming-baths. Sunday lunch was always a favourite feature in Helen's week. 'I don't feel much like lunch today, Mummy. In fact when I had only swum one length of the baths I couldn't breathe properly and had to gasp big gulps of air. I hope I haven't got cancer!'

Only a few days later Helen was waiting for a biopsy at the Royal Marsden Hospital in south London. The first task of the morning was to go for an X-ray, prior to going to the operating theatre. As we sat outside waiting to go in we discussed a mad scheme I had for making a film or major television documentary on the life and work of Rudolf Steiner. In connection with this, we discussed the difference between Newton and Goethe's theories of colour. Helen had just been learning about Isaac Newton at school. We were talking together animatedly, more like research students in a university canteen than two people filling in time before an ominous event. After Helen's X-ray we rushed back to her ward at the highest possible speed, not to be late for the operation. When we got up to the children's floor Helen suddenly spun her wheel-chair off at a tangent to take a quick look at a bazaar being held to raise money for Leukemia research. She bought a jigsaw puzzle and a colouring book for her little brother before zooming down the passage to her ward.

There had been no breakfast for her that morning and nothing to drink before the operation. Helen was desperately thirsty and justifiably furious with me when I said to her on entering the room: 'I must give your flowers a drink!' The porter arrived to take Helen down to Theatre. I took a small crystal with me and when Helen's eyes began to shut I held it up, it sparkled purple and blue light. 'Look!' I said, 'These are healing colours.'

Back in Helen's room I waited the prescribed twenty minutes. Then forty, then an hour. After what seemed an age a nurse came to tell me that Helen had difficulty in breathing and needed a tracheotomy in her throat. I rang my husband who was looking after the children at home. He left them with a neighbour and came to the hospital. We paced the ward together for another hour, then he said 'Where is this ****** operating theatre?' so we marched down the passage in search of it together. It was empty. Porters were putting away the linen. A nurse appeared from behind another door. She told us that Helen was in Intensive Care and being prepared for a lightning journey to Great Ormond Street Hospital at the height of the evening rush hour. One of us could travel in the police car behind the ambulance, which was crammed with vital equipment. Aydin returned home to the children. I entered Intensive Care where the most amazing scene lay before me. The room was full of people all concentrating on the silent figure in their midst. Helen was lying with her hair falling in a cascade of gold on her pillow. Her face was deathly white. The tracheotomy tube was plunged into her throat, surrounded by cotton wool, the centre of which was tinged with blood. 'She looks like a swan that has been shot in the throat by an arrow!' I thought. At that time I had not heard of the legend of Parsifal, let along read it.

Then the rest of the scene came clearly into focus and everything started to move very fast. Many different people were in the room with Helen, helping her in their various capacities. Nurses were busy connecting tubes from all sides. The Children's Floor Matron officiated. Ambulancemen stood by waiting for instructions, together with two policemen who would be in the squad car. Although the situation was grim, there was an urgency in the air which kept me going. I was ushered downstairs to the front door of the hospital. The ambulance stood waiting directly outside, the squad car in front. I climbed into the back of the squad car, watching over my shoulder for Helen's entourage to follow. They came out of the hospital and up into the back of the ambulance. The blue light began to turn. Then the squad-car radio was live and a voice described a list of roads and road-junctions. The policemen explained to me that two possible routes were being offered through the rush-hour traffic from the Royal Marsden in Sutton to Great Ormond Street in the centre of London. On both of these routes the traffic had already been halted. I was filled with awe and gratitude.

A route was chosen. The matron said goodbye from the kerb, the policemen turned to me in the back. 'Hold on tight, we'll be travelling close to a hundred miles an hour!' The sirens began to wail and we shot off, the ambulance and the squad-car like two arrows from separate bows. Despite the rush hour, the journey took less than twenty minutes. There were policeman at every road-junction holding back the pedestrians and traffic. All the way into London I was looking out of the back window watching the blue light on the ambulance and telling myself that while it stayed alight Helen was still alive inside.

We arrived at the doors of Great Ormond Street Hospital and I left the squad-car thanking the police for their great skill and perseverance on the journey. At that moment I was supremely grateful for the positive benefits of modern science.

Later I was told by the nursing staff in Intensive Care Unit at Great Ormond Street that there had been a 'Laurel and Hardy-type' scene in progress while our race into London was taking place. After they had received the phone call from the Royal Marsden in Sutton they realised that there was no bed available for Helen. Several of the staff rushed down to the basement of the hospital where they eventually found a bed lying in bits in a corner. They hurried upstairs again with the bits only to find that they didn't fit together when they tried to assemble them in the ward. More hilarious scenes followed which typified the human side of the experiences I was going through during the next two weeks in Great Ormond Street.

Alice came to visit us twice. She looked at Helen's palm for the first time since that day on 'Endless Summer'. There were many changes, several mystic crosses and stars had appeared. She left for a week's holiday in Italy, then returned to find that the lifeline that she had seen interrupted by illness two years ago had now grown very faint but the crosses and stars had increased in number in only seven days. Alice told me that the night before she had dreamed she was in a zoo, when suddenly a swan rose up high into the sky and flew away out of sight leaving Alice calling, 'Helen, Come back! Come back!' That evening I telephoned a friend from the upstairs kitchen. As I was speaking I glanced out of the window. The sky was filled with the pink and orange colours of a glorious sunset. Then a flight of swans flew across it and out of sight behind the dark edge of the hospital building.

Easter Day dawned and, as I made my way towards Intensive Care from the bedroom I had occupied for the last two weeks, I met a familiar nurse coming towards me down the passage. She very gently told me that the decision had been made to switch off Helen's machines as there was nothing more that could be done for her. I returned to my bedroom and a little later appeared in Helen's room with the Bible. I sat down and read to her from the Gospels for the first time ever. I read through the story of Easter morning from all four Gospel accounts. The day passed in a gentle, peaceful way. At about three in the afternoon the doctor in charge of the life-support equipment came to switch off Helen's life support. He was known to be very fond of 'his machines', yet as he leaned forward to flick up the switches, he muttered. 'Let's turn these b***** things off!' As this was happening I bent over Helen's head and said the Lord's Prayer to her, also for the first time. When the machines were silent and the prayer over I expected Helen to go. She was much weaker than two weeks previously when she had made the journey from Sutton to London because she could not breathe without the tubes thrust deep into her lungs; yet now she continued to breathe easily and deeply with no tracheotomy and no tubes. Many prayers had been said during those two weeks. A friend had suggested that as many as possible should pray for her every hour upon the hour. This message went out to ever wider circles of people, in many cases those I had never met. A Turkish friend of my husband's went to great lengths to keep to it, on one occasion suddenly pulling another friend to his knees with him, saying, 'We've got to pray now, I'll tell you why later!' When he told me he added. 'Maybe we've started a new religion?'

I laid my head beside Helen's in the welcome silence broken only by her gentle, easy breathing. Hours passed, and I was aware of the sun slowly moving around the corner of the building. Eventually a nurse came in with a jug full of diluted lime juice. Two weeks ago Helen had been longing for a drink before the biopsy at the Royal Marsden, and even though she had suffered considerable brain damage from loss of oxygen under anaesthetic that day, I had since been told it was very possible that her hearing was still unimpaired. Maybe she could hear the refreshing sound of ice clunking in the jug? I asked the nurse if we could put a few drops of the lime juice in her mouth now that it was clear of pipes and tubes for the first time in two weeks. The lime juice was siphoned into a clean syringe and then carefully dropped into Helen's parched mouth. She sighed deeply, not breathing again for what seemed like a full minute. She breathed a second time and paused again. Then she took a final deep breath and died.

After Helen's death the other children searched everywhere for photos of her; putting them up all over the house with flowers and lighting candles in front of them. My oldest daughter Yasemin found one of Helen with her younger sister, Suzie, sitting in the bath in brightly-coloured bath hats, a line of plastic ducks in convoy around the sides of the bath. The picture had been found inside a book of Christmas legends, the top of it underlining the words:

'Only a few drops touched his tongue, but more was not needed. As soon as he tasted the water, a delicious coolness surged through his body, and he felt no more that the helmet and armour burnt and oppressed him. The sun's rays had lost their power. His dry lips became soft and moist again, and the red flames no longer danced before his eyes.[2]

★

The following summer I took part in a week's conference at Michael Hall, a Steiner School in Forest Row, Sussex. I had taken various books with me to continue my Rennes-le-Château research. I was about to begin Arthur Guirdham's book on the Cathars: THE GREAT HERESY,[3] which lay unopened on my desk. The questions to which I hoped to find the answer were: What was the treasure of the Cathar stronghold, Montségur? Why did the besieged Cathars ask to remain in Montségur for an extended period of time? and Where was the treasure taken by the four *parfaits* who escaped with it on the last night before the remaining Cathars were taken down the mountain and burnt in the field below?

On the second to last day at the conference I discovered that I had to travel to London, together with my husband, in order to sign important documents in a London bank. As I had spent all of my cash on books at the conference I had to write a cheque for my ticket including the tube fare at East Grinstead Station. When I was asked for my destination at the ticket office I replied: 'St James's'.

A voice behind me echoed: 'There's a very lovely church at St James's!'

I turned round, finding a very venerable gentleman standing behind me who could have been mistaken for Merlin.

'I have a friend who does mime workshops there.' I replied.

'That's where I have given lectures on butterflies.' Merlin added.

'I was at a lecture on pine-cones last night.' I continued.

'Why don't we travel up to London together?' said Merlin, 'and then you can tell me about pine-cones and I can tell you about butterflies. Keep me a seat! I must say goodbye to the family I have been staying with.'

When he finally sat in the seat opposite me my new friend asked where the pine-cone lecture had taken place.

'At Michael Hall School,' I answered.

'I used to teach there' came the reply. 'I was an Anthroposophist once.'

'*Were?*'

'No longer, I subsequently became connected with the Cathars. Years ago I was staying with the family with whom I have just been staying again. Their two sons had two French boys staying with them on an exchange visit. They were all due to return to France together but no one was available to escort them back. I offered to take them as far as Paris, but when we got there, again no one was available to collect them, so in the end I took them all the way home. They were the children of Gérard De Sède.'

I knew that Gérard de Sède had written THE ACCURSED TREASURE OF RENNES-LE-CHÂTEAU,'[3] the book that began the whole 'Rennes Industry' and that Henry Lincoln had found in a magazine rack while on holiday in France in the 1970s. 'Merlin' described how through Gérard de Sède he was introduced to the twentieth-century head of a group of Cathars centred in Holland, of how he was taken to the caves of Lombrives. There he had stood in the pulpit of the huge cave church where the Cathars had sheltered for over seventy years from the Inquisition and from the 'Crusading' army assembled by Rome.

'As I stood there I realized I had stood there once before, and as the memory grew stronger I began to preach a sermon in the Occitan French that we used eight hundred years ago.'

Then he grasped both my arms firmly and said:

'Would you believe me if I told you I was one of the four who took the treasure out of Montségur on the last night of the siege?'

I was so taken aback that I immediately responded by asking the question I had been asking myself all week.

'What was it?'

'I can't properly remember. It could have been the Lost Gospel of St John. All I can remember is that we were being let down the steep side of the fortress in one of the huge wine-baskets that our provisions came in. As we descended I remember the bright moonlight illuminating the up-turned faces of the wild flowers below. I don't think I died that night but was hidden in the caves of Lombrives for the rest of my life'

We had lunch together at Victoria Station, exchanged telephone numbers and addresses, and arranged to contact each other at the end of the summer. I went to Turkey with my family, and while I was on the ferry between Izmir and Istanbul a possible solution to the mystery of the treasure of Montségur occurred to me. It involved a sketch I was idly drawing of a version of the Grail symbol: the Moon chalice holding the Sun with twelve stars around it. I looked at the Turkish Flag floating at the stern of the ferry with the moon sickle on its side holding one star. Some time later I looked at where I had drawn the symbol, on a guide book from Ephesus. The Grail symbol I had drawn was immediately below some printed words in the guide book: 'The Temple of Artemis Reconstructed'. The significance of this later led me to further conjectures!

That October Merlin came to stay at my home in Surrey. I related to him the solution to the mystery of the treasure of Montségur that I had come across in the summer. He was very enthusiastic about its validity. He reminded me that he was in touch with someone else, also named Sylvia, who had also remembered being one of the four who escaped from Montségur with him on the last night of the siege. He had known her for many years. She and her husband, Rob, had been troubadours in that incarnation and had both studied together at the Château de Chalusset near Solignac, taught by a knight who was *incognito* as a Cathar and troubadour. There they were taught knightly skills and the troubadour tradition. After they left they travelled south as troubadours to the main Cathar Country. He thought it was important that Sylvia and Rob should hear what I had to say about my interpretation of the treasure of Montségur.

A few weeks later he rang me to say that both of them were visiting London on their way to Rennes-le-Château. He gave me their home telephone number, suggesting we should arrange to meet when they arrived in London. I rang them, and told Sylvia (later named Jehanne) my interpretation of the treasure, at which she also became very enthusiastic. We arranged to meet half way between where they would be in London and my home in Surrey. When we met I handed over my version of the story. They took it down to a group of people at Rennes who again agreed with this interpretation.

Some months later Sylvia came to stay. On the first morning, while I was taking my children to school, she told me that Helen had appeared to her and asked her to ask me to tell her the story of how she died. She appeared to Sylvia later on her way back to her home in Stroud on the train, and again when she reached home there.

Merlin and Sylvia's visits continued. Some time later Sylvia discovered that important communications came through to her before we began discussion each morning. These began after a disaster–prone friend of my older son's accidentally drove through our very large sitting-room picture-window very late one night. Helen's message to Sylvia the next morning was 'This is a breakthrough!', which was followed by a series of pieces of information on some members of my family's troubled relationships, and their causes during Cathar times. This series of information ballooned into a story involving many people who remembered their involvement. One of these began to visit me and every time she stayed, when she awoke in the morning, she found red flame-marks on her arms. She told me that this happened whenever she stayed in a house with Cathar karma.

Her connection with the story was so strong that, on her way to Rennes-le-Château after I had briefly related its unfolding, she accepted a lift from a stranger who suddenly and unexpectedly gave her a curved scimitar with sun and moon emblazoned on its blade, which was connected with the story I had related of these happenings of eight-hundred years ago. When she reached her destination the people staying there with her also felt involved in the story. She visited the spot where the events had occurred and perceived them replaying and augmenting the story so far.

A year or so later Alice came down from London on a routine visit. The young daughter of woman she had recently met through a business contact had been killed in a car crash in France the year before. Alice thought it would help her friend to meet me. They both came down from London to have lunch with me a week or so later. During lunch Alice asked me how the book was progressing. The Languedoc was mentioned, and at this point Marina's knife and fork fell onto her plate.

'That was where the accident happened! I had taken my four-year-old daughter Hermione to Carcassonne a few days before. Suddenly she tugged at my hand and said "Take me away! The knights on horses are coming to get us!" She then insisted that she and I, and my husband, should travel to Andorra together along the old Roman Road. To arrange the trip it was necessary to have our Land Rover taxed and insured, which we did. The road was very straight and the route visible for miles: so typical of a Roman road.'

At this point in the story I interjected, 'Was the accident your fault?'

'It wasn't: a car was stationary at a road junction in front of us, and as we drove nearer, it drew out directly in front of us, forcing us to the side of the road and then sped away. I had multiple facial injuries, Hermione seemed unscathed but died in hospital of brain damage a few days later.'

Earlier, Marina had told Alice and I how she had been invited to the house of her husband's secretary for a lunch to meet a clairvoyant. The clairvoyant told her how two little girls with blonde hair had appeared to her. One of them indicated that she was looking for her mother, who was known by the secretary. She had then rung the secretary to ask, 'Do you know of anyone who lost a young daughter last year?' The secretary mentioned Marina, and subsequently invited her to lunch to meet the clairvoyant. The clairvoyant's description of the younger child fitted Hermione perfectly. At this point Marina turned to me and said, 'I'm sure that the other, older girl, was your daughter Helen.' I believe that this was later proven to be the case.

★

On a plane journey from Milan some time later, Alice decided she didn't like the seat she had been allocated and asked to sit somewhere else. Then she found herself next to a young man who during conversation appeared to be very interested in all of the subjects in which we were both presently absorbed. At the end of the journey Alice exchanged phone numbers, telling him that she would ask me to phone him. Within a short time we were involved in a three-hour phone conversation in which the young man, Richard, asked for contact details for 'Merlin'. Richard then invited Merlin to stay with him in London, during which time amazing synchronicities occurred. As a result of that meeting Richard asked me to gather together all of the people who had entered the story so far. One of these was Angela, a new friend of mine who had come to my house the previous year for a Christmas Festival meeting with another friend and, not knowing I was the host, came up to me and introduced herself by saying. 'I know you, but not from this time!'

Now, as I arranged the meeting Angela asked if she could bring two friends, one of whom had Cathar, the other Templar memories. As the meeting began I decided that I would begin by describing the Swan and Goose, connections with the time around Helen's death. As I did so I noticed that Angela's Templar friend had tears in her eyes. Afterwards she told me that her daughter, Clare, had been killed in a car in Brussels when she was just nineteen, ten years previously. The morning after her death two white doves had flown into her garden.

In October that year I rang both Richard and Marina and arranged for them to meet each other in London. At the end of the day we all met, together with other friends at a restaurant in Covent Garden. While the others were talking, Marina leaned across the table and asked me to travel with her to Carcassonne the following week, which would be the first anniversary of Hermione's death. Her husband wanted to be there with her to mark the anniversary, but she thought she could face it better if I came with her. 'I can't,' I protested – 'I'm totally stuck at home.' I then thought of Sylvia, who had recently changed her name to Jehanne,[5] and told Marina about her. 'I'm sure that she could help, I'll ask her to join me in sending you thoughts and prayers.' We did. Two weeks later Jehanne rang me asking for a description of Hermione, which I gave her. This verified the appearance of both Helen and Hermione to Jehanne on two occasions, Hermione emphasising that important Cathar work was to be done.

A few weeks later Jehanne was deep in thought, considering the clairvoyant process generally, when Helen and Hermione again appeared, this time joined by another older girl with dark hair. I checked with Jo, and the third girl fitted the description of her daughter, Clare.

Two years before Helen died she and I had begun organising Musical Christmas parties to which she invited all her friends who played musical instruments. We held them two years running, on both occasions we managed to scrape together recorder players, pianists, a very small violinist and a proficient banjo-player. Christmas Carols and popular music were interspersed together with a welter of iced buns, fabled chocolate-crispy-cakes, sandwiches and crisps.

After Helen's death the musical Christmas party metamorphosed into an annual Christmas gathering where I invited local Anthroposophical friends and people of like mind. These later extended to be held at the four main annual festivals, the other three being Easter, St John's-Tide and Michaelmas. Jo eventually joined us, and was with us for a Christmas gathering. We had just finished reading the lecture which preceded tea. I had slipped out to warm the mince pies and light the candles while the group was sitting discussing the lecture. Jo suddenly came into the kitchen behind me asking urgently for a pencil and paper which I hurriedly found for her. She then wrote down a message which was arriving from Clare.

'My dearests, Helen and Hermione have grown and grown in spirit. Together we are meeting those who have deliberately ended their earthly lives. We hug and give so much love for you, see slowly they will have to realise what they have left undone and, slowly knowing, they will have to return.

'The three of us crinkly with laughter, this may seem strange considering our work. The little ones will move to another place to meet another part of themselves. The three of us will have a fourth. And always our lives will intertwine....'

This reminded me that the kindly professor, living across the road who Helen had befriended, had committed suicide a year or so before Helen died. I wondered if she was helping him.. As if in answer, the professor's son rang me a few days later.

'Please come across and see me this evening! I have something of the utmost importance to tell you.'

I went to see him and he told me that early that morning he had seen his father standing at the French window to the garden, behind him was the rising sun; he had his arm around Helen's shoulders. He apologised for the sadness which his death had caused his wife and son. Helen had a message for me. 'Tell mummy, the squirrel in the garden!' Earlier that week I had been feeling very sad as I walked down the garden to the park with Helen's Labrador, Max. Suddenly a squirrel ran up a tree in front of us. For some inexplicable reason I thought of Helen and felt better immediately. I hadn't told anyone of the experience.

The day after this message from the professor's son, Marina rang me from London. She was in the middle of packing to go abroad. I told her what had just happened at the professor's house. No sooner had I told Marina than she replied in great agitation.

'Did Helen have shoulder-length hair and gappy teeth?'

'Yes, but why?'

'Because she's standing next to me looking into my open suitcase! What shall I do, she's going into my bathroom now?'

'Shall I put the phone down? Can you ask her a question from me?' I asked.

'I'm going into the bathroom after her, put the phone down and ring me back in a quarter of an hour.'

I asked Marina to ask Helen if I should tell my husband about something we had discovered about his incarnation in the thirteenth century. I then went into Suzi's room. 'I don't think Helen would advise you to tell Baba (Father.)' was her answer. After the agreed time I rang Marina. She was fairly shaken.

'She sat on the side of the bath stroking two frog bath toys as if they were real. I asked her several questions to which I needed answers which she answered very well, then I asked your question. She said 'Don't tell my father, he knows already. Then she said, 'Tell James (Marina's husband) to go to Sion in Switzerland tomorrow. I asked her why I had seen her and not Helen. 'Hermione is not in space and time now.' She answered.

As she turned to go, I said: 'Please don't do this to me again! I don't think I can take it!'

She smiled. 'You'll be alright!' Then Clare, Jo's daughter, was standing in the doorway ready to take her back.'

When I had put the phone down I rang Jehanne to tell her what had happened. As I was speaking to her in Stroud, she exclaimed that Clare had just appeared next to her on the bed on which she was sitting.

*

After Jo's message about a fourth member of the group I was not surprised at the next turn of events. I heard from Jehanne a short while later that she had heard from La Valdieu, near Rennes-le-Château, that someone suffering from melanoma had rung them asking if they were a centre for curing cancer. 'They weren't,' they had said, but someone had written about the possibility. (This was something I had written concerning the siege of Montségur some time before and had sent down to them, just after I first met Jehanne and Rob.) They then rang Jehanne asking her to contact me to find out if it was alright for this person to telephone me. Laurie, the person suffering from melanoma, subsequently rang me, telling me that he had lost his twelve-year-old daughter Ruth with cancer five years previously. He was flying out to Toulouse en route for La Valdieu in two days' time and invited me to meet him and his wife for dinner at his hotel near Gatwick Airport the following evening. Laurie and I found that we both had so much to say we had to keep putting a hand up to get our respective next bit of information into the conversation! In retrospect, my connection with Laurie seemed to have been mainly in order to put him in touch with 'Gerson Therapy'. Because of our meeting I was able to put Laurie in touch with Gerson Therapy which, he claimed, was to give him a few extra months of life. Laurie eventually died and we lost touch with his wife. Laurie had told me that, while on holiday skiing in the Pyrenees some years before, a clairvoyant had seen him dressed in the blue robes and white belt of a Cathar Perfect.

After all this it seemed to Jehanne and I that Ruth was the fourth member of the group that the girls had predicted. Ruth had contacted Jehanne telling her that she had collected 'simples' (herbs) and learned of their uses in the Cathar time.

That would have seemed to be the end of our search, had not another friend who was also connected with our story visited with a book which he thought I should read: LET THE PETALS FALL, by Margaret, Viscountess Long of Wraxall. Already inside the front dust cover was information that Viscountess Long had strong connections with the Cathars. Inside the back cover it was related how Margaret's nineteen-year-old daughter, Charlotte, had died after a lorry had plunged into her car as it stood on the hard shoulder of the M4. I read the book day and night until it was finished. Then I felt compelled to find Viscountess Margaret Long. For three days I searched but with no luck. The publishers had gone out of business and could not be traced. Housework came to a standstill. On the third morning I was driving home after taking the children to school when the thought came to me that 'Maybe Viscountess Margaret Long will find me!' I was amazed at my audacity. When I entered the house I found a strange envelope with beautiful writing in the letter-pile, undiscovered from the post a few days ago. It can't be, I thought. It wasn't, but was from a friend of Alice's, a 'thank you' letter for dinner at my house a week before; she had contacts with the aristocracy, and so I rang her and asked if she knew Viscountess Margaret Long of Wraxall. No, she didn't. Then I described a little of the story and mentioned that Viscountess Long had a daughter called Sarah. Light dawned.

'Oh, Sarah Long! Yes, I know Sarah, we are both in the art world, she sent me an invitation to her Gallery only yesterday. I'll look up her phone number for you.'

The next day she rang with the number. A year later she told me that she now remembered meeting a young Indian student years ago who had asked her if she knew Sarah Long. When she said she didn't he insisted: 'But surely you must know Sarah Long!'

Having obtained the number of the gallery I rang, but was told that Sarah Long was in Russia, she would be back the following day. I was therefore delighted when she rang me only a few hours later, she had just returned. In a short time I was speaking to Viscountess Margaret Long and within a few minutes we had arranged to meet Jo, Angela and Angela's husband Ken a few weeks hence at Jo's flat in Pimlico.

Margaret brought Charlotte's notebook with her. It had begun as a typical young girls' account of her daily affairs full of the observations, enthusiasm and humour of a lively young actress, and then, during the final few weeks before her unexpected death, the tone changed. Drawings of Greek Temples and a detailed description of the accident that hadn't yet happened. The sudden impact, the pain, the group of people looking down at her; then perfect peace and white doves flying. Jo's house was filled with white doves after Clare's accident: china doves, glass doves, mobiles of doves and doves in pictures. Jo had named the two that flew into her garden after Clare's death Charlotte and Charlie. 'Charlie' had been Charlotte's nickname for herself.

We kept in touch after that first meeting. Sometime later, just before Easter, I found a card with two girls in white shifts standing in front of a barn door which was slightly open. Light poured in from behind and there were white doves flying there. One girl was quite tall with dark hair, the other was smaller and blonde. I bought four copies of the card; one to keep and the others to send to Jo, Margaret and Marina as a surprise for Easter. When I showed them to Suzie I commented that there were only two girls in the picture, the dark one representing the two older girls, the blonde one the two younger ones. 'Maybe they are working in pairs?' I suggested. Before I had sent the cards, Jo rang to tell me that she had woken in the night hearing a clear cultured voice speaking to her. It was Charlotte: 'We are foursquare. We are working in pairs. Helen and I, Clare and Hermione.

At around this time I met a friend of my next door neighbour's, Rachel, who for some time had taught drama and ballet to the neighbour's daughter, Helen, and my younger daughter, Suzie. I went to have lunch with Rachel in the lovely Surrey Village of Brockham. At lunch she told me that she had always felt she had some connection to the Cathars, so I told her about Helen and the synchronicities. I rang Rachel a few hours after I reached home. She was very excited:

'After you left this afternoon a group of Canada Geese flew over my house, suddenly one of them separated from the others and flew into my garden. He's been sitting there all afternoon, the neighbours have brought him water and have been throwing bread over the fence for him.'

She had completely forgotten that I mentioned the swan and goose synchronicities while we were having lunch together earlier.

After meeting Jo for the first time and before learning about Margaret Long, I had arranged for Marina and Jo to meet. They got on extremely well and it even turned out that they had mutual friends. Jo wanted to take Marina to have lunch at De Beers, the diamond firm's main office in London to meet her husband who was a director. She needed an excuse. Then she remembered that a Canada Goose had made a nest on the balcony outside her husband's office window, their eggs had hatched out that week so there were goslings to show Marina!

The only time to date that all four of us have been together was at the occasion of Sarah Long's wedding. It was at the Russian Orthodox Church in Ennismore Gardens, with a reception at the House of Lords. It might be thought that such a moment marked the end of this story of 'Four funerals and a wedding', but Helen's story is ongoing. Looking at it in retrospect, the references to Cathar times are intermittent but unmistakeable, and the sense of the four girls foursquare in their work together feels deeply significant. I might add that my family as a whole has always had plenty of healthy scepticism about the whole idea of Cathars reincarnating today, on the quite reasonable basis that 'if you put an advertisement in The Times inviting everyone with a Cathar memory to meet at Piccadilly Circus one evening, the crowds would fill the West End'. Yet when we gain this sense of connection it is irresistible, and whatever its cause it is not to be dismissed. My other article in this publication arose as a result of direct indications from Helen to Jehanne about the events the night before the Siege of Montségur came to its awful end. These indications were later corroborated verbally by a statement originally made by Dr Walter Johannes Stein several decades ago and passed to me through a direct line of three Grail researchers, the last of whom had heard of Helen's version of the ceremony performed in Montségur on the last night of the siege.

To date, one event that took place near the beginning of Helen's story has worked its way into everydaylife and its product constantly spreads to ever-wider circles of people whom I may never meet. After one of Jehanne's visits in the early 90s, I was driving her to the station in Leatherhead, Surrey, for the train that would take her back to Stroud in Gloucestershire, when I suddenly remembered that the tune and first line of a song had been running through my head for several days. I said that I thought it might have been from Helen, and sang it to Jehanne who said: 'Leave it with me.'

A week or so later, just after my birthday, Jehanne rang me in quite an emotional state.

'It's here,' she said almost in tears.

'What's here?' I answered.

'Pipy's song', was the reply from Jehanne. She had been tinkering with

PIPY'S SONG

Every day of my life, every moment of the day
I am caught in the beauty of our love
For this love turned the key that has set my spirit free;
It is the fountain of everything I give.
Now my circle of freedom is as big as the world
And as small as the place on which I stand
And though nothing can shake it and no one can take it
We share it when I give to you my hand

When I walk in the forest every tree is a friend
And the roots are the guardians of my dreams
If I open my heart wide then I'll let the sun inside
And every pathway becomes more than what it seems.
Though the trees they may tumble and the branches may fall
I can still feel their blessing coming through
In my thoughts they still grow, in my dreams they still show
The pathway that is leading me to you

When the streets are full of strangers and the moments full of pain
And I seem to lose direction in the crowd
Then the song that we share bathes the world in light again
And I find myself singing it aloud.
And there's no need to give out my name to the world
No need to call attention to my face
When we meet we shall know, as so often long ago; My dear

For love is the temple of all peace.

Jehanne Mehta

(When sung, the first verse is repeated, along with the second quatrain of the last verse, and the last time the final line is sung it becomes 'That love is the temple of all peace'.)

a tune on the piano when suddenly all the notes and continuation of the song's lyrics flooded through, making it possible for her to play and sing the song almost immediately. 'Pipy' was Helen's nickname. Her full name was Helen Peri-Han. Peri–Han in Turkish can either mean 'fairy queen' or 'the angel that came to Earth'.

'Pipy's Song' has been sung and played many times at many varied events: weddings, funerals and concerts. Jehanne tells me that often people come up to her and tell her that it has had a very special meaning for them. It was included in a CD: 'Rose in Deep Water' that Jehanne and her husband Rob made in 1992. I believe that while the story continues, the song is a good way to leave it for now.

Notes:
[1] BBC2 *Chronicle*, second programme: 'The Priest, the Painter and the Devil', first shown in 1974.

[2] Selma Lagerlof, BETHLEHEM'S CHILDREN, one of a collection of 'Christ Legends'. Edinburgh: Floris Books, 1980.

[3] Arthur Guirdham, THE GREAT HERESY. Neville Spearman, 1977

[4] Gerard de Sède, THE ACCURSED TREASURE OF RENNES-LE-CHÂTEAU. DEK Publishing, 2001.

[5] The previous Easter, Sylvia had experienced a very bad bout of tinnitus – which, because of its connection with Cathar memories, prompted the change of her name to Jehanne, a Cathar name.

CATHAR

JEHANNE MEHTA

> *Cathar*
>
> Let me not escape from this moment,
> Keep me captive in your arms until I see,
> From under the wrinkled, earthen lids of time,
> The sudden eye of love wink blindingly
> And all that ever blossomed, blossom now,
> Radiant white, along the blackened bough.

WHEN I and my husband, Rob, first went to the south-west of France, the foothills of the Pyrenees, we both felt immediately at home, as if this was our country. The first experience of climbing Montsé-gur was powerful. While sitting near the edge of the big drop behind the castle, I suddenly had the experience of looking at little plants growing in a cliff face, directly in front of my eyes, and the sense of going down the cliff. From this I had the feeling that I was among those who were let down from the castle just before the *auto da fé*, carrying something of great significance to the Cathars who were besieged in Montségur. I may of course have been picking up something which was not my personal history, al-

---

Jehanne Mehta is a poet and singer-songwriter. She studied modern languages at Keele University, followed by a primary school teacher's certificate. She lives in Stroud, Gloucestershire, with her husband Rob, and has three children and two grandchildren. She writes poems and songs for the Earth, soul and spirit and also works with sound healing, using her voice. The lyrics of one of her songs are given on p. 220. Her life-experiences led her to develop an inner sensitivity. This allowed her, for a period, to bring through information concerning events in thirteenth-century France, the time of the Cathars, with which she felt a strong connection.

though subsequent experiences of riding, alone, eastwards away from the Languedoc towards Austria seemed to confirm something. It would have been necessary to take the treasure well away. I would certainly have not been the only one.

When Rob and I descended the mountain (this was in the 1980s) I was overcome with sorrow and loss. The sense was that, returning later in the thirteenth century and discovering the information about the burning, it was clear that someone, maybe several people who had been close, were now dead.

Back in England later I had an inner experience of our troubadour teacher who had also been the one who taught me and my husband the skills of knighthood, at a château further north, south of Limoges, which we had been able to identify and visit. On the same occasion I saw my own body, male, very dark and somewhat squat and I felt that I did not like my appearance. Memories suggested to me that I received the *consolamentum*, the Cathar blessing and initiation, (which was given to those among the besieged who were not yet full Cathars) shortly before leaving the castle by descending the cliff in some kind of basket.

When my husband, Rob, and I went later to the caves at Lombrives it felt to me that I had been in those caves with the surviving Cathars who took refuge there after March 16th, 1244. I also felt that I had eventually met my end somewhere near there.

THE CATHARS, MARY MAGDALENE AND THE TRUTH?

ALPHEDIA

A memory, but also a deep encounter with … Mary.

THE CATHARS, meaning the 'pure ones', have held a fascination for me for many years now. I have visited France only twice but both times it felt like home, invoking a familiarity and peace within me that I had rarely experienced outwith Scotland. I knew little about French history, especially its medieval history, but as I got older I started to read historical fiction, gathering my historical knowledge of countries through this medium. On occasion I noticed an emotional pull when reading these types of books, a connection when I was reading about certain historical periods or focused on certain people or locations. This was certainly the case when I started to read books about the Cathars. A curiosity was aroused within me. Who were these people? What did they stand for? And why was I so drawn to anything mentioning them?

When I was younger I had a very scientific mind and this influenced my beliefs about religions and the way I viewed the world. In my mid-twenties, however, I started to explore spirituality and became fascinated by not having to be confined to a religion to connect with the Divine (God), Angels, Nature Spirits and other 'supernatural' forms of Life. I became aware that when I felt emotionally connected to something there was more often than not a hidden meaning or message for me to explore spiritually.

Alphedia (Fiona Murray) is the author of MESSAGES FROM NATURE'S GUARDIANS. She is the founder of Elemental Beings, a Scottish mind, body and spirit business where she teaches people to communicate with beings in the other realms and about working with nature spirits to protect the environment. She has written in numerous spiritual magazines and has a documentary about her work with Nature Spirits that airs regularly on Sky TV. She has a degree from Edinburgh University in Geography and Environmental Studies and is a former political environment researcher in the Scottish Parliament.

At school I loathed my history lessons, yet as I grew older I came to understand why I disliked being taught 'history'. For starters, there is no definitive 'history': there are historical facts such as dates of events, but what we know of the events is often clouded by one person's dominant viewpoint and often what is written may be one person's truth rather than the ultimate truth. Perhaps that is why I like historical fiction; it isn't pretending to be the truth. We all view events and experiences from our own individual conditioning and belief structure, so one person's experience is never the same as another. However, even to this day many people have been ostracized, even persecuted for holding views that differ from the 'norm' or from the leading authority or political power of the time. Throughout history there have been those individuals who have sought to speak universal truths, who seek universal knowledge and who are often referred to as enlightened ones; pushing the boundaries or current paradigm of thought at that particular time. Invariably these people's way of being or teachings are accepted by some and are a threat to others. The Albigensian crusade is a representative case.

Remembering

As a mind, body and spirit author and a spiritual channel I use my sixth sense on a daily basis. I suppose I am a seeker of gnosis (by which I mean having personal experience, knowledge or insight into the spiritual dimension of the world). I am also a seeker of universal truths. My enlightenment happened when I was taken seriously ill at the age of twenty-three. This enlightenment, which for me was that the world is more than just physical, that subtle energies are around us all the time, and that I am here for a greater purpose – referred to in esoteric and new age literature as my divine life path. Like the Cathars, I believe in reincarnation. This was not always the case, as I was brought up a conventional Christian; yet through my work as a spiritual facilitator I have seen enough evidence of reincarnation now to convince me I have lived on Earth before.

My first past-life experience relating to the Cathars happened not long after I started to read mind, body and spirit literature. I had very recently accepted that I have a soul and that life does not end for my soul when my physical body departs. At this stage I had never had a past-life regression or read much about them, so the experience was rather odd for me. I was reading the bestselling novel LABYRINTH by Kate Mosse, which was about reincarnation and set in Carcassonne, one of the Cathar strongholds in southern France. One day as I was reading it, I got a vision of a person picking herbs and plants down by a river and taking them back to a walled castle to make medicine. I felt as though I knew this person, and over the next days of reading I got another vivid vision. This time I knew that it was me standing in a queue with others beside a huge fire at the bottom of a slope with a castle on the top. I didn't know what this vision meant and there was no emotion attached to it so I let it go.

Since then I have had past-life regressions under deep meditation and I have also had flashbacks and *déja-vu* moments, which often come up when I have been trying to release or clear a fear or emotional block in my life. There is a lot of literature and evidence now showing that we are affected by our past-life experiences in this current lifetime and that by clearing past-life problems or emotions we can clear up issues affecting us in the now.

I thought nothing more about the Cathars until I again found myself reading a historical novel on them in 2010, THE DAUGHTERS OF THE GRAIL by Elizabeth Chadwick. It was just a fortnight before I was intending to go on a tour of the Languedoc region of France on honeymoon. By now I had had many past-life memories, and I knew what these visions (which reappeared while reading this new book) meant: I had been burnt to death in another life, for my spiritual beliefs as a Cathar. However, the more I read about the Cathars in historical texts some of the truth seemed to be eluding me, the 'history' of them wasn't ringing true. I couldn't put my finger on it, but I started to get really strong negative emotions about the Roman Catholic Church around this time, as well as developing a fear of being unable to breathe! During a healing session, trying to clear this new fear which I started to realise I had always had, just not so extremely, I got a strong vision accompanied with the emotions and feelings of being suffocated by smoke. I intently knew I was being burnt in a fire at Montségur, the last remaining Cathar stronghold, and that in doing this I was willingly sacrificing myself for something greater. What that something greater was, I didn't know.

Not long after I was visited by Dave, the editor of this book, and he mentioned working on a project to do with the Cathars. I was able to tell him that I had a strong connection with them that was not yet fully explored, and he asked if I wanted to contribute to this book. I was not sure at the start what it was I was to contribute so I went into meditation and asked. The information that came to me was to do what I do best. I am known for my work as a spiritual channel and clairaudient. This means I can hear beings in the other realms. I run workshops all over the UK and many people come to me for Soul Channellings.

At first I was unsure of who to call upon to give information and guidance on the Albigensian Crusade but the more I read the more I knew within my heart I was to speak to Mary Magdalene. I have a strong connection with her and a beautiful painting of her by a psychic artist hangs in my living room. Mary was believed by many in New Age circles to have been the wife of Jesus Christ and the mother of their child Lady Sara. It is believed she fled to France after the crucifixion. I was curious to get her view on the Cathars and if there was any connection between them and herself.

No channel can claim to be one hundred per cent accurate. However when I channel I have little recollection of what words I have spoken until I listen back to them. These words will either ring true to you in your heart and resonate or they will not. When you read channelled information it is important to come out of your head – where most of us spend most of our waking hours – and read the words with your awareness in your heart centre so you can connect to your own inner truth and discern from there. I offer you Mary Magdalene's words as she gave them. It is up to you individually to learn and gather what information is relevant for you and your soul's journey in this incarnation.

The conversation with Mary Magdalene was performed as a series of questions and is reproduced exactly.

Mary Magdalene Speaks

Why has the 'Cathar consciousness' come so much into increasing public view at the present time and particularly in the last couple of decades or so?

'The Cathar consciousness has awoken in those who were of that faith at this time. The energies that are descending daily to planet Earth as part of the spiritual awakening process are allowing those who have past life memories from this era to resurface. The knowledge has always been in those who were incarnate during this period of time. However more and more souls are becoming enlightened and are therefore remembering their previous existences.'

What were the true origins of Catharism? Did it develop initially in the Languedoc region of South West France or was it imported from somewhere else?

'As with many faiths, the origins are dependent on what story you are told. The beginnings of faith begin with enlightened souls and these souls preach of their enlightenment. As with everything the humans have to deal with their ego sides. Many times profound deep spiritual meanings and messages are lost or distorted from the true original meaning. This is part of the human evolution of consciousness. The Cathar beliefs originated in the Middle East. They were spread by preachers of gnostic knowledge. The reason that the Languedoc region of France embraced Catharism was that at this time this state was independent of others' control. This area was rural and the teachings therefore appeal to this parish-type community, meaning that people lived as neighbours and harmonised as neighbours.'

I believe I died in the pyre at Montségur protecting something greater than myself. What was the nature of the 'treasure' allegedly spirited away via the cliff face at Montségur by four initiates just prior to the final capitulation of the two-hundred-plus Cathars at the end of the siege in 1244?

'The nature of the treasures spirited away were just the secret teachings. The Roman Catholic Church knew at this time of the Cathari belief that Christ was a father. The knowledge that the Cathars had were that I, Mary Magdalene, was the mother of Lady Sara [Daughter of Jesus]. They however wished to persecute this contradiction to the story being told. Teachings from myself, original teachings, had come to be kept by the Cathari Illumini.'

What is the connection between the Cathars, Mary Magdalene and the return of the Divine Feminine?

'The Connection is as I have just said. They [the Cathars] didn't acknowledge any difference between male and female. Their teachings were different from the teachings I carried to Southern France yet they became the guardians of the sacred knowledge of my existence and that of my child. The return of the Divine Feminine is a return of heart centred consciousness. At the time of the Cathar movement, the heart-centred consciousness was being suppressed from many different angles. The vibration was one of power, greed, need for control and curtailment of the masses.'

A troubadour quote from the Cathar era mentioned that 'At the end of seven hundred years, the laurel will be green once more'. Does this refer to current times?

'The people of this time were enlightened. They could see the destruction being wrought by the current regime. Too much is placed upon these quotes, but know that with everything, destruction of the current egoic systems on the Earth must occur. Greed, power at all costs is unobtainable that is why collapse in banking, media and justice systems is imminent if not already occurring. As we move into a heart-centred conscious awareness these vibrations and lies must combust. Earth is moving to a new phase of her development and we will see those who maintain the old way of being struggling at this time.'

How will the reintroduction of Cathar consciousness impact on the machinations of the Roman Catholic Church?

'All the energies are creating a situation, as I said, that untruths, deceits, egoic needs, desires and stifling of free expression of speech become unobtainable. The consciousness and awareness of the Cathari movement is one part of the puzzle. Those that are interested in finding more about this movement are already starting to seek truth, are already starting to question the foundations and structures of the world we live in. Know that this process continues.'

What was the nature and importance of the 'Book of Love', allegedly secreted away by the Cathars?

'The Book of Love was illuminated consciousness. At this time on the Earth the energies were dense and spiritual enlightenment was only sought and held by a few. As the book has since been named, it was teaching of love over fear. The teachings of the purity of God as they saw it and the knowledge and awareness of Oneness with the Creator. Miracles can be performed through the vibration of love within one's being. Only fear stops those who cannot find true connection to their heart centres and experience the gift of love. Love is unable to be controlled, love is pure and love is infinite.'

What is the main message left by the Cathars and how will it manifest now and in the future (if at all)?

'The main message left by the Cathars is that all souls have identity, all souls have freewill while they incarnate on the earth plane. Those that seek to control the freewill of others will struggle at this time in the ascension process.'

MINGLING OF THE CENTURIES:
A PERSONAL EXPERIENCE

VAL WINEYARD

The author's memories link her to actual historical lives lived in Cathar times.

MY INTEREST in the Cathars was triggered in a way that was itself unusual. A French woman that I hardly knew, called Elaine, suddenly told me I was reincarnated from a man called Jules Azéma. He had been the mayor in the village near Narbonne in which I now lived, a village called St. Celse. He died in the 1930s.

It was quite dramatic. We were walking together in the village graveyard and she suddenly declared; 'The man in this grave is now you!' She was white and shaking.

At that time I had no belief in reincarnation, but Elaine was so sincere I decided to research the life of Jules Azéma, the name on the tombstone.

I went to the village library, thinking they might have a book about him. In the history section I picked up a leather-bound book. Inside the cover was a dedication – to Jules Azéma. It was the first book I picked out, I was holding it in my hands, and it had belonged to the person who had been – me.

That was quite an emotional moment for me. The dedication translates: 'To my friend Jules Azéma in remembrance of the talks and laughs of our friendship on the banks of the River Aude, cordially yours, P. Estieu 27th March 1891'. (It is pictured in this book on p. 136.)

Later I was told by local people that Jules Azéma's ancestors came from the department of Ariège to the Narbonnais in the Middle Ages, the region around Narbonne in Languedoc, because they were looking for work. I knew little about the department of Ariège, but I had an English friend, David Warr, who had bought a castle there, the Cathar castle of Usson. 'You must find out about Montaillou, the village where the last Cathars lived,' David advised.

So I bought the book by Ladurie about Montaillou[1] – and there were

---

For a biography of Val Wineyard see p. 127; for accompanying pictures, see p. 136

the Azémas, two extended families of them, twelve people in all.

The ancestors of my previous life were Cathars.

The Montaillou Azémas lived there between 1280 and 1309, and after the Inquisition raided the village they were among those who travelled towards the Mediterranean coast. I found traces of this family and their descendants in various history books.

But another Azéma was involved in the story of Montségur – from which was taken (both history and legend tell us) a great treasure, shortly before the fortress surrendered in 1244.

The medieval castle of Usson is in the south-eastern corner of the area known as the Pays de Sault. In the north-western corner is the fortress of Montségur, and halfway between it and Usson, the village of Montaillou.

You can see the castle of Usson, perched high on the hill overlooking the River Aude, if you take the D118 south from Carcassonne through Quillan and Axat and arrive at Usson-les-Bains. The castle is just over the departmental border in Ariège (so is often not listed among Cathar castles, not being in Aude, *Pays Cathare*) and on the clifftop. It guards two valleys, those of the Aude and the Bruyante.

The Pays de Sault has never been greatly populated and the Cathars lived there in peace for hundreds of years. Many villages there are of Visigothic origin – Niort, Coudens, Montaillou – and the castle of Usson, with its Visigothic name, was built by the Visigoths.

David had bought twenty or so plots of land around the mountaintop castle, and spent the summer camping on one of his plots, the courtyard of the castle, where there were two houses with stables, abandoned in 1956.

Two years later he was sleeping in his tent in the courtyard when he was woken by people claiming he was camping on the site of an archeological dig and had to leave. In vain he protested that he owned the land; they wouldn't believe him. He went and checked it in the local town hall. His land registry entry was found to include three fields that hadn't been there before; but the courtyard was now mysteriously part of the castle.

Why had the village changed the land registry entries? Because they had heard the legends that the Occitan (Cathar) Gospel of St John was still there? 'The archeologists didn't find anything. I knew they wouldn't,' David told me, 'because the peasants stripped the castle bare during the Revolution.' After the archeology had been done, the houses in the courtyard were renovated and made into a museum that you can visit.

Some Ariège History: Usson and Montségur

In the twelfth century, David's castle of Usson was owned by the Alion family, the owners of the land called Pays d'Alion, which included Montségur and was part of the Pays de Sault, already mentioned. The Pays d'Alion was a large basin, between 1,200 and 1,800 metres above sea level, occupied by four villages, Comus, Camurac, Prades and Montaillou. The castle of Montaillou was at a crossroads of various territories and it played an important role in the history of Pays d'Alion and its surroundings. Montségur was some 30km north-west; a similar distance to the south-east was Usson.

Montségur fortress, perched on its 'pog', had been there since Visigothic times. By 1204 the half-stone, half-wooden castle of the Visigoths was in a poor state, and was rebuilt by Raymond de Péreille, at the request of the Cathars, as a place of refuge. Historically, the Crusade against the Cathars began in 1209; but the signs were there earlier.

Then the Inquisition began, in 1232, and the Cathar Bishop of Toulouse, Guilhabert de Castres, fled from Toulouse and asked for protection from the Alion family. He was hidden on their lands. When Guilhabert later took refuge in Montségur, Aton d'Alion was one of the suite who travelled with him to guard him. Guilhabert would be safe at Montségur and have a chance to stabilise his leadership and rebuild his church. Other Cathars followed him there for safety.

They lived quiet religious lives, in prayer and contemplation. They worked at making goods such as saddles and blankets to sell, or they became herbalists or doctors and tended the sick.

Bernard d'Alion and his brother Aton frequently visited Montségur from Usson. The Alions asked the *parfaits* for prayers and understanding. They had made submissions to the Catholics for political reasons, but couldn't, however hard they tried, change their Cathar faith. In 1234 Arnaud d'Alion offered his crossbow archer to the Cathars as part of their defence force. By then Bernard-Othon de Niort, the Alions' kinsman, was living permanently at Montségur. In that hard winter of 1234, Bernard-Othon arranged a collection of money and food for the *parfaits* of Montségur.

In 1236 the Alion family gave up pretending and effectively declared themselves Cathars, by the action of Bernard d'Alion marrying Esclarmonde, the sister of the Foix Count Roger Bernard II. (Not to be confused with Esclarmonde, the sister of Raymond Roger of Foix, the lady who was ordained as a Perfect in 1204, and who still appears in people's visions.)

Guilhabert de Castres died in 1240 and was replaced as a bishop by Bertrand Marty. The King of France, in 1241, asked Count Raymond VII of Toulouse to fight Catharism by destroying the castle. This he could not do, being a secret Cathar himself – they were his own people! He sent some troops and recalled them after three days. It was a token gesture.

By this time the Roman Catholics were calling Montségur the 'Synagogue of Satan'. It was necessary for Montségur to become a military fortress.

All food had to be smuggled in. They had a bread oven in the castle, so they baked their own bread. They had a cistern to collect rainwater. The *parfaits* didn't eat meat but the soldiers did, in the courtyard of the castle. They acted as escorts for *parfaits* as they went about the countryside converting and preaching. By 1240 they employed specialist crossbow archers called *arbalétriers*. One of the men who trained them was called Guillaume Azéma.

He was an ancestor of my previous life, who lived through the events of Montségur.

In May 1242 feelings against the constantly-harassing Catholics ran high all over the region and many Inquisitors were attacked and murdered. Maybe it was thought that guerilla tactics were all they had with which to fight back. Under Pierre-Roger of Mirepoix a group of men and soldiers of Montségur, including Bernard-Othon from Usson, moved under cover of darkness to Avignonet in the Lauragais and slaughtered members of the Inquisition. In retaliation, the Catholics arrested and hung several people who had nothing to do with the raid, and decided to destroy Montségur. They found it hard to assemble troops, for the minor nobility and the people of the villages refused their support.

But early in 1243, six thousand troops under Hughes des Arcis, Seneschal of Carcassonne, and Pierre Amiel, Archbishop of Narbonne, camped at the foot of the castle. Inside it, or living in the workers' cottages just outside, were five hundred people. They included more than two hundred Cathars and the garrison of a hundred and fifty men and fifteen knights and squires. The Catholics commissioned mercenaries from neighbouring villages including Camon, but these were Cathars and they played a double game. Messages, supplies and reinforcements continued to reach the castle of Montségur.

Continually throughout the siege, the Alion brothers of Usson offered effective support to Montségur. The Alion lands served as staging posts and as a refuge for the persecuted in the forests, as did the castle at Usson. The *parfaits* continued to travel and preach, with bodyguards with them. In Dourgne, between Fontanès and Usson, another thirty Cathars hid in the little castle there. There was coming and going between the two castles, passing through Montaillou. The house of Arnaud Bellon, a bailiff for Bernard d'Alion at Usson, became a 'safe house' for *parfaits*, as did the castle of Usson itself. Bernard d'Alion and his brother Arnaud d'Usson gave provisions of bread, wine and meat. They also gave their crossbow archer, Raymond de Belvis, to help defend Montségur.

Optimism ran high that they would survive the siege.

But at Christmas 1243, the besieging Catholics found some Gascon mercenaries who were prepared to climb the eastern end of the mountain under cover of darkness and make a surprise dawn raid. They were beaten off but the fighting was serious, and several knights and soldiers were wounded, including Guillaume Azéma. Others who died were buried within the citadel; their graves were found during excavations in 1965.

This surprise attack was the beginning of the end, and the Cathars knew it. Bishop Bertrand Marty assembled the gold and silver possessed by the *parfaits* and had it smuggled out by two Cathars, Matthieu Bonnet (a *parfait*) and his brother Pierre Bonnet. They hid the treasure in a cave on the south side of the Col de Peyre, near Caussou, while the men of Camon, their military escort, stood guard. The treasure including goods for trading and artisanal products, as well as gold and silver coins.

Zoé Oldenbourg, the French historian and novelist, says:

'This treasure consisted, in the first place, of money deposits, because for the defence of the castle and the Perfects considerable sums were needed and Montségur accepted help from military people in the region and those who had reason to support them. The treasure included other things; sacred books, perhaps old manuscripts. Cathar literature was abundant, and was not only the New Testament. The *parfaits* were altogether more passionate about theology than the Catholics. They cared about the purity of dogma and attached great importance to books which helped them maintain their traditional ideas.'

After hiding the treasure, the *parfait* Matthieu Bonnet was travelling continually, escorted by men of Camon. He travelled around Ariège and went, without doubt, to Usson. Fighting continued throughout the frosty winter in spite of a last attempt by Arnaud d'Usson and Bernard d'Alion to raise a fighting force. Matthieu Bonnet came back to Montségur between

February 14th and 21st, 1244, to see what he could do.

But all hope was gone after a hard winter and the Cathars started to ne-gotiate a surrender. Pierre-Roger of Mirepoix asked for a period of grace of fifteen days before the attackers moved in, so the soldiers, knights and simple believers could go free. One of these was Guillaume Azéma, who had recovered from his wounds. But he stayed to the end; he was sent to get oats, pepper, oil, salt and also wheat.

The Cathars spent the time in religious ceremonies, in saying goodbye and preparing for death. They gave all their material possessions to the soldiers who had defended them for ten months. These were personal pos-sessions, rather than wealth, although Zoé Oldenburg thinks that religious relics were given as well. Guillaume Azéma received a sack of grain from the *parfait*, Raymonde de Cuq.

Many in the castle were impressed by the faith of the Cathars at this time and by their goodness and kindness. Some people converted to Cath-arism knowing full well what fate would await them. On March 13th, twenty believers asked the *parfaits* to give them the *consolamentum*, includ-ing Raymond de Belvis from Usson, and there were more the next day. By this time the huge brushwood pyre had already been built and they could see it from the castle. But they became Cathars.

Meanwhile, on the night of March 14th, Matthieu Bonnet explained to the *parfaits* exactly where the treasure was hidden. near the Col de Peyre, and then he managed to get out of Montségur and across to Us-son. Back in Montségur, the *parfaits* agreed they should try and save their faith by preserving their sacred documents. If the words were destroyed so would The Word be.

Bertrand Marty persuaded Pierre-Roger de Mirepoix to hide four *par-faits* in a crack in the rock; they were lowered down on ropes with sacks on their backs and spent the night on the mountain. At dawn the next day, they managed to escape with the treasure.

On the morning of March 16th, 1244, the Archbishop of Narbonne and the Seneschal of Carcassonne took formal possession of Montségur. At the bottom of the mountain, in the field still called Prat de Cramats ('place of burning' in Occitan) was a stockade filled with resinous wood, mostly pine, and straw. Bertrand Marty, their bishop, led the Cathars and *parfaits* down the mountain. They were all barefoot and clad only in simple robes. They mounted the pyre voluntarily, climbing ladders to do so. There was no need for their prosecutors to lash them to the customary stakes.

The pyre was torched. The executioners had to retreat, so fierce was the heat and the smoke. The Cathars were heard praying. Then their voices died away. Two hundred and twenty-five men and women perished in the flames. The smell and smoke of burning bodies swirled around the castle and the countryside for several hours.

Was it seen by the four *parfaits* who escaped? Did they stop on their journey to rescue the treasure and look back at the pall of black smoke that hung above the mountain? We can imagine their feelings of horror and sickness. The four recovered the treasure at La Peyre and travelled via Caussou and Montaillou to meet with Matthieu Bonnet at Usson and the treasure was held there for a while, at what to me is 'David's castle'.

Two of the four *parfaits* who escaped were later known to be alive in Lombardy, Peytavi Laurent and Pierre Sabatier. At the same time, coins not previously known appeared in circulation. It's thought these were coins from Montségur. It's not known if the other treasure went there too.

★

A personal treasure for me was the knowledge that the great Cathar historian, Déodat Roché, was a friend of Prosper Estieu. You remember, Prosper Estieu was a friend of my previous life, Jules Azéma. As well as his Occitan poems, Prosper founded a magazine called simply *Montségur*. By this time the 'Occitan thing' was closely linked to the 'Cathar thing' as part of the courageous history of Langedoc.

Déodat and Prosper met each other at Rennes-le-Château, while Prosper was working there as a supply teacher. The two of them, therefore, would have been working colleagues with Bérenger Saunière, the priest at the time. I knew, from an old lady in my village of St Celse, who had known Jules Azéma, that Jules had visited Rennes-le-Château. The man that was me had known Rennes-le-Château and maybe had even shaken the hand of Bérenger Saunière....

An Unusual Postcript

One winter's day, here in France, I was making a bonfire to burn all the trimmings and leaves from the garden. Although it was cold, the autumn had been very dry. The fire got blazing well. Then I realised the dried grass between the clods of earth was burning, and the fire was following the underground roots. The wind was blowing and the flames were travelling rapidly towards the hedge; by reflex I ran forward to rake the fire into the centre and contain these tiny blazes. The wind suddenly gusted. Flames and smoke blew into my face. I was gasping, my eyes were streaming, I thought my chest would burst. *Christ*, I thought, *it happens as quickly as that.*

What happens as quickly as that? I think you know, as I did.

A hand over my face, I ran out of the fire, ran desperately for the hosepipe, dragged it back down the garden, and doused the fire before it reached the hedge. I sat down on a plastic chair, coughing for breath, gasping. The smoke had nearly choked me, I'd taken great gulps of it, my throat, chest and lungs felt scorched and burned.

I'd been in the small flames and blowing smoke for less than three seconds. I knew then that when one is burned at the stake, it is the smoke that gets you and you die very quickly, well before your body is consumed in the flames. Any clothes or hair burn off first, which is why one sees macabre images of people being burnt apparently naked.

Now I have a wood-burner in my house, and when the pine logs burn up and flare (as they did at Montségur), their yellow tongues licking the chimney, their fierce heat turning the chimney breast, in the room above, into a radiator, I am afraid.

*

Cremation is becoming more popular in France, but I want to be buried in the graveyard. I am adamant that I do not want to be burnt.

This is against all logic. When the body is dead, the soul has gone somewhere else. What on earth does it matter, the fate of our humans remains? Rotting in the soil, or burnt to save space in the cemetery?

There is only one solution to my insistence of being buried in the graveyard in the regular way. I do not want to be burnt. I am scared of being burnt. Maybe I have a memory of that.

I joined the church youth club to meet people many years ago. I was only 19 and in a strange town. One evening there was a talk. A young man stood up on the stage to bear witness about how he had come to Jesus. 'I used to mix in bad company', he said. 'I got introduced to drink and drugs. I had a girlfriend who was a bad influence on me. We were going to get married. Then I came to Jesus and immediately I ditched all my old friends and left my girlfriend ...'

Unlike everyone else, who thought this was the power of Jesus, I was totally shocked. Did loving Jesus meant you had to ditch your friends and throw aside the girl you had promised to marry? Jesus never bothered about respectability, every soul was valuable to Him.

The next time I went to church I felt uncomfortable, and so sat near the back. After a while I thought I might be ill. We were standing to sing a hymn.... I had to sit down, and then I felt a black blanket being thrown over my head and tied with a rope, pinioning my arms. I was suffocating and terrified. I stumbled to the door, out into the fresh air and sunshine. I sat on the grass until the shaking and cold shivers had gone. Deep breaths!

This experience only came to mind when I woke up from a bad dream in which I was dying, and the dying was like having a black blanket thrown over my head and I woke up because I was struggling against it.

When I worked as a tour guide, here in France, the customers often wanted to go to Minerve, the town in the Minervois where the wine comes from. I always resisted, because for me, to visit Minerve with my holiday-makers meant the shivers, and the hair standing up on the back of my neck, restlessness. Get me out!

This was ten years before I knew that many Cathars were martyred there during the Crusades against the Cathars. I found out later that a hundred and fifty people had been burnt alive in 1210. They went willingly to their terrible deaths. It was July 22nd, Mary Magdalene's day. But three of the women refused to go on the pyre and were manhandled, beaten into submission, and thrown into the flames. 'They fought like wildcats', the soldiers said. This incident is part of recorded history.

Imagine how I felt when I read this! Those shivers I had experienced in Minerve! I must have been one of those women, forced onto the fire. Did these soldiers at Minerve throw a black blanket over my head and tie it with rope?

One summer night about three years ago, a group of us were chatting on the terrace of the local café as the moon was rising. The conversation came round to the Cathars. One of the women said to me; 'I was one of the three women who struggled against the soldiers at Minerve, but was then burnt alive.'

She knew nothing about me when she said this, but then she looked hard at me, and then we knew each other.

[1] Emmanuel Le Roy Ladurie, MONTAILLOU, VILLAGE OCCITAN DE 1294 À 1324. Folio Histoire de Gallimard, 1975

VIII. BELIEF : 1

REDISCOVERING THE CATHARS
AND THEIR RELEVANCE TO THE SURGE OF
MATERIALISM IN THE TWENTY FIRST CENTURY

MARGARET LONG

Arthur Guirdham was a psychiatrist who came to discover an apparent collective memory of Cathar times among many of his patients. His numerous books include THE CATHARS AND REINCARNATION, WE ARE ONE ANOTHER, A FOOT IN BOTH WORLDS *and* THE LAKE AND THE CASTLE. *Margaret Long, who knew Arthur Guirdham well, writes about him as both friend and teacher, while taking a look at Cathar attitudes to problems such as evil.*

THE CATHARS left behind no magnificent church architecture, for they believed that the essence of Christ's teaching was humility and

Margaret Viscountess Long (nee Frazer) is the author of the spiritual classic, THE WEDDING PRESENT. She was born in Singapore, where her father was a Scottish rubber planter. Her mother died when she was a few months old and her father was taken prisoner by the Japanese in World War II. She was brought up and educated in Scotland before leaving for London to study music. One ancestor was George Bogle, an eighteenth century merchant and diplomat who was the first white man ever to stay in Tibet. Her great uncle was Sir James Frazer, OM, classical scholar and Fellow of Trinity College Cambridge, author of many books including the twelve volumes of THE GOLDEN BOUGH.

She married Viscount Richard Long in 1957. The marriage lasted for twenty-six years and they had three children, one of whom was killed tragically in a car accident in 1984. After a visit to Greece with her eldest daughter and the Orthodox composer Sir John Tavener, both she and Sarah converted to Orthodoxy and in 1986 were taken into the Russian Orthodox Cathedral in London by Metropolitan Anthony of Sourozh, who became their Spiritual Father.

an indifference to material possessions. The temple of God lay within us for He was approached through the heart.

It was a beautiful, pure, but dangerously simplistic faith, for it implied that we need no intermediary or Church Hierarchy between us and God. In many ways it was similar to the early Christians before the Crucifixion, but it would never have been tolerated by the power of the Roman Catholic Church in the twelfth- and thirteenth-century Languedoc.

Catharism is an oral tradition, in that most of the evidence about its practice was obliterated by the Inquisition, although by strange irony the Inquisition gives us an enormous quantity of data about the daily lives of Cathar villagers at the same time as it masks their deeply-held values. With any oral Tradition it is necessary from time to time to examine the source of its continuity, to assess those who are passing on the knowledge and to learn how they came about that knowledge in the first place. A heresy is easily dismissed because it is a threat to established dogma. It receives no safeguards, so information can be distorted, misinterpreted and misunderstood. The main source of information describing the Cathars can be biased because it was taken from the Inquisitorial records.

*

I was privileged to be one of Dr Arthur Guirdham's closest friends during the last years of his life when his research on the Cathars had moved from practical, historical evidence to a much deeper understanding of its philosophy, taken both from historical research and from people's reincarnational memories. He was the first person who made me think more deeply than I had ever done before. He had the capacity to ignite something dormant in people, whether it was far memory or a past existence. With me it was an ability to understand what I would never have considered in day-to-day living – an unexpected clarity, an accelerated way of thinking perhaps and how to apply the immense subjects of good and evil to the twenty-first century. I didn't read his books on reincarnation until after his death. I learnt from him as a person: his words, his teaching, his feelings and his enormous knowledge.

Arthur despaired about the evil in the world and how people were unable to recognize or discern it. Evil was of course important to the Cathars, who were dualists. Plato, Origen, Plotinus and Porphyry too had strong dualist leanings.

The early Fathers tell us that evil is not a nature but a state of nature. It is like bacteria or parasites, a negation of all light. We can see the whole gamut of man's evil in the extremes, from bizarre 'over the top' decadence and headline depravity to the other extreme, the narrowing-down mentality that reduces with unbending legalism. Both have the purpose of *breaking down*.

One day, many years ago, I was making a lemon soufflé, whisking the eggs and hoping that nobody would telephone or interrupt my concentration. There was a bluebottle flying around the kitchen that irritated me, and I thought briefly of the uselessness of it – feeling that it was a typical if trivial example of Arthur's idea of the manifestation of evil in nature. I opened the door to let it out and grabbed a shopping list, but instead of adding caster sugar or fly spray to the list of groceries I found myself writing the following words:

'The force of evil is necessary to the world of matter because matter has to be broken down. When this is understood only that which is necessary is broken down. When it is not understood the balance is tipped and there is chaos. In the realm of true spirit there is no evil because there is no matter.'

My definition might refer to the process of a bluebottle, black and unsightly, an analogy perhaps of 'evil' in nature, alighting on a decaying fish. However unpleasant a process, there is a purpose in its destruction of that decaying fish. If evil is a breaking-down process that destroys by negation, then it has a purpose in the destructive and regenerative forces of nature. Evil is maladjusted and unbalanced when it breaks away and becomes separate. Not only are the extremes of evil implicated in this concept, but evil involves all the negative and destructive traits of man from hatred to violence, from rudeness to cynicism, to domination, discourtesy, rage, indifference, lack of respect, vulgarity and all kinds and degrees of aggression which have a purpose of humiliating, reducing and ultimately, *breaking down*.

In my first book before becoming Orthodox, I had written about this, including the observation of the lemon soufflé and the bluebottle, and Arthur added a footnote to this.

'The idea that evil is necessary for the breaking down of matter is to me a revelation. What Margaret has written of the balance between good and evil has a neoplatonic flavour. I have a suspicion that it goes deeper than my (Cathar) dualist concept of good and evil. It is not opposed to it but amplifies it beyond my previous comprehension.'

Dualism was concerned with the emanatory capacity of man, places and atmosphere. You cannot always sense evil with sight for it is proximity that makes it apparent. Goodness too can be 'felt'. Arthur wrote that 'there are those people who lighten the dark corners of the world as a lighthouse illumines the sea.' You *feel* better, and safer, after seeing them. Sometimes it is in the tone of voice, sometimes it is in the eyes. It is like a 'vibration' or 'emanation', and you cannot define it but we have to learn the subtlety of discernment for if we don't understand evil we won't understand what good is up against.

All emotion, like metal, can develop in purpose but cannot change its substance. The purpose is freedom within the laws of the universe. If it goes outside these laws it is an unnatural negating process and is evil. We see this again and again in Nature, where there is no waste because each action is necessary to the survival of the other. When good and evil manifestations are perfectly balanced, they are perfect in the design of God. When the balance is maladjusted there is chaos, and chaos is the beginning of evil. This is why in some places we sometimes sense an atmosphere that is malign and in other places we pick up an atmosphere of peace and happiness.

Many years ago I parked my car in an underground car park beside Park Lane in London. For some unaccountable reason I felt so fearful that I could hardly walk. I drove away as quickly as I could and came off the motorway early, to see a friend who lived near Maidenhead. She said I looked as though I'd seen a ghost and I said I felt as though I'd seen a thousand ghosts. Later it was pointed out that it was close to the Tyburn gallows and nobody sensitive to atmosphere should go there. Of course I have also been in places that felt pure and holy, like walking into the Kingdom, but we are all responsible for our immediate surroundings whether we choose to transfigure them or contaminate them. It is perhaps wise to make sure we understand that energies once created can stay there for ever!

There are many ways, beyond the obvious, in which one human being can harm another. We *feel* the reaction. Arthur Guirdham used to say that in his experience as a consultant psychiatrist 'accidents' were often caused indirectly after such an attack of 'evil' as he put it. Extreme rage, or verbal abuse can be put down to a 'personality disorder' or a specific anxiety, but it can be 'demonic' in a way that leaves the victim shattered, off balance, unable to concentrate and sometimes ill. It is like a snake hissing poisonous venom. We do not feel comfortable after this sort of proximity, for it can damage the whole physical and spiritual equilibrium, as adrenalin is unnaturally activated in order to cope with the attack.

The side-effects come in when the adrenalin is withdrawn.

The words used to describe our adversary speak for themselves: the Enemy, Satan, the serpent, the Confuser, the Prince of Darkness, the Father of Lies, the Evil One…. *Diablos* in Greek means literally 'to tear apart' and if we do not understand our adversary that is what can happen.

The early Fathers were good psychologists. They understood our human weaknesses and used vivid language to illustrate our watchfulness in 'ascetic warfare' or 'unseen warfare'. St Hesychios the Priest wrote that 'one cannot befriend a snake and carry it about in one's shirt, for it is the snake's nature to bite whoever tends it…'

One night I had a dream, which I felt was showing 'evil' as a force before it had reached the human level. Looking back it seems to illustrate the same kind of primordial energy that enters into a mob when it spirals out of control – such as we saw in the London riots of 2010. The dream started with decay and water that was stagnant. I felt the water lapping towards me, children were bathing in the water, oblivious. I called to them to come out of the water before it was too late but they wouldn't come. The sky was a sulphurous dark negation of light. Then I could hear the force like thundering hooves, at first far away but coming closer. It materialised as huge herds of animals, cloven-hooved, were stampeding in a mindless mass. They were totally without direction and without control in the destruction of everything that lay in their path.

Forces of good and evil entered into the universe from the beginning of the world. The Devil has had a long and dramatic history and has been given different degrees of status through the centuries. For the Manichees, Cathars and Gnostics, who were dualists, the Devil was seen as a second power, subversive and insidious in its action to destroy from the inside. With the huge psychic forces of evil in the world today, it is perhaps a heresy that we can understand, but without the teachings from the ancient proven traditions, many are oblivious to the energies they are dealing with. Evil in its parasitic form is infectious and propagates itself by disfiguring and twisting all that it touches. With free will and ignorance we can add to the darkness and we certainly have the ability to make things worse. With knowledge we can restore the balance. There is a Greek word, *diakrisis,* which means discrimination or discernment. It is like a spiritual sense of taste.

When I first began to think about the evil in the world, long before I joined the Orthodox church, I found myself comparing it with a rather mundane and very simplistic analogy which seemed to clarify part of the dilemma. That I was studying music at the time might explain the subject used in the analogy. In the keyboard of the piano there is an extreme bass and an extreme treble. Ignoring these extremes, think of the framework stretching over two octaves only. The limited framework would not have the power or the capacity for great musical creation. It would be too bland. I took the analogy further. If the bass represented evil, the *breaking-down process*, and the treble represented good as *the perfecting process*, and if the two extremes were part of God's Creation – huge, all-powerful, unlimited in range – then extremes were needed: the mountains, the rocks, the volcanoes, the oceans, thunder and lightning from the skies…. Order was forged from chaos. As humans we cannot accommodate such extremes of creation and destruction. We are not meant to, for it is not in our nature or capacity to create on such a scale.

This very personal analogy is not to inhibit creativity in the arts or in music, although we seldom, if ever, use either the top or the bottom note on the piano! It might, however, make us see that there is unlimited freedom in everything we do, yet boundaries through which we simply cannot go. Although it was a heresy, discernment and sensitivity was certainly something understood and inherent in the philosophy of the Cathars.

*

I will now attempt to describe Arthur Guirdham as a man, before explaining the extraordinary events that led him to his role as a world authority of the Cathars in thirteenth-century France.

Scholar, doctor of medicine, a psychiatrist, scientist, philosopher, poet, writer and wit, Dr Arthur Guirdham was one of the most remarkable men I have ever met. Although he had written many medical books, including THE PSYCHE IN MEDICINE, A THEORY OF DISEASE, CHRIST AND FREUD and OBSESSION, he was known principally for his books on the Cathars: publications that included THE GREAT HERESY, THE CATHARS AND REINCARNATION, THE GIBBET AND THE CROSS and THE LAKE AND THE CASTLE.

Guirdham studied medicine at Oxford and Charing Cross Hospital, London where he won the Governor's Clinical Gold Medal in 1929 and was a senior consultant psychiatrist in the Bath area for over thirty years.

I knew almost nothing about him when we first met. I had seen his name in various journals and I think it was Rosamond Lehmann, the novelist, who first suggested that I rang Arthur Guirdham as a possible kindred spirit and interesting to talk to. I left it for a few weeks and then, realizing that he lived only a few miles away, I wrote him a letter and he eventually rang, asking me to tea in July 1981.

His tangled garden of old roses – *Celestial, Rosamundi, Souvenir de la Malmaison, Honorine de Brabant* – tumbled in masses of striped pink and purple around his grey stone house near Bath. It was like walking into a painting by Arthur Rackham.

He had the easy, impeccable manners of the distinguished medical consultant. But as our friendship grew I realized the more subtle qualities of this gentle and august man. His approach to sickness and the interpretation of dreams was a logical extension of the thinking of Freud and Jung. Johan Quanjer, editor of the spiritual journal *New Humanity*, for which Guirdham wrote regularly on science and philosophy, described him as 'a genius and one of the great men of our age'.

Guirdham, like the Cathars, saw the world as being in a cosmic battle between good and evil – and in many of his medical books he illustrates the psychic forces in the causation of disease – the principalities and powers, 'the rulers of the darkness of the world' of St Paul's epistle to the Ephesians. Both as a doctor and a philosopher Guirdham saw evil as a virus, or bacterium. Evil was highly contagious, 'a negation of all light', as I described the Fathers as calling it. The symptoms in people capable of transmitting evil had to be diagnosed, discerned and understood.

Like Plato and Plotinus, the Neo-Platonist, Arthur Guirdham believed in the pre-existence of the soul and that it was possible for the soul or psyche to be united in successive and different bodies. His philosophy, like that of the Cathars, was emanatory. He would use the word 'vibration' to describe an integration or disintegration between two people – whether they got on together, or not. There are some people in whose presence we feel happier and stronger physically, and others whose negative influence can actually destroy us. He felt that the deeper levels of integration or disintegration between people would not necessarily have been caused by the experience of one life only. This, to him, implied the concept of reincarnation. Life was much bigger than is superficially observed with the physical senses and this leads us to the circumstances that moved him towards dualism, and to the Cathars.

It all began when, as a consultant in Bath, a patient was referred to him concerning disturbing dreams and visions which had begun when she was in her early teens. There was one recurring nightmare, accompanied by such loud screams that she and her husband feared she would awaken the street.

On looking at her case notes enclosed by the doctor, Arthur saw that she had in her early teens a few attacks of unconsciousness and that she had been referred to a neurologist who ordered an encephalogram. She was diagnosed as an epileptic. Arthur felt convinced, for no entirely rational reason, that she was not epileptic, that epilepsy was out of the picture in spite of the previous positive encephalogram, and he advised that it should not be repeated.

Neither mediaeval history nor mediaeval literature were taught in school, nor was it a practice for English girls of thirteen to translate their thoughts, visions and feelings into mediaeval French or the quite distinct language of the Languedoc. But this is what happened.

Arthur began as an amateur historian in checking what his patient had revealed. Sometimes it made no sense to him, but when he wrote to Monsieur Jean Duvernoy, the chief authority in France, and probably in the world, on the history of Catharism, he experienced astonishment at this detailed knowledge of the subject. At this point Arthur did not tell him that he had obtained it from a schoolgirl's notes of her dreams and visions!

From this patient, and from others like her, he learnt that seemingly epileptic reactions in adolescents could induce a capacity to step out of time.

The European origins of Catharism were in Bulgaria, Macedonia and Dalmatia, and so were originally under the authority of the Greek Church. By the thirteenth century Catharism was scattered all over northern Italy as in southern France and was mainly concentrated between the Dordogne and the Pyrenees and in what is now known as Provence. It was already predominant in the Languedoc and in the other possessions and dependencies of the Counts of Toulouse, who at this time presided over the richest, most cultivated and most sophisticated civilisation in Europe.

The word Cathar, meaning pure, to some suggests a 'dour and self-mutilating asceticism', but as we shall see this is not a fair description. Certainly there were difficult areas of doctrine which would not have been accepted by the Councils of Nicaea (325–787) but Catharism was a coherent and motivated religious philosophy which, in the regions in which it was established, threatened the very existence of the Roman Catholic Church.

The Inquisition was instigated by Pope Innocent III against the Cathars, although it was foreshadowed by the preaching mission of St Dominic to persuade and convert the heretical Albigenses and their leader Count

Raymond of Toulouse. Cathar records and literature were as ruthlessly destroyed by the Church as were the living exponents of the faith. The Inquisitional recorders regarded themselves as confronted with a formidable opposition, yet Pope Innocent 'castigated frankly and without reservations the corruption and neglect of duty on the part of the Catholic Clergy whose defects he regarded as an invitation to heresy.'

It is only when we look again at the Cathar philosophy in much more detail that we are able to understand why, in spite of its virtual annihilation in the thirteenth century, there was such astounding evidence that came flooding to the surface around Dr Arthur Guirdham in the twentieth century. How did it happen, and what was it trying to tell us?

There was in Catharism the same pattern as that revealed in primitive Christianity, a limited number of individuals with special gifts preaching the word, healing the sick and igniting a number of others with the same capacity. Arthur used to say that one cannot explain why a body of people endowed with these special gifts should have assembled in the Languedoc, but adds that there are 'periods in history when the materialism of a disturbed world is offset by an enhanced spirituality on the part of a minority.' Some years ago Sir Steven Runciman said, with commendable prescience, that 'for many the way back to Catharism appears to be by way of the occult'. We are cautious now in using such a word, but bearing in mind the amount of evidence that was destroyed and that the Cathars were trained in clairvoyance and telepathy, particularly where the emphasis was on pure spirit, it may not be surprising that they have in some way broken through the distance of time. Arthur always felt that the purpose behind the dissemination of knowledge of Catharism was 'to resist, so far as is in our power, the engulfing tide of materialism.'

Cathar priests, or *parfaits*, always carried a copy of St John's Gospel. It was clear to them that Christ had this extraordinary emanatory capacity with the compulsion of His presence. His gift of healing was so developed that he could raise the dead. He was also clairvoyant, as witnessed by his conversation with the woman by the well. These words in their original and pure form need carry no fear for us. It was the way that early Christianity, an intensely spiritist religion, spread through the centuries.

The two most advanced civilisations of Europe at the end of the twelfth century, those of the Languedoc and Northern Italy, were largely given over to the Cathar heresy and the ruling classes were mostly on the side of the heretics. 'It should be clearly understood' writes Arthur, 'that except for recalcitrants and heretics and, at the opposite pole, the dregs of society, man in the Middle Ages was dominated by the fear of hell.'

The Cathars removed largely from the people the fear of hell. The *parfaits* (and there were women *parfaites* as well as the men) were purified by the *consolamentum*, which was the only sacrament recognized by the Cathars. The Cathars were by nature 'anti-clerical', partly because of the pressure of proselytising from the Roman Catholic Church. The Inquisition was originally recruited from the Dominicans, the Order of Preachers, and if words and persuasion failed then it was followed by the punishment of death; and death for the heretic was by burning.

In contrast to Roman doctrine many of the *parfaits* were drawn from those who had already lived a married life and had children. It was easier and more natural to be celibate at this time in their lives. From now on they chose to live at the 'level of the spirit'. They were vegetarian, although fish was allowed; they loved the beauty of nature, they loved animals and they were against all forms of violence.

There was always, in Catharism, the feeling of *longing*. Life on this planet was sometimes hell – the lowest plane of consciousness. They were too enlightened to think of hell as a 'spatial concept' and with their love of nature there was always compensation – the sunshine, the birds, the trees … but beauty was transient. It didn't last, and leaves fell from the trees in autumn…. After death, the psyche or soul would be freed, existing beyond time. We would live in a state of greater perception and the beauty we had found in the world would still be there, but without the agony of its passing. The Cathar who was trained to become a *parfait* at a younger age would, as a dualist, be capable of knowing and reconciling within himself or herself, the differences of spirit and matter.

In troubadour poems we can see a similar way of thinking. In their longing for what was unobtainable they expressed religious allegories rather than celebrations of carnal love. Catharism was concerned with life at different levels of consciousness. Being 'trapped in the flesh', in materialism, numbed the perceptions and impeded the capacity of clairvoyance, telepathy, and most important of all to the Cathar, the gift of healing, which takes place out of time. Arthur would explain that the human personality is riveted in time, it is moulded by regrets for the past and desires for the future. The psyche, or soul, on the other hand, though relative to the ego, is emancipated from time.

The selection of the *parfaits* was 'laborious, careful and intensely scientific', according to Guirdham. They were chosen for their capacity to emanate the energy of goodness and for their capacity to function outside the dimensions of chronology. Their training included meditation to give insight into the nature and potentialities of those who wished to be *parfaits*. It separated the sheep from the goats. 'Some were especially destined for preaching, others for scholarship, others as seers, prophets, and students of philosophy, a large number as technicians in the Cathar workshops, but larger than any other category, those to be trained as healers'.

In many ways there are further similarities with classical Greek philosophy – initiation, serenity, and a vast and tolerant culture with the capacity to see life as a whole. The Cathar view on Christ, though it accepted that he was the Son of God, was more in accordance with St Paul when he spoke of the body spiritual as distinct from the body corporal. It was questioned then – and it is questioned now – 'if God is at one and the same time all powerful and all merciful why do such appalling things happen to people and, above all, to innocent people?' The dualist maintains that, so far as this world is concerned, good and evil are primary and opposed energies. This, perhaps, is one of the main difficulties of doctrine and there would have been obvious disagreements over the theology of the Fall and the origins of evil.

Philosophy to many is an intellectual process. To the Cathars philosophy was essentially 'a transcendental experience of revealed truth. It was something acquired through the last refinements of perception. Philosophic truth was revealed to the mind as a landscape might be seen by the eyes'. To the Cathars what we call poetic vision was not an imaginative experience or a flight of fancy. It was an insight more intense, more real, more utterly truthful than intuition. It was a piercing into the very nature of truth and it was for this reason that an elite among the *parfaits* were especially trained.

We can now see the polarity and gulf between this way of thinking and the temporal power of the Roman Catholic Church at that time. Here are just a few dates and events to remind ourselves of the tragedy and ruthlessness of the Inquisition.

In Béziers on July 22nd, 1209, all the inhabitants in the city were massacred. The number has been put at thirty thousand. The carnage was indiscriminate, Catholics and Cathars. It is recorded that when one of the

Catholic Knights of the Crusade wished to know whom to kill, the order was 'Kill them all. God will know his own'.

Guirdham points out that it was possibly the most appalling massacre Europe had seen for centuries. Its magnitude has been 'conveniently forgotten'.

An arguable defence of the Catholic apologists is that the Crusaders themselves were not responsible, and that their paid mercenaries, called *routiers*, got out of hand. Yet in forgiving in advance the sins of all those who took part in the Crusade, Pope Innocent III was perhaps inviting atrocities.

After Béziers came Carcassonne, which was the greatest Cathar fortress of its day. Pope Innocent desired nothing more than the complete extinction of heresy from the Languedoc and he removed from power the nobles who had been protecting the heretics. The young Viscount of Carcassonne and Béziers was imprisoned in a tower of his own fortress and died shortly afterwards.

The new Viscount of Carcassonne and Béziers was a person 'of brutish religiosity, avarice and aggression, which made him not only an ideal hammer of heretics but the perfect instrument for the consolidation of stolen territories.' He was to become leader of the crusaders and his name was Simon de Montfort. As the war continued de Montfort took the stronghold of Catharism with increasing barbarism. In the early April of 1211 he laid siege to Lavaur. Guirdham writes: 'It was defended by Aimery de Montréal, son of Blanche de Laurac, a *parfaite* noted for her piety and kindness, and brother of the chatelaine Guiraude, whose charity equalled that of her mother. The town was taken by storm. Aimery de Montréal was rushed to the gibbet with eighty knights who had fought with him. The gibbet collapsed and the victims were slaughtered like cattle. The mass slaughter of the aristocracy was unusual even for the Middle Ages. The châtelaine was offered for the amusement of the soldiers. She was then thrown down a well and buried under an avalanche of stones.

Four hundred Cathars were burnt at Lavaur. This was followed by Muret and Fanjeaux, and later at Montségur. The devastation caused by de Montfort was immense. It is estimated that four hundred villages and towns disappeared from the map.

Montségur is sometimes thought of as the culminating tragedy. 'So it was,' writes Arthur, ' in that it involved the destruction of a great spiritual bastion, but the *parfaits* burnt at Montségur were only half the number of those who died at Lavaur.'

By the late 1230s Montségur had become the main administration centre for the Cathars. When it fell, the *parfaits* were dragged down and burnt, it is said on the lower slopes of the mountain. Through prayer and meditation they would have prepared themselves for death and would have received the *consolamentum*, which was a deeply spiritual process communicating a capacity 'to slip into a timeless sphere beyond the reach of human agony.' Arthur comments that Catharism was linked more directly to primitive Christianity than many have imagined.

Two hundred *parfaits* were burnt at Montségur .

*

What was the Montségur treasure? There is strong evidence that the Grail legend had roots in Cathar country, but Arthur points out that 'none of this justifies for a moment the speculation that the treasure of Montségur was a sacred Chalice.' This was a faith which did not build Churches and rejected sacraments, although the Chalice, with the dove and the rose, was one of the visionary patterns which have appeared regularly to Cathars and other dualists.

Arthur assumes that the treasure consisted of sacred writings which would have had a limited circulation among the initiates. It is also known that the Cathars possessed a special version of the Gospel of St John and they would have had a collection of rare books which included the Works of Greek philosophers from Pythagoras to Plato, the neo-Platonists, Plotinus and Porphyry and books from the Alexandrian School. The works of Valentinus and Basilides were also included in the Cathar library.

The treasure of the Cathars would have included money. Although they had built no Churches, there were Cathar houses where the *parfaits* were able to stay. They travelled long distances on horseback and payment for horses and the expense of keeping them is mentioned in the records. There was also the upkeep of the convents for women and for workshops where 'young artisans were instructed in weaving, leather-making, and in other trades'. For centuries people have searched around Montségur, along the slopes of the Pic de St-Barthélemy and in the valley of the Ariège for the Cathar treasure, but nothing has ever been found.

For those of us in the West who are familiar with Patristic vision and the writings of the early Fathers there is sometimes a feeling of having been 'amputated from our Christian roots'. Since the great schism and because of our separate historical journeys the western approach gives priority to historical accuracy and Christian ethics but seems uncomfortable with the depth of spirituality.

Dualism, of which 'Catharism was the last openly and widely asserted example' is the oldest-established philosophy in the world. Catharism was concerned with life at different levels of consciousness. To its exponents, this world was hell because in it we achieved our lowest level of sensitivity. That is what is meant when it is said of the Cathars that to them matter was intrinsically evil. This was nothing to do with the 'special sinfulness of sexuality'. The Cathars never used sexual morality as a yardstick by which to separate good and evil. Knowing what was right and what was wrong would come to them naturally, for they were sensitive, tolerant and compassionate. Discernment developed with their belief in emanating *goodness* and their understanding grew from the purity and spirituality of higher consciousness. Many were doctors and the philosophy has been described as 'an amalgam of mysticism and common sense.'

Holiness is an irrelevance to our present culture, for it is a word used to describe something that is no longer understood. Either it has turned into extreme fundamentalism, in which case it is not holiness, or a bold but sometimes aggressive moralism which we are seeing so much in modern Protestantism, the movement within Christianity that originated in the sixteenth-century Reformation. Our religious language has been reduced to the banal, and we try to materialize what is immaterial. Many learn about Christianity with words that have been sanitised into clichés and platitudes that cannot begin to describe the depth and beauty of Divine wisdom and knowledge.

It is said that we are reaching the 'limits of the intellect' – a saturation of factual information – but what does this teach us about the highest knowledge that enables us to touch God? There is no longer a sense of the sacred, for we are obsessed with glamour and triviality, cynicism, violence and the need for constant distraction. What kind of progress is this? What kind of culture? There is no suggestion here that we should return to a heresy but with discernment we should be able to see some of the wisdom in the philosophy of the Cathars.

Part of this article began as a biographical tribute to Arthur Guirdham prepared for the website of the Research into Lost Knowledge Organisation (RILKO).

GNOSTIC CHRISTIANITY REBORN

JAAP RAMEIJER

The author sees Catharism as a flower that sprang to life in the middle ages from a bush planted in the times of Jesus and Mary Magdalene. He believes that the teachings of Mary Magdalene – her message of love, hope, spiritual growth, wisdom and forgiviness – was particularly instrumental in bringing the sweetness of the true Christian faith to the Languedoc, a faith which he calls Gnostic Christianity.

TRUE CHRISTIANITY, by which I mean Esoteric Christianity, Gnostic Christianity, the original teachings of Jesus and Mary Magdalene, was almost completely destroyed during the Albigensian Crusade (1209–1229), which was meant to stamp out Catharism. It was a ruthless campaign ordered by the pope in which more than 100,000, some even say 300,000, Christians were murdered or burned alive. Sometimes even the dead were dug up and burned! Fortunately Pope John-Paul II apologized in 2000 AD for this outrage. The Crusade was followed by the French king conquering the rest of the Languedoc, mainly the lands of the count of Toulouse. This campaign was then followed by the Church further enslaving the people with the harsh Papal Inquisition.

Catharism is a dualistic religion. A religion of good and evil, light and

---

Jaap Willem Rameijer was born in 1945 in Utrecht, the Netherlands. He served for eighteen years in the Royal Netherlands Navy. He has master's degrees in Law and in Business Management. He worked for ten years at Fokker Aircraft Manufacturer. From 1992 on he had several jobs, such as director of a Health Insurance company, director of a psychiatric hospital, vice chairman of the University of The Hague and director of a high school. He retired in 2004.

In 1999 he bought a *domaine* called Les Labadous in Rennes-le-Château, the magical village in the French Pyrenees. He has written books about Rennes-le-Château and Glastonbury, as well as JAMIE ON HIS CLOUD, MARY MAGDALENE IN FRANCE and THE BEAUTY OF ORBS. *For accompanying pictures, see colour section pp. 4–5.*

dark, body and spirit, differentiating between the immortal soul and the mortal body. Cathar reasoning is as follows. How is it possible that evil came into this world if God is only goodness and love? There must have been, next to God the creator of the spiritual world, the world of light and beauty, a second God, the creator of the material world – the world of materialism, power and flesh. This God was known as Yahweh, Satan, or the Demiurge. The God of the Old Testament, the God who rules over a depraved, materialistic world.

The idea isn't new. There had been other dualistic religions, like Mazdaism. Its prophet Zoroaster preached more a way of living than a religion. People should have good thoughts, speak good words, and do good things. By living a good life they would get closer to God. Catharism is a Gnostic religion, Gnostic meaning 'knowledge'. It is a religion aimed at enlightment, at personal growth, at gaining knowledge, at spiritual development. It is a religion of direct contact with God, the creator of the spiritual world, a religion of love and knowledge.

No so long ago people thought that Catharism originated spontaneously in regions like the Rhineland in Germany, Lombardy in Italy and the Languedoc in France – regions that were prosperous, where women were respected; regions that knew a certain amount of religious freedom and were reasonably tolerant. They thought that Catharism was a natural reaction to the utterly corrupt and power hungry Church – a church of fear, sin, penitence, dogmas, indulgences and excommunication. The church that was doing nothing for her believers; the church that had positioned itself between God and the people, where priests were striving for material gain and where bishops, cardinals and popes were striving for secular power.

Others thought that Catharism had come gradually to these regions, originating in the Middle and Far East, from religions like Mazdaism, Buddhism and Hinduism and then slowly spreading to the West – creating religious trends like Manichaeism (third century AD), the Paulicians (sixth century AD) and Bogomilism (tenth century AD).

But a few people think otherwise, including myself. I think that Catharism is, and was, a continuous, Gnostic undercurrent – a current that was kept alive through the ages because the message was so good, so clear and so powerful, and because the preachers were sincere. They lived the life they preached. The people who listened to Mary Magdalene, to the teachings of Jesus and herself, treasured these messages. They were messages of love, of hope and of understanding. Messages that touched the soul. Messages that were embedded in the hearts of the people, in spite of the efforts of the church to stamp them out.

Many of these messages were contained in the more than sixty Gnostic writings scorned by the Roman emperors and the early Church Fathers. They were the gospels that were not selected for the New Testament during a series of unruly councils in the fourth century AD. Gospels, the words of Christ, that were later declared heresies! Fortunately the Roman Catholic Church was, at least until the Albigensian crusade and the Papal Inquisition, not very strong in the Languedoc. The Languedoc was a region that knew powerful rulers like Alaric the Visigoth, Clovis and Dagobert I and II the Merovingians, Charlemagne the Carolingian and the kings of Septimania – rulers who did not care too much for Rome and did not easily bend to the will of the Church.

Catharism sprang, in my view, and I know this is subjective, but it is my view, a feeling from the heart, from the seeds sown by Mary Magdalene in the south of France. A similar process took place in England, where Joseph of Arimathea also preached the teachings of Jesus, resulting first in Celtic Christianity, a much more Gnostic and 'natural' religion than the orthodox teachings of Rome. In later centuries the English monarchs and priests clashed regularly with Rome. There was always friction between Rome and England – over issues as Pelagianism, disputing the rightful succession of the popes in Rome, over Thomas à Becket, who refused to acknowledge the law of the king in crimes committed by priests, over the Dissolution Act of Henry VIII, disbanding all abbeys and cloisters, frustrated as he was by the arrogance of the Church and the refusal of the pope to annul his first marriage. It resulted finally in the establishment of the Anglican Church.

What did the Cathars believe? Or rather, what did they not believe? Well, they didn't believe that Jesus was the Son of God. They didn't believe in the virgin birth. They didn't believe he died on the cross. Jesus was a prophet, yes, and a teacher, a very important teacher, showing the people the way to enlightenment and reminding them of their divine nature. They didn't believe in original sin. Jesus didn't come to free the people from their sin, but from their ignorance.

They didn't like the Church as an institute – the Church with her relics, her saints, her sacraments. To say nothing of the infamous trade in indulgences or its excommunication practices. They did not accept the celebration of the Eucharist. How could bread and wine turn into the body and blood of Christ? They didn't believe in heaven and hell, or in the last judgment. Hell didn't exist, unless it was the imprisonment of the divine spark of every human being in his or her physical body. They believed in reincarnation. Each life on earth was a step towards enlightment. By living in poverty, love and compassion, never using violence or lying to other people, they hoped to get closer to God, their Spiritual God. Their religion was not based on the Old Testament, but on the New Testament, mainly on the Gospel of John and, most probably, on the forbidden Gospels of Thomas and Philip too.

There are scholars who think that Mary Magdalene wrote the Gospel of John, and that John the beloved disciple was none other then Mary Magdalene, the dearly beloved disciple. They think that John was invented by the Church to get Mary Magdalene out of the way. This hypothesis was strengthened by the many 'curious' changes that were made in the Gospel of John – changes that could only prove that the Church wanted to hide something. Sometimes the effort to hide things is the best way to attract attention to them – just the attention they wanted to avoid. The Gospel of John, or Mary Magdalene, is also the most trustworthy gospel. It reads like an eyewitness's account. And what better eyewitness than Mary Magdalene?

The word 'Cathar' means pure or clear. There were different "grades" in Catharism. The *auditeurs* were the people who listened to the message of the Cathars. The *croyants* were the believers. At the height of Catharism about fifty per cent of the population was said to be 'believers'. The *Chrétiens* were the priests, those who had received the *consolamentum*, the sacred blessing. They were later called *les parfaits*, 'the perfect ones', by the inquisition, a name that stuck and was carried with pride. The local people called their priests *bonshommes* and *bonnesfemmes*, meaning 'good men' and 'good women', for men and women were equal in the eyes of the Cathars. Men and women could both be priests and very good priests they were. They lived an exemplary life. The *parfaits* were highly respected. They included skilful craftsmen, good weavers and excellent healers. They had to and wanted to. For they worked for their living.

The *parfaits* are said, for example by Antonin Gadal, to have undergone a severe training. Some say this training took place in the Holy Mountain in Ussat-les-Bains, a mountain full of caves and tunnels. Even now the caves are very impressive and carry a special atmosphere. They are eerie sometimes. I have visited the caves many times, guiding people around. And every time when my friends got there, they were very quiet, impressed. Or scared and crying. Some of the caves are huge, like the Hermit cave – not as big as the Lombrives cave on the other side of the river Ariège, but still huge. Some caves are highly energized, like the Église Cave or are filled with happy higher energy forms, called Orbs, like in the Bethlehem cave.

The Cathar church was nothing like the Church of Rome. It had not even one special building, and certainly nothing resembling the beautiful cathedrals, basilicas and churches built for Rome – blinking with gold, 'received' from grateful and fearful believers. No, the Cathars met in the houses of the people, or out in the open. There was no hierarchy and there were no relics, statues or other religious artifacts.

The Cathars believed themselves to be the true successors of Jesus and his disciples. They 'operated' in exactly the same way. The Cathar church had no managerial or hierarchical function, but a spiritual one. The Cathar bishops initiated their *parfaits* by the ritual of *consolamentum*. An initiation, or baptism, performed by the laying of hands on the head. The *parfaits* obeyed strict rules: no earthly possessions, no intercourse, no meat or cheese, eggs and butter. No killing of men or animals, not even in self-defence. Always telling the truth. No financial support, no taxes, only gifts and legacies. There were in 1226 AD five bishops in the *Pays Cathare*.

It's not so difficult to see what danger Catharism constituted for the Church of Rome. And their religion was spreading. The Roman Catholic Church tried, it really tried – that must be said – to bring the Cathars back to 'true' Christianity. But to no avail. The differences in belief systems and attitude were too great. After that it needed only a single incident to spark the wrath of Rome. On January 14th of the year 1208 AD, the papal envoy Pierre de Castelnau, who had terribly misbehaved in Toulouse, was murdered in St-Gilles-du-Gard – probably by a soldier of the count of Toulouse, who was however far too clever to have ordered such an act. The furious Pope Innocent III then called for a crusade against the Cathars – on June 24th, the feast day of John the Baptist. He excommunicated all Cathars and all those who helped them, including Raymond VI, count of Toulouse and Raymond-Roger Trencavel, viscount of Carcassonne. Being excommunicated meant being labelled 'outlaws'. And outlaws, even Christian outlaws, could be killed without committing a Christian sin! How very convenient.

A huge army was assembled at Lyon, some say 300,000 men. Some knights, some clergymen and a lot of brigands, bandits and ruffians, who had all received forgiveness from the Pope for their previous sins! Yes, the ways of the Church are at times incomprehensible. The Albigensian crusade had started. The crusade was officially led by the papal envoy Arnaud Amaury, with Simon the Montfort as military leader. It would turn out to be an incredible cruel and brutal crusade. A crusade of Christians against fellow Christians. Some even called it a genocide.

On July 22nd 1209, on the feast day of Mary Magdalene, the city of Béziers was conquered. Everybody was killed, more then 20,000 people, including the people who had taken refuge in the *Église Madeleine* and in the cathedral. They were all killed. The churches were set on fire. The papal envoy Amaury, when asked how to discern between true Christians and Cathars, is said to have answered: 'Kill them all. God will know his own'. It was the day when the Church lost the respect of its people.

After that, Carcassonne and Toulouse were conquered. The country was plundered and devastated. More then four hundred villages were burned. Hundreds of people were burned at the stake. In 1210, a hundred and forty Cathars died at the stake in Minerve. A dove hewn in the rock still reminds us of that horrible fact. In 1211, 400 Cathars were burned alive in Lavaur. I will not recount the whole gruesome scenario of the Albigensian crusade, with its kings, its counts, its popes, its bishops, its battles, its treason, its changing alliances, its treaties, its convictions and its cruelty. It is too horrible to contemplate. Just a few highlights.

In 1229 the treaty of Meaux was concluded, officially ending the Albigensian crusade. However, not being able to eradicate Catharism from the Pays Cathare, Pope Gregory constituted in 1233 the Papal Inquisition. A more horrible institution can hardly be imagined. The task of finding and persecuting the heretics was given to the Dominicans. In the same year the castle at Montségur became the official seat of the Cathar church. It has been called by many names, like the Vatican of the Cathars, the Grail castle, the Temple of Light, the Pyramid of the Pyrenees. The castle was fortified.

However the actions of the newly installed Inquisition were so brutal that the country revolted. New armies were assembled, new alliances formed. But it was too late. The Albigensian crusade, which started as a religious war, had now become a secular war as well, with the king of France participating in the campaign and occupying the lands of the count of Toulouse, comprising roughly the present-day Languedoc.

In 1243, siege was laid to the last fortress of the Cathars, the famous Montségur. The head of the Cathar dragon had to be cut off. There was fierce resistance from the soldiers defending the castle, and the fortress was practically impregnable – until the water supply was poisoned. Negotiations about surrendering the castle were started. The castle would be surrendered on March 16th, 1244. All who renounced Catharism would be spared. In the weeks before surrendering the castle, special ceremonies were held. So special were they that several soldiers converted on the spot to Catharism, knowing full well that a certain death awaited them.

On the night before the surrender four Cathars left the castle. They silently descended the mountain, taking with them the most precious treasure of the Cathars. Nobody knows what that treasure was. Surely not gold or precious stones. The Cathars didn't care much for material wealth. It could however be the location of their 'treasure', for they had gathered quite a lot of money, meant for sustaining the defence of Montségur and for buying off the victims of the Inquisition. Gold and silver would be far too heavy to get them safely down the steep rock. It could have been *The Book of Love*, a supposedly heretical booklet written by Jesus or by Mary Magdalene. It could have been documents proving the marriage and genealogy of Jesus and Mary Magdalene. It could have been the knowledge that Jesus and Mary Magdalene were deeply in love with each other. And had children, even. Or it could have been any of the forbidden gospels. Maybe even the second gospel of John, the beloved disciple. Or the *Cène Secret*, the most treasured secret book of the Cathars, *cène* meaning the last supper. Or special rituals and ceremonies. Or sacred numbers and symbols. Or documents proving the true origins of Catharism. Maybe even the sermons of Mary Magdalene herself. Highly explosive material at that time. And even now, in this time, we don't know what the treasure was. It could even have been the knowledge stored in the heads of the *parfaits* themselves. The treasure was never found. And no one knows where the four *parfaits* went. Some say to Spain, to Montserrat, others to the initiation caves near Tarascon-sur-Ariège. Others say they went to Limoux or to Rennes-le-Château.

On March 16th, 1244 some 225 Cathars were burned alive at the stake in the field at the foot of the 'Pog' of Montségur. In 1960 a memorial stone, a stele, was placed at the site, with a text which translates: 'To the Cathars, to the martyrs of the pure Christian love, 16 March 1244'. If you climb Montségur, it takes about half an hour and it is something of a pilgrimage;

then stop and stay for a while at this memorial. Think of all the Cathars who died there, singing. Lay a flower, a rose, at the monument. At that time, in 1244, one hopeful statement was made. It stated that in seven hundred years' time, the laurel would blossom again at Montségur.

And it does bloom again, literally and figuratively. For Catharism is alive, very much alive. It is like a religion reborn, thanks to a few French scholars. Now there are museums, magazines, bookshops with hundreds of books and beautiful pictures of the Cathar castles. Thousands of tourists visit the *Pays Cathare* each year. It has even become a brand name in the Aude department. With Cathar restaurants where plenty of wine and meat is served, Cathar accountants, Cathar garages even Cathar undertakers! Just south of Narbonne, on the *Autoroute des deux Mers*, the autoroute leading into the *Pays Cathare*, now stands a monument dedicated to the memory of the Cathars.

Catharism is a religion reborn. Maybe it is still the same, continuous Gnostic undercurrent that surfaced in the time of the Cathars. A religion that is surfacing again in our time, just in time to save the world. This pure and Gnostic religion is 'calling out' to more and more people. It is as if *l'Histoire se repète*, as if history is repeating itself, as if this beautiful religion is replacing the old and outdated doctrines of the Church of Rome and the conservative protestant churches. For Catharism represents, in my view, the original message of Jesus and Mary Magdalene: a message of love, enlightment and spiritual growth. A message to take to the heart. No more striving for power and materialism. We have had enough of that.

The twentieth century was the most violent century in living memory. But now, now that we have found our freedom, the heritage of Jesus and Mary Magdalene and the heritage of the Cathars is coming to the surface again. It is now that we can create a new religion, with Catharism as a wonderful model. For we all long for the return of universal love and sacred femininity, for harmony between the sexes, for female priests. For churches preaching the original message of Jesus, like in the time of the Cathars. We long for a religion that teaches us respect for nature, for each other and for Mother Earth.

TO GO TO THE WALL

MORAG FOSTER

*Could it happen again? Morag Foster asks questions
about society, pacifism and aggression.*

'TO GO to the wall!' How often has that phrase been heard in connection with the demise of a company or institution?

In the case of the Good Christians, or Cathars as they are now known, it meant exactly what it said on the tin. Many are said to have been walled up, literally, for their heresy and left there. Imagine if you will, the sheer physical, mental and emotional terror of such a deed. Eventually, as a group of believers, the Cathars were extirpated totally.

The Cathar story is part of the story of man's inhumanity to his fellow man throughout the whole of known history. It is the story of control of the masses, keeping them in a state of fear, not only for their lives but also for their immortal souls.

The Cathars practised a simple theosophy, close to that of the early Church and were pacifists and healers. Throughout the centuries such simplicity and pacifism has aroused passion, resentment and hatred, even in

---

Morag Foster graduated from Edinburgh University and Moray House College, eventually becoming Head Teacher in a school in the Highlands of Scotland, a post from which she has since retired.

She has had a lifelong interest in psychic phenomena and healing modalities and was indeed cured of ME by a complementary practitioner. Over a considerable number of years she has trained in a variety of therapies, including Reiki, Karuna Reiki, EFT, Psych-K, Emotrance, Metamorphic Technique, Indian Head Massage and Remote Viewing (RV). She is a member of the British Society of Dowsers (BSD) and has dowsed for health and wellbeing as well as for information connected to RV. Her website is www.treehousecentre.co.uk.

At the present time she has a particular interest in the development of behaviour and attitudes in preschool children.

the hearts of the seemingly devout. The overwhelming question is, why should the story of the Cathar massacre stir people so much?

Could it be because it took place in a land romanticised by the troubadours, a country separate at that time from France, a country full of music, laughter and a gentler ruling class, or so history tells us? A land renowned even now for its beauty and the majesty of its mountains, making the atrocities seem even more marked as a result?

The Cathars also believed in two Gods, a benevolent one and a destructive one. To understand their belief we need only read the Old Testament and compare it with the New. There can be very little argument that the writers have interpreted them as different beings. There are even theories, however seemingly far-fetched, that the God of the Old Testament was an alien 'Lord' who kept humanity in thrall through fear of punishment.

It's hard for us in the twenty-first century to contemplate such barbaric acts as were perpetrated then, especially those that were in the cause of the Church – or is it? Have we learned anything at all in the intervening seven hundred years? In today's so-called civilized and enlightened world, such cruelty still persists. In Guantanamo Bay, Iraq, Syria and many other parts of the globe atrocities occur daily, but somehow we seem to be able to distance ourselves from the horror.

Have we become so desensitised by the deluge of media information that we no longer pay much attention to the coverage of such events?

I first became aware of the Cathars on reading the book by Arthur Guirdham, WE ARE ONE ANOTHER. It resonated with past feelings of 'knowing' a place or a person, even knowing in some cases that death was imminent. Such feelings are not readily shared in normal, everyday conversation, for fear of ridicule.

Later, when I began my healing work, visions of countryside, mountains and people being tortured or persecuted would appear in my consciousness, depending on the client. Whether or not this could be linked in any way to past lives continues to be debatable. Such visions of course were never disclosed, for obvious reasons.

Still later, after my training in Remote Viewing, it became apparent to me that there had to be some substance to so many people's claims of such visions, past, present and future. I began to look differently at our notion of time, measured as it is in linear fashion. Certainly the pattern of the seasons, and of birth, life and death, lends itself to this interpretation, but I began to wonder if there could possibly be different kinds of time. Perhaps time outwith our physical or conscious awareness, which could have a parallel existence, yet still have an effect on our lives here on earth.

Various personal experiments with Lucid Dreaming produced visions of distinctive landscapes and mountains. As I 'flew' over this land every detail was clear, including what I came to realise later, on seeing photos of the Languedoc, was the ridge of Montségur. The scenes also bore an uncanny resemblance to the landscapes of the Harry Potter films.

Could these visions be merely the product of a fertile imagination or was time being manipulated in some way in order to reveal the past or even the future?

Looking backwards to a childhood which featured the stories of Jules Verne and the like brings the realisation that the world as we know it has changed more rapidly in the last fifty years than in the past few thousand. What was once regarded as science fiction is now accepted as reality. Science is progressing faster than the ability of ordinary people to comprehend. Powerful microscopes reveal hitherto hidden worlds within and around us. Knowledge has become fluid and changeable, science pushes the boundaries of possibility hour by hour.

Communication in all its forms has led to a shrinking world, metaphorically. Information can be instantaneous, travel effortless.

Why then, in spite of these meteoric changes, have we been so reluctant to accept such things as telepathy, distant healing, hands-on-healing and complementary therapies? Has there been an inbuilt 'failsafe' – to protect the human brain from information strain and sensory overload? We talk casually about 'not getting our head round things'. What will it take to open up our heads, our brains, our imaginations and accept immeasurable, unlimited possibilities of human abilities? Healing has been handed over to the physicians and surgeons as if they have all the answers. Healing ourselves and others has seemed up until now to engender ridicule or fear in the majority of people. What are we afraid of and why?

Has the primitive part of our brain acted as a brake on our potential power and, if so, why?

Experiments are taking place, as we speak, which appear to prove that we are wired for peace not war.[1] Sooner rather than later we may come to realise that there is enough on our planet, physically, mentally, emotionally and spiritually, for everybody.

These experiments remind me of experiences I had while doing a Remote Viewing experiment on the Isle of Skye. As a teaching Head Teacher I had been encouraged to take part in various 'enterprise' projects, one of which involved taking part in an archaeological dig in the south of the island.

Although protocol states that RV(Remote Viewing) should be done using coordinates and not on site, I decided to ignore this and see what would happen if I focused on the area of the excavation of the Iron Age cave since not a lot was known about it. My reckoning was that if RV's other name was Psychic Spying, then the psychic part was important and should not be bound by mere man-made rules.

On my first site-based RV I obeyed most of those rules – date, time, place, etc. – and settled down to write and draw as I had been trained to do. The results amazed the archaeologists, since they revealed things I couldn't possibly have known about, for instance a lozenge with a snake shape on it that they had found the week before but hadn't yet shown to anyone. There were many other such 'coincidences', enough to make them accept the possibility that what I 'saw' held credence.

I did two such 'viewings' onsite. The images appeared in my mind as if I were watching an old-fashioned sepia movie. It felt like I was watching and being a part of it at the same time. The prevailing sense was one of a peaceful community working together for the benefit of all. Cooperation seemed to be key.

I received a clear impression during the session that their system of justice, here on the island, included the practice of cutting off the tip of a finger as punishment for a serious misdeed. It provided a constant reminder of the deed to the perpetrator and the community but did not prevent the person from continuing to contribute his or her skills to the group. My archaeologist friends confirmed that bony tips have been found in middens all over Europe, with no explanation as to where the rest of the bones were. This apparent revelation seems to make sense of those finds.

The cave and its surrounds appeared to have been the ancient equivalent of a Community Centre, church and pharmacy, with an industrial estate nearby. Guiding the whole way of life seemed to be a Wise Woman who was district nurse, herbalist and mother-figure all rolled into one, aided by Elders whose main aim was the smooth running and health and wellbeing of the village.

Running through the smaller cave at the back was a stream which was part of a birthing rite of passage. When a pregnant woman entered the environs of the cave itself, she was ministered to and the newly born child was then washed and prepared before being brought from the bowels of the earth into the light of day. A powerful symbolism.

The sense of peace during this time was in stark contrast to my growing 'awareness' towards the end of the viewing of the intrusion of warlike strangers intent on plundering and destroying the land and its people. Indeed the people eventually gave up resisting and moved on to settle elsewhere.

As we are beginning to realise, the end of this age heralded a more aggressive one dominated by weapons made of newly discovered stronger metals. Patterns of any kind, whether behaviour or thought, can either be maintained or disrupted. According to the ideas of the Mayan End Times, perhaps the pattern/habit of this aggressive energy which has lasted over two thousand years is now ready to give way to a gentler, feminine, more inclusive one. Not an end as many would believe, but a change, a metamorphosis, a new beginning.

In conjunction with the destruction being perpetrated around the world at present has come a surge of interest in healing. There is a growing awareness that healing has to start within each of us and that as we heal ourselves we heal each other and our environment. This seems to echo the Cathar quest for perfection all those centuries ago. Modern science and technology will give us advantages that were not available seven hundred years ago. As science continues to prove that we are indeed linked to one another and that the 'ether' does exist, perhaps peace will be the only solution. War will become obsolete and barbaric, simply a memory of a distant more primitive past.

The Cathar model, all those centuries ago, embodied the essence of a tolerant, caring, peaceful society. Perhaps when we accept that there is much we don't know, but are beginning to have the means to find out, then we may realise that we are indeed all inextricably linked together. Through this realisation we can work with one another to be worthy custodians of our planet. To behave with tolerance and understanding towards all living things, including Gaia, Mother Earth, is the only hope for the future of humanity.

[1] Hamilton, Dr David, WHY KINDNESS IS GOOD FOR YOU. London: Hay House UK, 2010

VIII : 4

SOME ASTROLOGICAL NOTES
ON THE IMMOLATION OF THE CATHARS AT
MONTSÉGUR ON MARCH 16th 1244 (OS)

SIMON BENTLEY

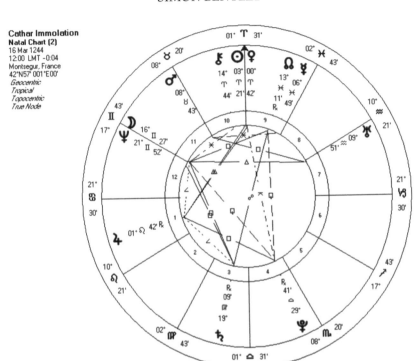

Cathar Immolation
Natal Chart (2)
16 Mar 1244
12:00 LMT −0:04
Montsegur, France
42°N57' 001°E00'
Geocentric
Tropical
Topocentric
True Node

W HAT FOLLOWS is a response to a request to set up a chart for the recorded day that Cathar *parfaits* were finally taken from the châ-teau of Montségur for burning in the meadow at the foot of the 'pog' or peak. While it has not proved possible to determine the exact time of day at which the fire was lit, the date itself is well known and beyond doubt, as

Simon's interest in astrology began long before he went to university and studied, among other subjects, the history of science. Graduating from Cambridge, he trained in horticulture and then took up astrology professionally. He became Principal of the White Eagle School of Astrology in 1995.

is the place. The chart used for these notes is cast for local noon.

What immediately strikes the astrological eye is that while the Dominicans saw their work as being to bring the Cathar heresy to an end once and for all, the chart shows not an ending but a beginning. The Sun and Venus are in conjunction at the beginning of Aries, traditionally the first sign of the zodiac; the so-called 'wounded healer', Chiron, is also in that sign. The latter is a perfect symbol for either wounding or healing by fire, according to your point of view, Aries being one of the fire element signs. It is also about the overcoming of the ego, very important for the Cathars. The Sun and Venus meanwhile are the two planets which one would naturally link with the heart of the matter – they are associated with the heart chakra in the human body – and at the beginning of the first sign they show, in a way, the start of a journey of the heart as well as an illumination of the head, the part of the body ruled by Aries.

In esoteric terms this configuration indicates an initiation, which the fire undoubtedly was, both for those within it and those who witnessed it. It is perhaps easy to say this with hindsight, but the Sun and Venus are beautifully supported by a strong and harmonious link from Jupiter, itself placed in Leo, the sign that rules the heart both physically and spiritually. Jupiter is the planet that above all helps humanity to expand its consciousness, another result of this apparently terrible event. This event not only freed, in every sense, those who were in it, but it also ensured the immortality of the Cathar movement both in human memory and spiritually. Today, Cathar principles inform us probably more than they have ever done since that time.

The chart also illustrates very well the attitude of the Cathars to what was happening to them. Mars, the ruler of Aries and long associated with fire and war, is, as it were, 'trapped' in Taurus, symbolic of the earthly life – it is the 'fixed earth' sign – while the Aries planets and indeed Jupiter all demand a release from that entrapment, which of course the fire gave them. Meanwhile the Moon, always symbolic of the earthly personality and life, is conjunct Neptune. Above all, this shows not only the dissolution of the earthly, but also that the Cathars simply didn't care about what happened to their physical selves, their eyes being so firmly on the things of the spirit. Also highly symbolic is the fact that this conjunction is in Gemini, illustrating beautifully the dualism fundamental to their beliefs.

Of course it was this very dualism that was such a red rag (Mars again!) to the 'bull' (Mars in Taurus) that was the established church. The chart shows this further through the uncomfortable and indeed uncompromising square between the Moon–Neptune conjunction and Saturn, in Virgo with the Moon's south node. This Virgo influence signified for the Cathars themselves their relentless quest for perfection, a quest expressed in the very terminology used to describe those who totally committed themselves to its path. For the Dominicans, however, this signified their dogma, narrow-mindedness and a ruthless quest for 'purification' of religious belief. The clash and outcome were both inevitable: on the one side a church that could not tolerate anything seen as remotely deviant, on the other, a group that had already freed themselves from all materialism and were in conscious contact with the divine. By accepting God's will and walking willingly into the fire which they knew would bring them their freedom, the Cathars won the battle (Aries) so overwhelmingly that they will probably be remembered and their principles acted upon long after the church that persecuted them has faded into obscurity.

An interesting astrological rider to this is the close square between Mars and Uranus, the latter in its own sign of Aquarius, signifying perhaps that in their obedience to the Will (Uranus / Aquarius) of God they made an enemy of the established church (Taurus). Uranus is the planet of the rebel, the revolutionary, the self-willed, often less than obedient to physical law, which is of course how the Cathars were seen, but the planet teaches humanity about 'willing the Will of God', as indeed do the fixed signs, of which Aquarius and Taurus are two. As the old saying has it, the Cathars were in truth 'obedient unto death', epitomizing the saying in physical as well as spiritual reality.

Pluto, at the end of Libra, linking with both Jupiter and Venus, shows the inevitability of the final outcome of that 'aweful' day, while Mercury and the Moon's north node in Pisces really show where the protagonists, the Cathars themselves, were going – back to a world of spiritual freedom and direct communion with the Divine Source.

The fact that the chart symbolizes so clearly the situation shows us, among other things, that there are no accidents. The nature and timing of what happened was clearly ordained for purposes we may even now only dimly comprehend. That it was a total victory for those who lost their physical lives is not to be doubted. The Sun in Aries is said to teach the soul the lesson of love in action. The Cathars who walked into the fire demonstrated in the most overt manner possible both love of God and love of humanity through that action. It will never be forgotten.

IX. CONNECTIONS : 1

THE ABC OF INITIATION
A JOURNEY OF SYNCHRONICITY VIA
'ACD', BACON AND THE CATHARS

DAVE PATRICK

The phoenix rises from the ashes.

WHAT WE ARE witnessing in these times, beyond any shadow of doubt, is emerging evidence that, while the Catholic Inquisition may have succeeded in ruthlessly suppressing the Cathar 'heresy' through the burning of the Cathar people, their sympathisers and their books and manuscripts, the Cathar consciousness has lived on and shines ever more brightly as we stand, tantalisingly, on the cusp of what may be the next prodigious step in human evolution. A wait of seven hundred years is but the blink of an eye in the spiritual realms....

Many contributors to THE CATHAR VIEW have shared their heartfelt, often deeply personal stories; yet the poignancy and sorrow encapsulated within them, intertwined with the joy and the laughter, provides a refreshing glimpse into a period and a people long gone, and visionary insights into events already happening, and those yet to manifest. The process of editing this book and its two predecessors has projected me into a whole new world, completely unknown to me just a few years ago, of wonderful and passionate people – published writers who have become valued friends, and valued friends who are now published writers. I thank them

---

Dave Patrick is the editor of this volume. For his biography, see p. 1

all, not forgetting my '444 connection' with Shannon Andersen (see 'The Call of the Cathars').

I have called this chapter a 'journey of synchronicity'; it is about learning to pay attention to 'meaningful coincidences' as Carl Jung referred to them. When I take action guided by these subtle nudges my life seems to flow more easily and I know at a deep level that I am being true to my soul purpose.

What follows is my story, and the 'story behind the story', of how the three books (so far) in THE VIEW series came to be written – THE VIEW: FROM CONAN DOYLE TO CONVERSATIONS WITH GOD (2009), THE VIEW BEYOND: SIR FRANCIS BACON – ALCHEMY, SCIENCE, MYSTERY (2011) and, now, THE CATHAR VIEW: THE MYSTERIOUS LEGACY OF MONTSÉGUR.

Sir Arthur Conan Doyle

As I outlined them in THE VIEW, my spiritual adventures kicked off in earnest only in 2005, a combination of life circumstances conspiring to relocate me from Aboyne in Royal Deeside to Nairn in the Scottish Highlands. I had started taking an active interest in the life and works of Sherlock Holmes' creator Sir Arthur Conan Doyle (ACD), and knew about his commitment to Spiritualism. However, as someone brought up in the Church of Scotland tradition, I did not anticipate becoming involved in Spiritualism myself, yet started attending the local Spiritualist Church in Inverness, and other Spiritualist groups in Nairn and the surrounding area, initially 'out of curiosity'. I received 20 messages from different mediums over a 40 week period, nearly all consistent with each other and talking about my writing and healing work.

A defining moment occurred in 2007 when the librarian at the Inverness Spiritualist Church said to me one evening, 'You have an interest in Sir Arthur Conan Doyle, don't you?', as she thrust a copy of THE RETURN OF ARTHUR CONAN DOYLE, by Ivan Cooke (originally published 1956), into my hand. I had never heard of this book before, nor had I heard of Ivan Cooke.

Reading it was a massive revelation and it changed my views on life (and the hereafter) forever. Already comfortable from my two year immersion in Spiritualism with the idea that we are eternal souls who reincarnate over many lifetimes, I discovered that THE RETURN OF ARTHUR CONAN DOYLE contained the channelled messages of ACD over an eighteen-month period in 1931–32 (he died on July 7th, 1930) via the Spiritualist medium Grace Cooke (wife of Ivan), with the help of her spirit guide White Eagle and involving a group of sitters, often including ACD's second wife Lady Jean. Also instrumental in getting these messages through were the Polaire Brotherhood, a group also with Cathar connections.

These sessions created the foundation for what became the White Eagle Lodge in 1936, Grace and Ivan Cooke being the founders. So inspired was I having read THE RETURN OF ARTHUR CONAN DOYLE that I joined the White Eagle Lodge the following year, 2008. Many synchronistic occurrences happened throughout that year, detailed in THE VIEW, leading to my meeting Grace and Ivan Cooke's grandson Colum Hayward, and then to the publication and launch of THE VIEW on the 150th anniversary of ACD's birth, 22 May 2009, at the White Eagle Lodge in Hampshire.

ACD's main messages taken from THE RETURN OF ARTHUR CONAN DOYLE, plus Ivan Cooke's previous book on the subject, THY KINGDOM COME (1933) and Colum Hayward's more recent update ARTHUR CONAN DOYLE'S BOOK OF THE BEYOND (1994) I condensed into a fictional Sherlock Holmes pastiche in THE VIEW, in a chapter titled 'The Mystery Of Sir Arthur Conan Doyle's Vital Message'. At the end, having solved the mystery in his usual inimitable fashion, Holmes turns to Dr Watson and proclaims, 'You see what the essence of Sir Arthur's message is, Watson, he is showing us the way. It is the 'Way of LOVE'. What greater message, what greater legacy, could he leave for humanity?'

It should be remembered that ACD was brought up a Roman Catholic, yet renounced his faith in favour of Spiritualism later in life. And an interesting question emerges – does 'The Way of LOVE' not hold more resonance with the Cathars' approach to spiritual matters compared to that of the Roman Catholic Church?

In THE RETURN OF ARTHUR CONAN DOYLE ACD states that it is the quality of our thoughts which determine whether we create heaven or hell for ourselves in the hereafter. He also says we do not have to wait until we die to go to heaven, we can create heaven on earth during our physical lifetime – again, is this not what the Cathars sought to do?

Somewhat ironically, it appears that the majority of modern-day Spiritualists, aware of ACD's advocacy of Spiritualism during his lifetime, nevertheless remain blissfully unaware of his channellings with Grace Cooke after his death, and the events leading up to the founding of the White Eagle Lodge.

'A Dry Run for the Real Work...'

Having been guided to contact Strathpeffer-based channel and healer Shirley Kilday in October 2008, I underwent a series of channelled sessions with her (Shirley also contributed to THE VIEW with 'The Journey of the Soul').

Shortly after THE VIEW's publication I had a my fourth session with Shirley. She informed me while I was in a deep trance state that Sanat Kumara had come in and that he was pleased THE VIEW had been published; he thanked me for my role in it, and that it was a 'dry run for the real work they wanted me to do' – to 'create a living testimony to the truth of the existence of the Masters'.

At that time I had no idea who Sanat Kumara was, my knowledge of the [Ascended] Masters being very limited. Shirley said not to worry as the right people, information and circumstances would be brought to me, which is what happened, involvement with THE VIEW trilogy being a crucial part of the process.

To help with preliminary research on the Ascended Masters I read a small book, MASTERS OF THE SEVEN RAYS: THEIR PAST LIVES AND REAPPEARANCE, by Phillip Lindsay. This provided an excellent introduction, as I discovered that Sanat Kumara is the Planetary Logos, also known as the Ancient of Days – I hadn't initially noticed that Francis Bacon was included, as part of an esoteric lineage of Ascended Masters which includes Roger Bacon (no relation) and Saint Germain.

I also found a second-hand copy of THE MASTERS AND THE PATH, by C.W. Leadbeater (published by The Theosophical Society in 1925) in a local Forres bookshop. I opened to the contents, and the title of Chapter 1 jumped out – 'The Existence of the Masters'!

Sir Francis Bacon

In February 2010 Colum invited me to edit a follow-up book to THE VIEW, to mark the 450th anniversary of the birth of Elizabethan genius Sir Francis Bacon (b. 22 January 1561). I was delighted to accept this invitation but had to admit, having been brought up in the Scottish educational system, that I had never heard of Sir Francis Bacon! And although I had covered the Shakespeare plays as part of the English curriculum, I was not aware of any debate or controversy about who might have written them. I now believe, supported by a combination of intuition and research, that Shakespeare's plays were written by different, overlapping groups of writers, the whole 'veiled' enterprise being masterminded and coordinated by Sir Francis Bacon.

The following week another incredible series of synchronistic events was triggered. A friend in Nairn, Phil Andrews, suggested I search for two terms on the internet – 'the Dagobert Documents' and 'Le Serpent Rouge'. Independently, the same day, we both spoke about a BBC documentary programme being shown that evening on the nature of infinity. As we watched it in our separate homes, I jokingly texted Phil to say 'the answer's 42' (referring to a quote from Douglas Adams' book THE HITCH-HIKERS' GUIDE TO THE GALAXY); Phil's response was 'Number 9'. Puzzled by this (my house number was 9), I started playing with numbers and texted Phil again, saying 3x3=9 and 4+2=6 (9 upside down).

When the programme finished I searched for the terms Phil had mentioned. I was stunned to be led to a website, www.montaguekeen.com, containing a book review written by Peter Welsford, Chairman of the Francis Bacon Society (FBS), of a book written by Sylvia Francke entitled THE TREE OF LIFE AND THE HOLY GRAIL: ANCIENT AND MODERN SPIRITUAL PATHS AND THE MYSTERY OF RENNES-LE-CHÂTEAU. The website is operated by Veronica Keen; each week she posts a message passed to her by her deceased husband Montague, who died in 2004 (a great quote of Monty's I often use is 'Nothing is as it seems').

The following is an extract taken from the book review:
'How Steiner predicts the hidden forces and the history of the creation of the cosmos is fully explained in terms of the formative processes of Warmth, Light, Chemical and Life ethers – where the chemical tone ether is the living, breathing substance of the earth itself. This she calls the science of the Grail – perhaps Sylvia is presenting here Steiner's premonition of the same forces which themselves may lie hidden and are still awaiting a full decode – in the underlying and mysterious workings of our DNA? She highlights this idea in the colour photos, following page 116 in her book, of The Apprentice Pillar at Rosslyn Chapel near Edinburgh in Scotland showing refined helical workings in the ancient stone pillars, compared with models by Mark Curtis of the images of DNA.

Sylvia elaborates the details of how these mysterious 'streams' have passed into and out of the wrong hands, over the centuries. Where are we now, she asks? The true Grail knowledge, THE TREE OF LIFE AND THE HOLY GRAIL is then more fully explained in a metaphysical context. She tells us that this is the most ancient life-line of energetic forces which ray up and down from the planets, interacting with all of us, as human beings.

Bringing matters up to date since Steiner, Sylvia re-focuses our attention on the mysterious document mentioned in THE HOLY BLOOD AND THE HOLY GRAIL – called Le Serpent Rouge (The Red Serpent), originally deposited in a Paris library. Various attempts have been made to decode the contents, unsuccessfully. A most enigmatic 'quatrain' headed Virgo (one of the astrological signs referred to) contains the following statement:

There is the seventh sentence which a hand has traced; 'DELIVER ME OUT OF THE MIRE, AND LET ME NOT SINK. Two times I.S embalming and embalmed'.

Where is the corresponding sentence? It can be 'traced', none other than to: THE RETURN OF ARTHUR CONAN DOYLE (ACD) and his teachings... through 'the hand' of Grace Cooke, the well known medium and clairvoyant, founder of The White Eagle Lodge.

On page 139 in that book there is recorded the following communication through Grace Cooke by 'automatic writing' (the seventh sentence is in italics) which reads as follows:

'...Now I must describe to you a vision. I have to indicate to you the numbers 3 and 9, which are of very great importance: 3 x 3 = 9. There is the entrance to a cavern. On the dark rocks shines the six-pointed star. On the floor a sword in its scabbard. A serpent entwined about a staff. The creature speaks: Man has descended through his own self-will into THE MIRE. He has now to break loose from his circle of sorrow and darkness. Of his own freewill he 'lost' his paradise, and he will not regain it save by his own will and by an immense effort.'

[This vision is identifiable with: L'hiver ou Le DÉLUGE, (1660-1664) Toile, by Poussin. Collection de Louix XIV].'

I couldn't believe my eyes as I scanned down Peter's review and noticed his reference to THE RETURN OF ARTHUR CONAN DOYLE and 3x3=9! The next day I found Sylvia's telephone number, we spoke at length about the synchronicities affecting each of us, and agreed to swap copies of our books.

Since then Sylvia, Peter and Veronica have become firm friends of mine, valued members of my expanding network of like-minded people. Synchronicity operating at its highest level, sparked by two seemingly random and unconnected events (thanks, Phil!). Sylvia and Peter were contributors to THE VIEW BEYOND, and Sylvia is also in THE CATHAR VIEW.

Over the next couple of months another remarkable sequence of synchronistic events led me to Fiona Murray, involving information in Sylvia's book, a green crystal and a remote location on the West coast of Scotland – plus a 'chance meeting' with a friend of Fiona's at Edinburgh's Botanic Gardens. I am delighted that Fiona is also a contributor to THE CATHAR VIEW. At our first meeting she was asked unexpectedly to channel a message from ACD, saying we had to visit Spiritualist Churches, and particularly speak to mediums, to say that providing evidence for the afterlife is not the be-all and end-all of their work as there is more than enough scientific evidence. What was more important, according to ACD, was spiritual development in this lifetime. This aligns with the principles of the White Eagle Lodge, where the emphasis is on meditation rather than mediumship. It is all about reclaiming our personal power at an individual level, making our own sacred contact with spirit through our hearts, rather than giving away our power to intermediaries, be they the priesthood or mediums. Is this not consistent with the Cathars' approach to their spiritual life?

As Summer 2010 approached, and after preliminary research, I had to decide what to write about Sir Francis Bacon for my chapter in THE VIEW BEYOND. Two areas of possibility piqued my interest – the possibility of buried treasure associated with him, and how his visionary ideal for a future society, detailed in his fictional book *The New Atlantis*, had panned out in the context of the United States of America, widely thought to be where his vision was directed.

In June 2012 Peter Welsford invited me to attend an FBS talk by Mark Finnan on the Oak Island treasure hunt, ongoing since 1795 on a small island off the coast of Nova Scotia. The other North American location with potential hidden treasure connected to Bacon is at Bruton Vault in Williamsburg, Virginia, where Marie Bauer (later Marie Bauer Hall when she married esoteric author Manly Palmer Hall) carried out a preliminary excavation in 1938. Several groups continue to press for a full archaeological dig, unsuccessfully so far.

Concerning Bacon's vision for the new world, as applied to the United

States of America at its inception and guided by the Founding Fathers (and purportedly aided by Saint Germain, 'the professor') a key question arose, which has been echoed by many others: '...if 'The New Atlantis' really was a vision of a scientific revolution which would benefit the whole of humanity, why do we appear, in the United States and Europe at least, to have what amounts to a scientific dictatorship, operating through a banking and corporate global elite, influencing governments to often push forward policies to the detriment of the wider society?'

These two areas were investigated in my chapter 'Bacon, Buried Treasure and a Burning Desire to Help Humanity' in THE VIEW BEYOND, written in collaboration with fellow dowser Mark Harris; we used dowsing and other associated techniques (high sense perception, remote viewing) to check out the Bruton Vault and Oak Island locations at a distance from our base in the Scottish Highlands. The results at the time were surprising and formed the basis for further research.

Phillip Lindsay, mentioned earlier, became another contributor to THE VIEW BEYOND after I 'bumped into' him at the Universal Hall in Findhorn, close to the hall entrance featuring a plaque containing a Bacon quote – recognising him from an online video interview I had watched only days before....

Following the launch of THE VIEW BEYOND on January 22nd, 2011, I was invited by Peter Welsford to give a talk to the FBS in London. I named my talk 'Is Now the Time for Bacon's Hidden Messages to be Revealed? – A Personal Journey of Mystery, Synchronicity and Spiritual Unfoldment'.

The FBS was founded in 1886 and is reckoned to be the oldest literary society in England, the venue for my talk being Canonbury Tower, Islington, where Bacon lived for ten years in the seventeenth century. An interesting sidenote is that 1886 was the year Sir Arthur Conan Doyle was formulating the character of his master detective Sherlock Holmes, as well as being around the time when priest Berenger Saunière started to dig deeply into the mystery of Rennes-le-Château.

The FBS talk provided a good opportunity to weave together the connections between ACD and Bacon, more information coming to light since the publication of THE VIEW BEYOND – especially the Shugborough Hall 'decode(s)', the continuation of Marie Bauer Hall's legacy regarding Bruton Vault (see www.godasmother.org) and a remarkable book I found on the Internet by Richard Allan Wagner, THE LOST SECRET OF WIL-

LIAM SHAKESPEARE (www.thelostsecretofwilliamshakespeare.com), centred on the Winchester Mystery House in California. I knew of this house, and that it had been widely regarded as an extravagant folly built by Sarah Winchester after the death of her husband William, whose company made the infamous Winchester rifles. Wagner suggests that the house is actually constructed in alignment with Bacon's higher-level mathematics, codes, ciphers, symbolism and the principles of Sacred Geometry, all seeking to point mankind towards higher-dimensional forms of consciousness.

Links with the Mayan Calendar?

While preparing for my FBS talk I came across some fascinating information on Dr Carl Calleman's website, on the History of Writing: '...the development of the means of communication is very directly linked to the evolution of consciousness, and to consciousness of time in particular. To the Maya writing was considered as a gift of the gods...'

Calleman believes the end of the Day 7 Baktun of the Mayan Calendar occurred on 28 October 2011 – regarding writing he believes the final period ran from 1617 to 2011, a period during which daily newspapers and the mail service were introduced. From a Bacon standpoint the year 1617 is notable, as this was about the time when Bacon was at the height of his powers and influence in government, and a year after the death of William Shakespeare.

Dr Calleman continues:

'Why then is writing linked to the evolution of consciousness in such a way that it clearly follows the evolutionary progression from seed to mature fruit? This may be understood in the following way: Writing to a large extent has been developed in response to a need to 'preserve' information through time...With the beginning of the baktun-based National Cycle, change in human society however began to take place at such a high frequency that 'preservation' became a necessity in many contexts. Thus writing is ultimately a function of the higher frequency of consciousness change carried by the National Cycle. In this way we may realize that writing was not just some kind of technical invention, but a reflection of an increased frequency of the divine process of creation.'

Serious Mayan Calendar researchers are aware of a significant divergence of opinion about when the 'end date' actually lands. Dr. Calleman reckons 28 October 2011 – others go with 21 December 2012 (at time of writing exactly 100 days to go). Does it matter? Will there be a set time and date when everything will suddenly go ... (what?) This is highly doubtful, but there have been strong indications that the period 2011 / 2012 is significant concerning the raising of human consciousness.

Another important cornerstone of my talk was inspired by a quote by Werner Heisenberg: 'It is probably true quite generally that in the history of human thinking the most fruitful developments frequently take place at those points where two different lines of thought meet.' In a contemporary setting these 'different lines of thought' translated into *spiritual awakening* and *corruption exposure*. My conclusion from the overall talk was that both ACD and Bacon stood for Truth and Justice, and the concept of Divine Love, 'Love in Action'.

Now taking the Cathar perspective into account it seems clear that Divine Love / 'Love in Action' was part of their daily living – they were know as the 'Church of Love' or 'Amor', as distinct from the 'Church of Roma', the Roman Catholic Church. And who were the greater purveyors of Truth and Justice, the Cathars or the Vatican-controlled Roman Catholic Church?

The Cathars

Following the publication of THE VIEW BEYOND, Colum suggested the Cathars as our next book's topic. My knowledge about the Cathars moved up a gear when I went on a retreat at the White Eagle Lodge centre at New Lands, Hampshire, in July 2011 on the Ancient Brotherhoods. Led by Colum, the specific groups covered were the Essenes, Cathars and Polaires (which connects us back to our old friend ACD).

In May 2012 I joined a dozen-strong group, mainly from the White Eagle Lodge, organised and led by Colum, which visited the Languedoc. Our base was Bédeilhac, near Tarascon, in the Ariège region. In the first couple of days after arrival some of us went to Montségur and climbed to the top of the pog, after taking time for contemplation at the Cathar memorial honouring the two hundred or so Cathars and sympathisers who bravely met their deaths on a blazing pyre on that fateful day, March 16th, 1244.

The day was overcast but that did not diminish the sense of awe I felt as we ascended Montségur. Prior to this Cathar trip my friend Cate, whom I had met at the July 2011 retreat, and I, had been guided to go to Sandwood Bay, remotely situated in the North West Highlands of Scotland, the previous October (we chose the Calleman Mayan Calendar 'end date' of October 28th) with a set of crystals which we were to position, using our intuition, in the sandy beach and in the adjacent Sandwood Loch. While there we wondered if any Cathars, escaping from the relentless persecution on the European mainland, had made it up to this magnificent beach. A beautiful rainbow broke through making us believe that something meaningful was taking place as a result of our actions. Although the esoteric nature of this ritual largely passed me by at the time, apparently it was connected to Arthurian Legend and the Grail Quest. I am only going by what I was told at the time, although I have no 'scientific' way of verifying what may or may not have happened at an esoteric level. What I can say with clarity is that having walked the four miles in to Sandwood Bay along the bumpy track, I was kept very grounded when I had to walk back the four miles with soaking wet boots, the result of standing too close to the waves lapping in to the beach.

Cate was also a member of the group which went to the Languedoc and again we were guided to take a number of crystals with us to leave at specific spots as our intuition (my dowsing pendulum came in handy!) instructed us. One of the crystals I flung over the sheer cliff from the top of Montségur approximately where I thought the four Cathar *parfaits* had descended that mysterious night in March 1244.

After the first couple of days into our trip, we visited the ruined castle at Lordat, scene of the exploration carried out by Grace Cooke and members of the Polaire Brotherhood in 1931, having visited the Bethlehem cave near Ussat-les-Bains earlier that day. The Bethlehem cave is famous for the irregular pentagon shape indented in one of the cave walls, and many visitors have commented on how their photographs of this cave show the phenomenon of Orbs.

As I was ascending the path up to the castle ruins at Lordat, now operating as an eagle sanctuary, in my mind's eye I asked for a sign that we were on this magical trip for a purpose. I glanced down at the pathway and picked up a small, pentagon-shaped stone strangely reminiscent of the shape we had witnessed in the Bethlehem cave wall. At the end of our visit, where with a noisy group of French schoolchildren we enjoyed a display of eagles and other birds of prey swooping and soaring across the surrounding valleys, we spent some time in individual meditation before returning down the hill to our waiting cars.

The following day was of special interest to me, as we were scheduled to visit Rennes-le-Château, a village which shot to prominence particularly in the early 1980s thanks to the seminal book HOLY BLOOD, HOLY GRAIL by Henry Lincoln, Michael Baigent and Richard Leigh; its notoriety was compounded with Dan Brown's fictional book THE DA VINCI CODE twenty years later. Some of the group decided to visit Cathar castles in the area first and then journey on to Rennes-le-Château later in the day; I joined the other group going straight there as I wanted to spend time in the village and visit the church, Tour Magdala, Villa Bethania, museum, bookshops, etc.

Part of our group – Cate, Philippa and myself – sat on a bench beside the village car park at the highest point of the village with the Tour Magdala to our right and a stunning panoramic view of the landscape immediately in front of us, the gentle breeze blowing across the wheatfields in the valley below, under a blue and cloudless sky.

Having eaten a light picnic lunch we closed our eyes and devoted a few minutes to our own individual journeys of inward reflection, absorbing the beautiful energy of our surroundings. As I was coming out of my reverie I looked down at the ground and spotted a beer bottle top embedded in the sandy ground. As I looked closer it revealed the name Grimbergen (I later found out it was a Belgian beer), and a date 1128, obviously when the brewery was founded. The fact that this date was during a time of high Cathar influence seemed significant.

As I was contemplating the bottle top Cate suddenly asked me to look at the image on it – it was a phoenix sitting in the middle of a huge bowl of flames. All at once my consciousness shot me straight back through history to those Cathar souls who had so bravely gone to the stake. I involuntarily burst into tears as these memories etched into my imagination, and I saw that the phoenix rising from the ashes symbolised the Cathar consciousness resurgence happening now.

Cate and I were guided to leave two crystals in Rennes-le-Château; I dowsed to see where they should be positioned. One was for healing the earth and we placed it under the outside wall of the Tour Magdala; this had a direct connection with a similar feature, now demolished, in Girona in Spain, on the other side of the Pyrenees. The line between the two goes through the sacred mountain Canigou, and the three form a central feature of Patrice Chaplin's books, CITY OF SECRETS and THE PORTAL: AN INITIATE'S JOURNEY INTO THE SECRET OF RENNES-LE-CHÂTEAU'. Patrice also lends her expertise to this book.

The second crystal we left in the Church at Rennes-le-Château where we lit candles and meditated for a short time. This was to give positive energy towards the healing of humanity in the world, especially the Cathars who had undergone such horrific treatment all those years ago. The flickering of the candles served to denote that our actions were being acknowledged.

When the three of us left the church we bumped into someone speaking English giving a guided tour to a small group. It turned out to be writer Val Wineyard, visiting from her home outside Carcassonne. We introduced ourselves, Val kindly gave us a copy of her book, LOOKING FOR MARY M; THE MARY MAGDALENE RESEARCH KIT. And Val became another contributor to THE CATHAR VIEW!

The day was becoming quite surreal. We made our way to Rennes-le-Château's beautiful garden restaurant 'Le Jardin de Marie', relaxing in the afternoon sun drinking coffee, unaware of the events shortly to unfold. As the time approached 6 pm, Colum and his group had still not connected up with us after their tour of Cathar castles, Bugarach and the Gorge de Galamus, and there was not enough room for the other group to go back in one car. I offered to stay behind and wait, the couple who ran the restaurant saying it would take them another half hour to clear up so there was no rush for me to go. I welcomed their hospitality and sat with a carafe of red wine in front of me. I was in no rush to go.

As the proprietor walked by I casually asked him if he had any interest in the Cathars. He smiled and said it was their interest in the Cathars and connected esoteric matters which had attracted them to come from Germany to Rennes-le-Château. He introduced himself as Tobias Dobler, and he and wife Gerda joined me at my table. When I explained that I was part of a White Eagle Lodge group Gerda in particular became very enthusiastic as she knew all about Grace Cooke and the Polaires, and their explorations at Lordat in 1931.

Colum's group arrived from their castles sojourn and joined us at the table, simultaneously filling it up with more people and more carafes of red wine. We were now certainly in no rush to go! We shared our stories and when Colum and I said we were preparing a book on the Cathars Tobias and Gerda said there were two people in particular we should meet – Christian Koenig, who looks after the Gadal house at Ussat-les-Bains, and Ani Williams, an American who splits her time between Sedona and Rennes-les-Bains. We were given Ani's contact telephone number but for Christian we were given directions to the Gadal house and told we should just turn up there and take our chance that he would be in.

The following morning Colum, myself and a fellow group member made our way to Ussat-les-Bains and located the house. Luckily Christian was in and he welcomed us into his lounge where he introduced us to four friends from the Netherlands who were staying there at the time; he explained that he was scheduled to take them for a tour of some of the Cathar caves that morning – *and would we like to join them?* Among the four, Peter and Anneke run a tour company in the region, and Anneke has written her first novel, WHITE LIE, under the pen name of Jeanne D'Août. Of course, Anneke/Jeanne had to become one of our contributors to this book!

As Christian led us to the caves above Ussat-les-Bains (our White Eagle Lodge contingent had by this time doubled in size) he explained that in the years before the Catholic Inquisition the Cathars lived peacefully here with other peoples in a region criss-crossed by different trade routes. The peace and serenity which exists today is palpable.

We were led into three different caves, the middle one being the Bethlehem cave we had visited a couple of days earlier. In the pitch blackness of the other two caves we had head lights and torches to light the way. Christian had taken his pan pipes with him into the caves and we were treated to some wonderfully mystical Cathar music, Christian being accompanied by his Spanish colleague Alicia on accordion. As we journeyed through the cave complex, at times feeling like potholers, it really was like a journey of initiation, providing a sense of wonder about what the Cathars must have experienced all those centuries ago.

The following night Ani joined our group for dinner at our Bédeilhac base, afterwards entertaining us with Cathar and troubadour music on her harp. Ani also agreed to contribute to our book and, a month later when Colum and I returned for a follow up visit, she introduced us to her friend Henry Lincoln, who lives near Rennes-les-Bains. For me it was a fantastic opportunity to spend time in the company of this wise and sincere man, and I felt as though I had come full circle from my earlier interest in HOLY BLOOD, HOLY GRAIL thirty years ago.

I'd really like to thank all the people that I've mentioned - they made our trip truly memorable. But I'd also like to thank those who were actually on the trip and (maybe more to the point here) all the contributors to this book that I haven't met. I look forward to making their acquaintance, and maybe working with them again, in the future. There's a synchronicity about everyone's connection with this book!

Convergence

We appear to be heading for a convergence point where underground streams of true Christ Consciousness are coming together, with the Cathar resurgence very much at the heart of this profound shift, now breaking through to the surface. ACD and Bacon (and countless others, including the Ascended Masters) have been playing their parts in helping to propel humanity forward to what could be a new Golden Age.

Isn't it exciting that ACD, Bacon and the Cathars have all been rising to prominence in people's consciousness at this time? I'm thinking particularly of ACD and the recent major films and television series featuring Sherlock Holmes, Bacon through the 'Who Wrote Shakespeare?' debate, which has now found its way into feature films – and the Cathars via the burgeoning number of books being written about them and the pilgrimages being made to Cathar locations in South West France.

The following ACD message via Grace Cooke summarises one of the key challenges to be overcome, however:

'The Medieval Church without question functioned under the ray of power, qualified perhaps by some wisdom but little love. Power without love inclines to ruthlessness. Love without wisdom or power becomes mere sentimentality minus achievement. One wonders at the power displayed, and shudders at the ruthlessness of the Church's history…. Might one suggest … that the Church of Rome still vibrates to the ray of power, as those who know something of her activities will readily admit.'

THY KINGDOM COME, Ivan Cooke (Wright & Brown, 1933), pp. 252–3

It is perhaps worth repeating the Jimi Hendrix quote I used at the end of THE VIEW: 'When the power of love overcomes the love of power, the world will know peace'. This is a message for the Church, institutionalised religion generally, governments, banks, corporations and other powerful institutions. Is anyone out there listening...?

What About the Treasure?

One of the consistent strands continuing along our historical timeline, linking ACD, Bacon and the Cathars, is the notion of hidden or lost treasure. Is there a connection between them?

With the ACD connection we have the treasure hunting adventures of Grace Cooke and the Polaires at Lordat in 1931. Bacon is widely thought to be the person behind the Oak Island and Bruton Vault hidden treasure mysteries. And in our Cathar story we have the spiriting away of the Cathar 'treasure' down the cliff face at Montségur by the four *parfaits* before the capitulation of their colleagues after the Montségur siege of 1244.

What was this Cathar treasure? Traditional, material treasure such as gold and silver, ancient manuscripts containing sacred knowledge, a way of using psychic abilities to enable access into higher dimensions? Mysterious alchemical powers? A person? Something or someone hidden in another dimension? Is there something hidden inside Montségur itself? The list of possibilities is endless.

In my own contemplations I developed an inkling that there could be something hidden underwater. This led to the idea it might have something to do with crystals. Is it associated with the Blue Stones of Atlantis believed by researcher William Henry to be '...sapphire crystals containing cosmic secrets 'etched by the hand of God' ... [which] were used to open gateways or passages to other realms ... they were in the possession of the Cathars who were taught the secrets of the blue stones by Jesus...'? (http://www.bibliotecapleyades.net/sumer_anunnaki/esp_sumer_annunaki13.htm).

Whatever physical treasure may be out there, is it not about seeking the 'treasure' within ourselves? Perhaps we are the ones who have been holding the keys to unlock the code all along! Might this help explain Grace Cooke's vision at Lordat as she came to some profound self-realization, sitting quietly meditating on the hillside?

As the end of 2012 approaches there is much talk of ascension, with humanity shifting from third dimensional reality up to fourth and fifth dimensions. If this process takes place and we have more strands of DNA activated within us, who knows how far we might evolve in the coming years?

We should be extremely thankful to the Cathars for the seeds of Love they planted way back in the mists of history. And to all the others who have played their part in restoring Love to the Earth.

Let us not fear the future. Let us embrace the Love. We have reached the end of seven hundred years and the laurel is green again....

INDEX TO CONTRIBUTORS

THE VIEW

MIND OVER MATTER, HEART OVER MIND

FROM ARTHUR CONAN DOYLE TO CONVERSATIONS WITH GOD

"An essential read for anyone interested in the future of humankind and spirituality". Kate Hartley, *Kindred Spirit*

THE 'VITAL MESSAGES' OF
NEALE DONALD WALSCH, ERVIN LASZLO,
PETER RUSSELL, DOROTHY MACLEAN
AND TWENTY OTHER PIONEERS OF THE NEW SPIRITUALITY

THE VIEW, edited by Dave Patrick. 288 pp, 156 x 234 mm, ISBN 978-1-905398-18-8

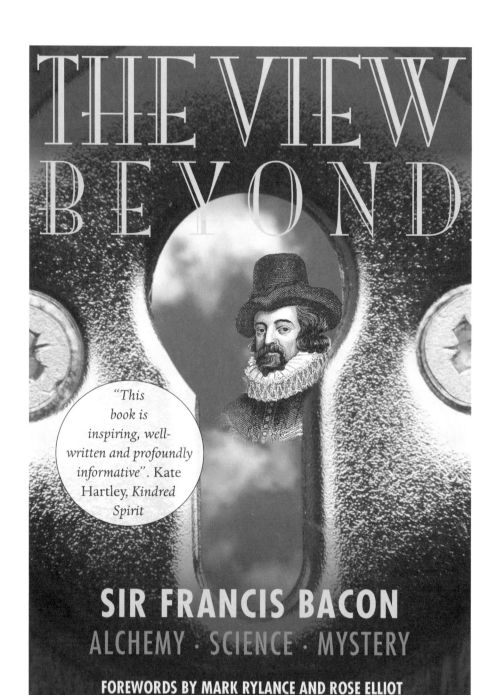

THE VIEW
BEYOND

"This book is inspiring, well-written and profoundly informative". Kate Hartley, *Kindred Spirit*

SIR FRANCIS BACON
ALCHEMY · SCIENCE · MYSTERY

FOREWORDS BY MARK RYLANCE AND ROSE ELLIOT
OVER TWENTY VISIONARY CONTRIBUTIONS

THE VIEW BEYOND, ed. Dave Patrick. 288pp, 156x234mm, ISBN 978-1-905398-22-5